Books are to be returned on or before
the last date below.

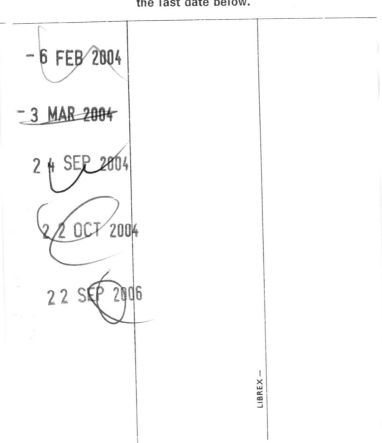

- 6 FEB 2004

- 3 MAR 2004

2 4 SEP 2004

2 2 OCT 2004

2 2 SEP 2006

LIBREX —

D1447642

WITHDRAWN

Do Political Campaigns Matter?

In recent decades, political actors of all sorts – parties and candidates, governments and other political institutions, interest groups and social movements – have increasingly come to view political campaigning as an essential supplement to their engagement in the process of policy-making. By investing ever more efforts and resources into political campaigns, they seek to mobilize support among the mass public, to persuade citizens of their causes and to inform the citizenry about public policies and political procedures.

So far as the practitioners are concerned, such campaigns matter a great deal. Each year, billions of dollars are spent on political campaigns. The sophisticated services of specialist agencies and campaign consultants are engaged; candidates are sent on television training courses; glossy literature, advertisements and campaign gimmicks are produced. While parties, candidates, interest groups, governments, media and – perhaps – voters all seem to be strongly convinced of the notion that campaigns do indeed matter, the collective views of the academic community can perhaps best be summarized as undecided.

This book, in bringing together some of the leading international scholars on electoral behaviour and communication studies, provides the first ever stock-take of the state of this sub-discipline. The individual chapters present the most recent studies on campaign effects in North America, Europe and Australasia. As a whole, the book provides a cross-national assessment of the theme of political campaigns and their consequences.

David M. Farrell is a Jean Monnet Professor of European Politics at the University of Manchester, UK. A co-editor of *Party Politics*, his research focuses on campaigns, electoral systems and representation in the European Parliament. He is also the author of *Electoral Systems: A Comparative Introduction*.

Rüdiger Schmitt-Beck is Scientific Director at the Centre for Survey Research and Methodology (ZUMA), Mannheim, Germany. His research interests are in the areas of comparative political behaviour, public opinion, political communication, electoral behaviour, political culture, social movements and political participation. He is also the author of *Politische Kommunikation und Wählerverhalten*.

Routledge/ECPR Studies in European Political Science

Edited by Jan W. van Deth, *University of Mannheim, Germany*
on behalf of the European Consortium for Political Research

The Routledge/ECPR Studies in European Political Science series is published in association with the European Consortium for Political Research – the leading organization concerned with the growth and development of political science in Europe. The series presents high-quality edited volumes on topics at the leading edge of current interest in political science and related fields, with contributions from European scholars and others who have presented work at ECPR workshops or research groups.

Do Political Campaigns Matter?

Campaign effects in elections and referendums

Edited by David M. Farrell and Rüdiger Schmitt-Beck

Routledge
Taylor & Francis Group
LONDON AND NEW YORK

First published 2002
by Routledge
11 New Fetter Lane, London EC4P 4EE

Simultaneously published in the USA and Canada
by Routledge
29 West 35th Street, New York, NY 10001

Transferred to Digital Printing 2003

Routledge is an imprint of the Taylor & Francis Group

Selection and editorial matter © 2002 David M. Farrell and
Rüdiger Schmitt-Beck; individual chapters © the contributors

Typeset in Baskerville by BC Typesetting, Bristol
Printed and bound in Great Britain by
Antony Rowe Ltd, Chippenham, Wiltshire

British Library Cataloguing in Publication Data
A catalogue record for this book is available from the British Library

Library of Congress Cataloging in Publication Data
A catalogue record for this book is available from the Library of Congress

ISBN 0-415-25593-7

Contents

Figures

Tables

Contributors

André Blais is Professor in the Department of Political Science at the University of Montreal and he holds a Canada Research Chair in electoral studies. His research interests cover voting and elections, public opinion, and electoral systems. He is the principal co-investigator of the 1997 and 2000 Canadian Election Studies. His most recent book is *To Vote Or Not To Vote? The Merits and Limits of Rational Choice Theory* (2000).

Michael Bützer is Assistant at the Research and Documentation Centre on Direct Democracy (c2d.unige.ch) at the University of Geneva. He has studied the public opinion formation process in Switzerland and is currently involved in a research project on local democracy.

David Denver is Professor of Politics at the University of Lancaster. He is the author of *Elections and Voting Behaviour in Britain* (1994) and (with Gordon Hands) *Modern Constituency Electioneering* (1997). He has edited (again with Gordon Hands) *Issues and Controversies in British Electoral Behaviour* (1992). He convenes the elections group of the Political Studies Association and is a frequent commentator on elections in the press and on radio and television.

David M. Farrell is a Jean Monnet Professor of European Politics at the University of Manchester. A co-editor of *Party Politics*, his research focuses on campaigns, electoral systems and representation in the European Parliament. His most recent book is *Electoral Systems: A Comparative Introduction* (2001).

Elisabeth Gidengil is a Professor of Political Science at McGill University. She has been a co-investigator on the 1993, 1997 and 2000 Canadian Election Studies and has published widely in the areas of voting behaviour, public opinion, gender, representation and the media. Her most recent book is *Unsteady State: The 1997 Canadian Election* (1999), with Neil Nevitte, André Blais and Richard Nadeau.

Gordon Hands is Head of the Department of Politics and International Relations at the University of Lancaster. He is co-author (with David

Denver) of *Modern Constituency Electioneering* (1997) and has also edited (again with David Denver) *Controversies in British Electoral Behaviour* (1992). He has written widely on British electoral politics and political sociology. With David Denver he is currently pursuing research on constituency campaigning in the 2001 British general election.

Romain Lachat is a Research Assistant and a PhD candidate at the University of Geneva. His main research interests are in the fields of electoral behaviour, public opinion and methods of data analysis.

Lawrence LeDuc is Professor of Political Science at the University of Toronto. His publications include *Comparing Democracies: Voting and Elections in Global Perspective* (1996, co-editor) as well as articles on voting and elections in a number of North American and European political science journals. His most recent book is *Understanding Referendums: Direct Democracy in Theory and Practice* (2002).

Ian McAllister is Director of the Research School of Social Sciences at the Australian National University. He has held appointments at the University of New South Wales, the University of Strathclyde and the University of Manchester. He is the author of *Political Behaviour* (1992), *Dimensions of Australian Society* (1995, co-author), *The Australian Political System* (1995, co-author) and *How Russia Votes* (1996, co-author). His research interests are in the areas of comparative political behaviour, political parties, voters and electoral systems.

Lionel Marquis is Assistant in the Department of Political Science at the University of Geneva. He has contributed to several publications on Swiss direct democracy, including voting behaviour, foreign policy and far right activism.

Mikko Mattila is Lecturer in the Department of Political Science at the University of Helsinki. His main research interests include the European Union, comparative politics and political economy. He has published articles in *European Union Politics*, *British Journal of Political Science* and *West European Politics*.

Richard Nadeau is Professor in the Department of Political Science at the University of Montreal. His research interests cover voting behaviour, public opinion and the media. He has been a co-investigator of the 1997 and 2000 Canadian Election Studies and has published extensively in academic journals such as the *American Political Science Review*, *American Journal of Political Science* and *Journal of Politics*. His most recent book is *Unsteady State: The 1997 Canadian Election* (1999), with Neil Nevitte, André Blais and Elisabeth Gidengil.

Neil Nevitte is Professor of Political Science at the University of Toronto. He was co-investigator (with André Blais, Elisabeth Gidengil and Richard

Nadeau) of the 1997 and 2000 Canadian Election Studies, and is principal investigator of the Canadian World Values Surveys. His recent publications include *Unsteady State: The 1997 Canadian Federal Election* (1999, with Blais, Gidengil and Nadeau), *The Decline of Deference* (1996), *The North American Trajectory* (1996, with Ronald Inglehart) and *Political Value Change in Western Democracies* (1996, with Loek Halman).

Pippa Norris is Associate Director (Research) at the Joan Shorenstein Center on the Press, Politics and Public Policy at the John F. Kennedy School of Government, Harvard University. She has published more than two dozen books and the most recent include *A Virtuous Circle* (2000) and *Digital Divide* (2001).

Marina Popescu is the Senior Research Officer of the ESRC-funded project 'Elections and the Political Transformation in Post-Communist Europe' and a PhD student in the Department of Government, University of Essex. Her main research interests are comparative politics, electoral behaviour, the mass media and public opinion.

Ilkka Ruostetsaari is Senior Research Fellow of the Academy of Finland in the Department of Political Science and International Relations at the University of Tampere. He has published studies in the field of elite structures, the recruitment of MPs, the professionalization of politics, energy policy and local democracy.

Rüdiger Schmitt-Beck is Scientific Director at the Centre for Survey Research and Methodology (ZUMA), Mannheim. His research interests are in the areas of comparative political behaviour, public opinion, political communication, electoral behaviour, political culture, social movements and political participation. His most recent book is *Politische Kommunikation und Wählerverhalten* (2000).

Pascal Sciarini is Professor at the Graduate Institute of Public Administration (IDHEAP), Lausanne. He has written on Swiss politics (direct democracy, political parties, European policy), political behaviour, European integration and comparative political economy. Recent publications include 'Referendums on European Integration: Do Institutions Matter?', *Comparative Political Studies* (2000, co-author); and 'The Political Economy of Budget Deficits in the European Union: The Role of International Constraints and Domestic Structure', *European Union Politics* (2001, co-author).

Gábor Tóka is Assistant Professor of Political Science at the Central European University, Budapest. He has published mostly on public opinion, parties and electoral behaviour. He is co-author of *Post-Communist Party Systems: Competition, Representation, and Inter-party Cooperation* (1999) and author of *Inventory of Political Attitude and Behaviour Surveys in East Central Europe and the Former Soviet Union 1989–97* (2000).

Series editor's preface

In his seminal work on public opinion and democracy Walter Lippmann observed already in 1921 that 'the art of inducing all sorts of people who think differently to vote alike is practiced in every political campaign'. The development of mass participation and mass media in representative democracies in the last decades has underlined the importance of campaigning. Modern political campaign strategies increasingly rely on the use (and manipulation) of media presentations of candidates and their personal characteristics and background. Television, cable, telephone banks, the internet, direct mailing enterprises and other new technologies make it possible to reach quite literally 'all kinds of people' and sophisticated campaign tactics and techniques take full advantage of the opportunities to 'induce' citizens 'to vote alike' in the way Lippmann meant.

Despite the fact that the development of political campaigning in representative democracies is hard to overlook, campaigning has not drawn major attention from the scholarly community. The traditional division of labour in political science and an evident US bias in studying campaign effects certainly explain much of this astonishing situation. As the editors of this volume indicate in their introductory chapter, campaign effects are 'located at the interface of various sub-disciplines' and a multi-disciplinary approach is required to do the subject justice. The development of political campaigning and campaign effects, then, cannot be understood within the conventional conceptual borders of electoral studies, party sociology or communication research, or by relying on American experience only. What is needed is, first of all, a rethinking of concepts like communication and effects, allowing much more analytical depth and detail than is usually provided in disciplinary approaches. Second, the scope of research should be broadened considerably not only to cover US campaigning and campaign effects, but to deal also with developments and specific circumstances from comparative and longitudinal perspectives.

The contributors to the volume differ in their research interests, study designs and selected material, and in the scope of the analyses presented, but they all cope with the impact of political campaigning in representative democracies from a broad perspective. Before these specific analyses are presented, Rüdiger Schmitt-Beck and David Farrell summarize the major questions and approaches in their introduction by elaborating typologies of political campaigning and of campaign effects (Chapter 1). The four subsequent chapters are addressed to campaign effects in elections in several countries. Ian McAllister examines the timing of voting decisions – the 'rise of the late decider' – and its political consequences in Australia, Britain and the United States (Chapter 2). Results from a Swiss election study are presented by Romain Lachat and Pascal Sciarini showing that increases in campaign activities stimulate voters to reassess their usual party preferences (Chapter 3). Marina Popescu and Gábor Tóka focus on the role of public television in Hungarian elections. Their remarkable conclusion is that government-controlled television makes partisan use likely and functions as a boomerang; that is, re-election of incumbents may be endangered by the use of public television instead of enhanced (Chapter 4). The much-debated 'priming' efforts of candidates and parties are traced by Elisabeth Gidengil and her colleagues in a study of the dominance of the free trade issue in the 1988 Canadian elections (Chapter 5). The next two chapters deal with campaigning in districts instead of countries. Ilkka Ruostetsaari and Mikko Mattila describe the Finnish electoral system, where candidates compete not only with contestants from other parties but also with competitors from their own party. In this situation, too, media coverage appears to be an important factor in winning elections (Chapter 6). In a similar way, David Denver and Gordon Hands discuss the development of constituency campaigning in Britain (Chapter 7). Before the last two contributions redirect the attention to campaigning in referendums, Pippa Norris argues convincingly that the decline of civic engagement in the United States – a 'campaign-induced malaise' – cannot be attributed to the way American journalists and politicians deal with campaigns (Chapter 8). Lawrence LeDuc examines campaign effects in twenty-three referendums held in fourteen different countries or regions. He comes to the rather surprising conclusion that attitudes towards the issue at stake establish only one of the factors determining the vote (Chapter 9). Concentrating on the Swiss case, Michael Bützer and Lionel Marquis follow this line of argument and point out the importance of elite discourse as an important determinant of individual vote decisions (Chapter 10). Finally, Rüdiger Schmitt-Beck and David Farrell return to the major problems and prospects in the concluding chapter by warning against simple and rather naive conclusions in this area. Campaigns do matter, but the specific impact depends much on particular circumstances, strategies and techniques (Chapter 11).

The spread of communication facilities and the decline of persistent party loyalties have made political campaigning increasingly important ever since Walter Lippmann defined 'inducing all sorts of people' as the common characteristic of these ventures. Sophisticated campaign strategies and techniques may not have the unambiguous and fashionable consequences presumed by most critics of representative democracies. Yet the prospects of democratic decision making depend heavily on the chances of improving campaign strategies and reducing abuses. Technical progress has not alleviated these tasks. On the contrary. In a digitalized and networked world with ample opportunities for 'many-to-many' communications political campaigning presents much more serious challenges and pitfalls than even Walter Lippmann could have imagined.

Jan W. van Deth, *Series Editor*
Mannheim, November 2001

Preface and acknowledgements

There are occasions when it is evident that a theme is ripe for more scholarly attention. Perhaps the echo of our call for papers for a workshop on the political consequences of modern electioneering, held in Copenhagen in 2000 under the auspices of the European Consortium for Political Research (ECPR), is just such an indication. This stimulated more than forty proposals – twice as many as we could accommodate in the workshop. In their turn, the number of papers presented at the workshop were twice as many as we could eventually include in this volume, given the space limitations and the need to provide a reasonable balance of coverage in terms of themes and countries. Difficult choices had to be made about which papers to include, but we want to stress at the outset that this volume has resulted from a group effort, and therefore we should record our thanks to those workshop participants not included in this volume whose presentations and comments helped to stimulate so much of what is included. These were: Kees Aarts, Wolfram Brunner, Rachel Gibson, Christina Holtz-Bacha, Hanne Marthe Narud, Henar Criado Olmos, Geoffrey K. Roberts, Patrick Seyd, Henry Valen, Philip van Praag, Paul Whiteley and Michael Wolf.

We also wish to express our thanks to the chapter authors who put up with our requests (sometimes several) for revisions and redrafting. That this volume was completed on time is testimony to their speed, efficiency and good humour throughout. We are grateful to the series editor, Jan van Deth, to our referees and also to Shaun Bowler and Barbara Pfetsch for their helpful and constructive comments, and to our Routledge editors, Craig Fowlie, Heidi Bagtazo and Belinda Dearbergh, for their guidance and support throughout. Thanks also to Oxford University Press for allowing us to reprint Table 1.1, originally published in R. Dalton and M.P. Wattenberg, *Parties without Partisans*, Oxford University Press, Oxford, 2000.

Tanja Pagel (ZUMA) was invaluable in helping us to prepare the manuscript for publication and we wish to record our particular gratitude to her for this. Thanks are also due to the Centre for Survey Research and Methodology (ZUMA) at Mannheim, which hosted David Farrell for a visit in summer 2001, enabling us to take big steps towards completing the final editing during a week of intense work.

Modern information technologies are a great asset not only for campaigners, but also for political scientists. Mindless counting is what computers are particularly good at. Hence, thanks to the automatic book-keeping functions of our e-mail programmes, we are able to record that the correspondence surrounding this book amounted to just short of 1,000 messages accumulating in our respective folders over two years. This volume is the result of a genuine collaborative effort on the part of both editors, as reflected in the altering of our name order, allowing David to take top billing on the title page and Rüdiger in the introduction and conclusion.

D.M.F.
R.S-B.
Manchester and Mannheim

1   Studying political campaigns and their effects

Rüdiger Schmitt-Beck and David M. Farrell

Political campaigns are treated as occasions of immense importance by politicians, and never more so than today. In recent decades political actors of all sorts – parties and candidates, governments and other political institutions, lobby groups, social movements and other kinds of citizens' associations – have increasingly come to view political campaigning as an essential supplement to their engagement in the process of policy making. By investing ever more efforts and resources into political campaigns they seek to mobilize support among the mass public, to persuade citizens of their causes, and to inform the citizenry about public policies and political activities. So far as the practitioners are concerned, such campaigns matter a great deal. Those waging campaigns firmly believe that these efforts help them to achieve their political goals and thus count in the political process. Each year, literally billions of dollars are spent, mostly in election campaigns (at all levels), but increasingly also in other kinds of campaigns, such as referendum campaigns, policy-related information campaigns, or image campaigns. The sophisticated (and thereby costly) services of specialist agencies and campaign consultants are engaged; candidates are sent on television training courses and are suitably colour-coded; glossy literature, advertisements of many forms and items of campaign gimmickry are produced. While parties, candidates, interest groups, governments, media and (some) voters are apparently strongly convinced of the notion that campaigns do indeed matter, the collective views of the academic community can perhaps best be summarized by the word 'undecided'.

The issue is certainly of relevance to a number of fields in political science. There have been countless studies in the voting behaviour literature on the ingredients that voters take into account when deciding which party or candidate to vote for at elections, or which proposal to support at referendums. But with few exceptions there has been little analysis of how these factors are connected with the communication activities of political parties and other campaign organizations. There is also a large body of literature in the area of communications studies, examining the effects of the news media's political reporting on the opinions and attitudes of their audiences during campaign periods. In a number of cases these show how media reporting to some degree reflects the campaign activities of political actors. But the media are by no means the only channel through which campaigns reach their audiences. While inquiries into the effects of political campaigns cannot ignore the mediating role of mass communication, equally they cannot restrict themselves to looking only at the media. Finally, there is a growing body of research in party sociology (and also in the study of social movements) on how political organizations plan and implement their campaigns. This usually starts from the premise that campaigns are important, although there have been few attempts to prove this assumption empirically.

To be sure, recent years have seen an increased effort to go beyond the limitations of these strands of research with the aim of producing firmer conclusions about whether and how political campaigns matter. A fairly large range of specialist studies of campaign effects have accumulated, although these have tended to be very specific in scope. Most have dealt only with election campaigns – zeroing in on a particular campaign in a particular context – and their findings, therefore, have tended not to be easily generalizable. Furthermore, the study of campaign effects has been predominantly focused on a small number of national contexts, above all the United States, with a much more sporadic coverage of trends in Britain and a few other cases.

This book represents the first cross-national effort to take stock of the state of this sub-discipline. The nine chapters which follow examine campaign effects in a range of different national contexts, using a range of different methodologies. In this introductory chapter we set the scene for what is to follow. We start, in the first section, by outlining the field of study of campaign effects, setting out a definition of campaigning, and reviewing the types of campaigns that can be included in this area of analysis. The subsequent sections concentrate on campaigns for elections and referendums, exploring the core features of contemporary campaigns and discussing the range of likely ways in which these campaigns might be said to have some influence. Finally, we provide a short section reviewing the main trends in the study of campaign effects, before concluding with an outline of the rest of the book.

The rise of campaign politics

Campaigning is a core feature of the political process in contemporary democracies. Election campaigns see parties and their candidates wage battles for votes and political office. Referendum campaigns see proponents and opponents of the relevant issue seek to steer the vote in their preferred direction. Issue-based campaigns see government agencies or interest groups attempting to have an issue or policy placed high on the political agenda, and to have it favourably framed in public debate. Image campaigns see efforts to paint the public perception of some political actor in a more favourable light. In the past few decades campaigning has assumed increasing relevance as a mode of political mediation, in part reflecting the growing volatility in the electoral process, in part also reflecting a general shift towards issue-based politics and a greater emphasis on alternative modes of political participation. If the first of these indicates a greater role for 'policy mediation' – consisting of top-down flows of strategic communication originating from the political elite – the second is more suggestive of a process of 'interest mediation', in which, in particular, the political elite face ever more competition for agenda setting from interest groups and lobbying organizations (Edelman 1985, 1988; Sarcinelli 1987, 1998; Röttger 1997; Bentele *et al.* 2001).

Campaigns occur not only in the political realm; they are increasingly important in all walks of life: for instance, a company mounts an advertising campaign to promote its product; a charity seeks to raise money for an overseas aid programme; a city engages in 'city marketing' in order to attract investors and new businesses. Since the focus of this book is specifically on *political* campaigns, it is useful to start with a basic definition. The objective of a political campaign is to influence the process and outcome of governance. It consists of an organized communication effort, involving the role of one or more agencies (be they parties, candidates, government institutions or special interest organizations) seeking to influence the outcome of processes of political decision-making by shaping public opinion. Political actors are campaigning because they hope that the support of the public, or of relevant segments of the public, will help them to promote their political causes. Often such public support, at least in the short term, may help political actors to attain their goals, most notably in those cases where the public itself takes the relevant decisions, as in elections or referendums. However, campaigns are also gaining importance as a tool of the political craft in many other scenarios in which favourable opinions on the part of significant publics are believed to lend causes legitimacy, thereby furthering their chances of success. This is shown, for instance, by the case of public interest groups striving to elevate particular issues on to the decision-making agenda, or by the case of government agencies seeking to produce legitimacy for policy programmes during the implementation phase. To such ends, these political actors mobilize strategic resources of varying kinds and to varying amounts. They do so within institutional and situational contexts that may entail both constraints and structures of opportunity (Farrell 2002).

What the agency is seeking to influence can vary widely. If it is a political party fighting an election campaign, it may want to maximize the number of seats it wins, or, indeed, it may as, say, a Green party, be seeking to influence the political agenda. In both cases the party's target for influence is voters (though, in the latter case, the expectation is that any influence over voters will also have a bearing on the attitudes of the established political

		Campaign focus	
		Single issue	Range of issues
Constellation of campaign actors	Competing actors	Referendums	Elections
	One actor	Information Interest-based	Image

Figure 1.1 A typology of political campaigns.

actors). In the case of a special interest group during a referendum campaign, its focus will be on achieving victory for its side, and again the principal target will be voters. By contrast, in the case of a special interest group seeking to raise the profile of an issue by placing it higher on the political agenda and framing it in particular ways (e.g. in the hope that a party might take it on as an issue, or that a referendum might be called) the principal target is the established politicians, with public opinion functioning as the connecting hinge (Schmitt-Beck 2001).

Figure 1.1 attempts to simplify the discussion somewhat, by reducing the wide range of different campaign scenarios to a simple two-by-two typology based on the constellation of actors involved in the campaign and the focus of the campaign. This suggests four main types of political campaigns, two of which are considered in this book. The first, and most obvious, type is the election campaign (dealt with in Chapters 2–8) which is characterized by a set of competing actors (political parties/candidates) each campaigning on a range of issues (as well as a focus on candidate and party image), with the principal goal being electoral success. To be sure, this is an ideal-typical simplification, as, for instance, in the case of certain minor parties, particularly those with a strong ideological bent, electoral gains may actually be given a lower priority. In addition, by waging campaigns, parties may also seek to serve internal party purposes, like maintaining party unity, attracting new members, fund raising, nurturing potential coalition links and so on. Yet success at elections, and the chance to occupy government positions that it provides, is clearly the core objective of parties and their candidates (Downs 1957; Weber 1980 [1921/22]: 840–1; Schumpeter 1994 [1942]). Second, there are referendum campaigns (dealt with in Chapters 9–10), which share with election campaigns the fact that there are competing sets of actors (although here there is greater likelihood that not all of these actors are parties), but in this case the campaign is focused on just one issue, and there is not even the 'distraction' of a political candidate.

Third, there are single-issue campaigns unilaterally launched by just one actor. Such campaigns are often implemented by government agencies, in order to inform the public (e.g. 'drink and drive' campaigns), and/or to mobilize support and raise acceptance of particular policies. Notable examples are the campaigns on privatization policies and the poll tax in

Britain, launched by the Conservative government in the 1990s (Newton 2000), or the campaign of the European Central Bank to ease the implementation phase of the euro. In the same category we find also interest-based campaigns by pressure groups aimed at influencing the political agenda and the way political problems are framed; a prominent example with transnational reach are the activities of the anti-globalization movement and its member organizations. This category shares with referendum campaigns the focus on a single issue at a time. A distinguishing feature of this type is that there is generally just one actor in the fray: a government department, perhaps a religious or consumer organization, or other public interest groups and lobby organizations. While starting with activities launched by just one actor, such campaigns may easily lead to competitive battles for public opinion as other actors, feeling challenged by the points of view raised by the first actor, wage counter-campaigns. Finally, completing our typological matrix, there are image campaigns. These are also launched by single actors, but may involve a range of issues, wrapped together with various kinds of emotional appeals. Their purpose is to raise the public esteem of the actor in question. An example is the campaign of the Conservative government to improve the 'uncaring' and 'cold-hearted' image of Prime Minister Margaret Thatcher (Newton 2000). These latter two types of campaign are dealt with only in passing in the remainder of this chapter, since our focus is on campaigns for elections and referendums.

Political campaigning here and there, then and now

Election and referendum campaigns can be seen as complex processes of purposive political communication that are essentially 'top-down', originating from campaign organizations like parties, candidates' support organizations, government institutions or interest groups, and aimed at the mass public in its entirety or at specific 'target' segments. Yet, as visualized in Figure 1.2 by means of broken arrows, campaigns also entail 'bottom-up' components, since political actors constantly seek feedback by monitoring their target audiences in order to assess whether their strategies are working. Election returns, for instance, are routinely interpreted as indications of the quality of election campaigns. In addition, campaign organizations increasingly rely on techniques for the systematic observation of public opinion like surveys or focus groups to plan their strategies and calibrate their campaign instruments (Rose 1967; Kavanagh 1996). The mass media are also utilized as sources of feedback. Guided by the assumption that the media are powerful agents of influence, political actors constantly screen their reporting in order to anticipate what media audiences think. In addition, when several actors wage competing campaigns each of them may use the media as a source of intelligence about its opponents.

Ultimately guided by their political goals, but taking into account their assessment of the specifics of the current situation, political actors like party

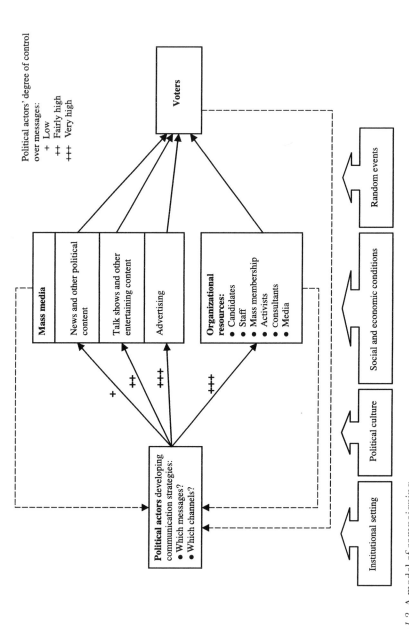

Political actors' degree of control over messages:
+   Low
++   Fairly high
+++   Very high

Voters

Mass media

News and other political content

Talk shows and other entertaining content

Advertising

Organizational resources:
● Candidates
● Staff
● Mass membership
● Activists
● Consultants
● Media

+

++

+++

+++

Political actors developing communication strategies:
● Which messages?
● Which channels?

Institutional setting

Political culture

Social and economic conditions

Random events

Figure 1.2 A model of campaigning.

Source: Adapted from Schmitt-Beck and Pfetsch (1994: 117).

leaders or candidates develop strategies for their campaign communications. They must determine which messages may be most helpful to achieve their goals, and which channels to use to get these messages across. Since material and non-material resources may be available in varying amounts to different political actors, but are in any case always inherently limited, decisions must be taken about how these are best to be allocated. Difficult problems must be solved. Should one wage an expensive advertising campaign, or rather rely on the manpower of the organization's rank and file? If advertising money is laid aside for 'paid media', should it be spent on a large number of newspaper ads, or on a few television spots? Should one seek the costly help of a prestigious advertising agency, or economize by financing training seminars for local volunteer canvassers? Such questions are not easy to answer, and a lot of experience and expertise, but also creativity and perhaps even luck, are necessary to arrive at the right answers.

The mass media are a very important channel of campaign communications, and increasingly so, but they are usually not the only means by which campaigners can reach their addressees. In election campaigns, most political actors traditionally rely on their own organizational resources. Only a few actors, like the independent presidential candidate Ross Perot in 1992, rely exclusively on the media to communicate to voters. But for other candidates it is still common to travel the length and breadth of the country, delivering speech after speech on public squares and in town halls, and meeting citizens in the back rooms of smoke-filled pubs. Local voluntary activists canvass the neighbourhood and seek face-to-face discussions with their fellow citizens at street stands. They are also a human resource important for organizing the local rallies for candidates and party leaders. Entering the age of mass parties, these organizations equipped themselves with permanently employed professional staff, among whose most important organizational tasks were activities connected with campaigning. In recent years, in addition to the organizations' own personal resources, the services of hired specialists have been quickly gaining importance for all kinds of sub-tasks within the increasingly complex business of campaigning. Political consultancy has become big business in the United States, but to some degree it is gaining ground in most contemporary democracies, leading to increasingly professionalized campaigns (Farrell and Webb 2000; Farrell *et al.* 2001).

In most countries, the days are long gone when parties owned their own general readership newspapers and thus had at their disposal a convenient medium of campaign communication. The party press, where it still exists, has mostly turned into an instrument of internal communication. Yet nowadays modern communication technologies offer new opportunities for campaign organizations to free themselves to some degree from the constraints that arise from the necessity to rely on independent media to get their messages across. Within a few years political actors' use of the internet has spread extensively. Most parties as well as government agencies and all kinds of other citizens' associations now operate professional websites as a means of circumventing the filters of the news media to communicate directly with voters (Bieber 1999; Margolis *et al.* 1999; Norris 2002).

Naturally, for political actors it is important to exert as much control as possible over the ways their messages are conveyed to the electorate (Zaller 1998). As far as they can use their own organizational resources for that purpose, thus directly communicating with voters, they enjoy considerable (though perhaps still not full) autonomy in designing and disseminating their messages. Constraints may arise to the degree that leaders are dependent on their organization's activist members. An important part of campaign strategies, therefore, focuses on efforts to mobilize the membership. This implies that political actors must be careful not to offend their followers by proposing unpopular ideas or violating esteemed traditions. In this sense at least, members can be a force of inertia, limiting the freedom of action of the leaders. Yet, despite all the changes in how campaigns are waged, political organizations continue to be one of the most important channels for political actors to reach voters directly. Another channel of direct communication with the electorate is advertising. Through printed advertisements, billboards or television spots political actors are able to convey (almost) any message they like to (almost) anyone they like, up to the limits of the audience's attention, and their personal budgets.

Advertising is expensive, especially on television. Therefore, political actors have a strong incentive to supplement these 'paid' media by 'free' media (in Table 1.1 we refer to these, respectively, as 'indirect' and 'direct' media), through appearances in the news and other political programmes on television as well as in the press (Salmore and Salmore 1989). Carefully staged 'pseudo-events', custom-designed to attract the attention of the media, have become a staple of contemporary campaigning. Although journalists are usually well aware that they are being instrumentalized they often report on such events, thus giving political actors a stage on which to present themselves to voters, free of charge. Yet this kind of media presence still comes at a price, in terms of a lack of editorial control. The conditions under which politicians attain visibility through the media differ widely across countries, depending on the nature of media systems (Semetko 1996). For instance, in West European democracies some media are to varying degrees affiliated to specific parties or at least certain ideological tendencies. This is usually favourable for parties, as long as they have allies in the media. In many new democracies across the world, it has been noted that government parties regularly seek to exploit the public media for campaign purposes (Milton 2000) – an issue discussed by Popescu and Tóka in Chapter 4 of this volume. In the United States, by contrast, the media are increasingly criticized for their general 'anti-political' stance: here the accusation is that, rather than showing favouritism towards particular candidates or parties, there tends to be a general air of negativism against all politicians, regardless of party (Patterson 1993), giving rise to worries over an increasing 'media malaise' among the general public, as discussed by Norris in Chapter 8 of this volume. The presence of political actors in the news, then, can be a two-edged sword.

Small wonder, therefore, that political actors seek to gain more control over their media images, bypassing formats where the conditions of their appearance are ultimately controlled by journalists. In recent years 'talk show campaigning' has become very popular among politicians, particularly in the United States, but increasingly also in other countries. The independent candidate Ross Perot gained a reputation for his particularly skilful use of this medium in his campaign for the 1992 presidential election (Lemert *et al.* 1996).

As indicated in the bottom of Figure 1.2, there are a range of political, social, economic and cultural contextual factors, and random events, which influence the nature of campaigning (for further discussion, see Bowler and Farrell 1992b, 2000; Schmitt-Beck and Pfetsch 1994). As an illustration of this, we can refer to some of the more obvious political institutional factors. For instance, in consensus democracies, where multi-party politics and coalition governments are the norm, the terms of the electoral contest can differ markedly from majoritarian systems, where politics is more of a zero-sum game (Lijphart 1999). In the latter case, much more is at stake for the competitors and there are no incentives for campaign alliances between party coalitions. Electoral systems are also known to play an important role in campaigning, for instance with regard to the potential for certain electoral systems, such as the British single member plurality system, to promote local, candidate-centred campaigning (Katz 1980). The Finnish open-list system provides an interesting example. Here candidates are required to mount personal campaigns, with their electoral fate dependent on their personal resources, as shown by Ruostetsaari and Mattila, in Chapter 6 of this volume. Despite a general trend towards deregulation, the extent to which the broadcast media may be used for political advertising also differs widely across today's democracies (Kaid and Holtz-Bacha 1995), in turn influencing the incentives to allocate resources to this medium of campaign communication. Regulations on the financing of political campaigns and of parties can also vary (Farrell and Webb 2000), and, depending on whether campaigners are legally allowed to raise and spend substantial sums, the campaigns themselves will manifest very different features when compared cross-nationally.

Obviously the way campaigns are conducted has been, and will continue to be, subject to a process of constant change. The past few decades have seen an important dynamic in the nature of campaigning generally, namely the fact that it has been going through an extended process of 'modernization' (Bowler and Farrell 1992a; Butler and Ranney 1992; Swanson and Mancini 1996). Various labels have been given to the new style of electioneering, referred to as 'stage III' campaigning in Table 1.1 (Farrell 1996; Farrell and Webb 2000). In her most recent study, Norris (2000; see also Chapter 8 of this volume) refers to this stage as 'post-modern campaigning';

Table 1.1 Three stages in the development of election campaigning

	Stage I	Stage II	Stage III
Technical developments			
Campaign preparations	Short-term; *ad hoc*	Long-term; specialist committee established a year or two years in advance of election	'Permanent campaign': establishment of specialist campaign departments
Use of media	'Direct' and 'indirect' Direct: party press, newspaper ads, billboards Indirect: newspaper coverage	Emphasis on 'indirect' Direct: ad campaigns Indirect: public relations, media training, press conferences	Emphasis on 'direct' Direct: targeted ads, direct mail, video-mail, cable television, internet Indirect: as before
Resource developments			
Campaign organization	Decentralized Local party organization Little standardization Staffing: party/candidate-based, voluntary	Nationalization, centralization Staffing: party-based, salaried professional	Decentralization of operation with central scrutiny Staffing: party/candidate-based, professional, contract work; growth of leader's office

Agencies, consultants	Minimal use; 'generalist' role Politicians in charge	Growing prominence of 'specialist' consultants Politicians still in charge	Consultants as campaign personalities International links 'Who's in charge'?
Sources of feedback	Impressionistic, 'feel' Important role of canvassers, group leaders	Large-scale opinion polls More scientific	Greater range of polling techniques Interactive capabilities of cable and internet
Thematic developments			
Campaign events	Public meetings Whistle-stop tours	Television debates; press conferences 'Pseudo-events'	As before; events targeted more locally
Targeting of voters	Social class support base Maintain vote of specific social categories	Catch-all Trying to mobilize voters across all categories	Market segmentation Targeting of specific categories of voters
Campaign communication	Propaganda	Selling concept	Marketing concept

Source: Farrell and Webb (2000: 104).

Denver and Hands (Chapter 7 of this volume) refer to this stage, particularly in the context of the local campaign, as 'post-Fordism'. While the process of change has been most prominent in the case of the national electioneering strategies of the parties and the candidates, obviously it has not been exclusive to the election campaign. Indeed, since a major feature of the 'modernization' of campaigning has entailed the emergence of what has become known as the 'permanent campaign', then, by extrapolation, we can also see evidence of such changes more widely, and certainly also in the cases of referendum, issue and image campaigns.

'Professionalization' and 'scientification' are other core characteristics of 'Stage III' campaigning, arguably the latest step in the process of 'rationalization' of party politics and political competition which was first diagnosed by Max Weber eighty years ago (Weber 1980 [1921/22]: 837–68). An important driving force behind this process is the logic of competition itself. In order not to lose ground in the contest for public support, political actors are forced constantly to adapt to environmental conditions that change with increasing rapidity. Much like commercial producers in the market place, political actors campaign to remain or become visible in an ever more crowded public space. As media systems develop in the direction of commercialization, diversification and fragmentation, it becomes more difficult for political actors to instrumentalize the media for the purpose of gaining favourable publicity. The underpinning of a political system by layers of social cleavages that characterized democratic politics from its beginning until well into the second half of the twentieth century provided a stable foundation for mainstream political actors. In today's democratic societies this can no longer be taken for granted, either because of processes of dealignment (Dalton and Wattenberg 2000), or perhaps because the country, as a new democracy, missed out on the party-aligned stage altogether (McDonough and López Pina 1984).

At the same time, in the realms of technology and business, new marketing tools are developed that can be adapted for the purposes of political campaigning (to a degree, this can even be a two-way relationship, see Farrell *et al.* 2001). Direct mail, telephone banks, inexpensive computer technology, the internet, cable, satellite and digital television, are just a few examples of the new means of targeted two-way communications. Faced with innovative potentials like these, political actors – not unlike antagonistic nation states enmeshed in an inescapable 'security dilemma' (Herz 1950; Buzan and Herring 1998) – operate under the assumption that their opponents will at all times seek to maximize their power potential by taking advantage of any innovative tool available to them, in order to prevail in the contest. Under such circumstances, the competitive pressures inherent in elections and referendums create an autonomous dynamic towards an 'arms race' between 'campaign warriors' (Thurber and Nelson 2000). As no party or candidate campaign organization can ever expect that its competitors will deliberately abstain from using the newest material and latest technologies of influence, strong incentives are built in to do the same, if only not to fall behind in terms of 'firepower', and to avoid giving anyone else a competitive edge. A spiralling arms race is set in motion, constantly infusing innovative methods into the conduct of campaigns, thus driving campaigning to ever higher levels of sophistication, and cost.

How can political campaigns matter?

All campaigners share in common the desire to have some influence over events; they also share in common a belief that they can, indeed, have some influence, that their campaign can 'matter'. The $64,000 question to be answered in this book is whether the belief is well founded – do political campaigns, more specifically campaigns for elections and referendums, actually matter? Yet, when thinking from a political science perspective about this question, we need to transcend the narrow instrumental focus of the political actors waging these campaigns; we should also take into account that campaigns may matter in ways not intended by these actors. In order to answer this question, we need, therefore, to flesh out in some more detail the notion of 'campaign effect', which can be seen to encompass a number of dimensions (see Figure 1.3).

First, there is the question of levels of analysis, in which we can distinguish between micro- and macro-effects. Micro-effects are, for the most part, short-term or immediate, referring generally to tangible effects resulting from a particular campaign. By contrast, macro-effects, for the most part (though not always), refer to the longer-term consequences campaigns may have for societies and the political process.

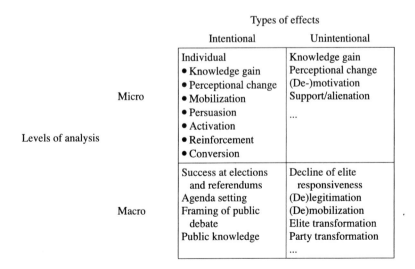

		Types of effects	
		Intentional	Unintentional
Levels of analysis	Micro	Individual • Knowledge gain • Perceptional change • Mobilization • Persuasion • Activation • Reinforcement • Conversion	Knowledge gain Perceptional change (De-)motivation Support/alienation ...
	Macro	Success at elections and referendums Agenda setting Framing of public debate Public knowledge	Decline of elite responsiveness (De)legitimation (De)mobilization Elite transformation Party transformation ...

Figure 1.3 Variations in campaign effects.

A second distinction can be made between the manifest and latent functions of campaigns (Merton 1968). The former refer to the campaign goals of the relevant actors, and the question here is whether or not campaigns really achieve the aims for which they are waged. Can political actors affect the course of governance in democratic societies in ways favourable to them by building up public support through campaigning? From the political actors' instrumental perspective, if a campaign does not deliver the desired results, this amounts to little more than a waste of resources. However, it is conceivable that campaigns, or certain activities within campaigns, may have counter-intentional effects, which actually represent a 'backlash' against the relevant actor. For instance, German voters in 1990 actually evaluated the CDU/CSU's leading candidate more negatively after having watched his party's television spots (Kaid and Holtz-Bacha 1993). Another example is the pro-Maastricht campaign of Danish government parties in 1992 which actually stirred up anti-Maastricht sentiment (Franklin *et al.* 1994a). Popescu and Tóka, in Chapter 4 of this volume, also discuss the case of a campaign that produced what they call a 'boomerang effect'. While such occurrences certainly are not what political actors desire, they have a clear relation to the purposes for which campaigns are waged, albeit a negative one. Actually, as Popescu and Tóka's findings suggest, they may even be a perfectly understandable consequence of certain campaign strategies applied within specific situational contexts. Yet, since campaigning in many ways changes citizens' communication environments, they may also have a range of other consequences – consequences which were not intended, or anticipated, by the actors, and which concern realms of the political process that they did not take into account when they waged their campaigns.

At the micro-level it is of interest whether campaigns reach their intended goals by persuading individuals to vote for particular parties, candidates or referendum alternatives (Burnell and Reeves 1984; Mutz *et al.* 1996). Such outcomes entail many components. Citizens may not initially be aware of all the alternatives they can choose from. Hence unknown candidates must seek to attract the attention of voters and to make themselves known, if they are to receive any consideration when these voters make up their minds about whom to support. Many citizens need to be mobilized before taking part in certain activities like turning out to vote. Latent predispositions to decide in certain ways must be activated, and already formed preferences must be reinforced and stabilised. The ultimate, and certainly most difficult to reach, goal of campaigners, however, is political conversion – attracting undecided voters to one's own fold, or, even more difficult, getting people to decide in ways other than their initial predisposition (Lazarsfeld *et al.* 1968 [1944]). To win electoral support, political actors may also find it important to shape voters' perceptions of their own electoral prospects, in order to stimulate 'bandwagon effects' or tactical voting (Schmitt-Beck 1996a, b). In so far as campaigns concern issues, political actors aim at an increased saliency of certain problems among their target audiences. In addition, they promote particular frames for these issues in the hope that these gain general acceptance as the way they should be depicted. With regard to information campaigns it is worth considering whether or not citizens actually learn what they are intended to learn through exposure to campaign communication.

In some respects, the unintentional effects of campaigns may be even more interesting. From being exposed to campaign communications, voters may become motivated to follow politics more closely on the news, and thereby become better informed about politics more generally (i.e. about a wider range of issues than those focused on in the campaign). On the other hand, as discussed by Norris (in Chapter 8 of this volume), concern is often raised that the on-going transformation in the nature of campaigning (and its reflection in the media's political reportage) may have had a detrimental effect on citizens' attitudes towards the political process and its actors (Patterson 1993; Cappella and Jamieson 1997). Levels of political cynicism may be on the rise as a result of certain styles of campaigning, so that voters eventually become de-motivated. In particular the recent trend towards negative campaigning, especially pronounced in the United States, has given rise to such worries (Lau *et al.* 1999).

At the macro-level, looking at election and referendum campaigns from a Schumpeterian/Downsian perspective, the straightforward goals of maximizing vote shares, electoral/referendum victory and taking control of government come into perspective. In this sense the macro outcome of a campaign is the aggregation of myriad individual occurrences of learning, mobilization, activation, reinforcement and conversion as depicted above, and it is interesting to explore in what ways specific individual-level effects combine to produce particular patterns of results. Do campaigns, for instance, primarily activate latent predispositions so that election results are to be understood as the manifestations of latent socio-political cleavage structures of societies, as proposed, for instance, by studies in the Columbia tradition (Lazarsfeld *et al.* 1968 [1944]; Finkel 1993; Finkel and Schrott 1995)? Or can they bring about real aggregate changes in support shares for the various parties and thus be decisive for winning or losing an election, as is suggested by recent theorizing about the increasingly volatile electorates (Dalton and Wattenberg 2000)? While many campaigns are waged primarily to reach immediate tangible results at crucial decisions like elections or referendums, issue-based campaigns aim rather at long-term changes of public opinion. They are conscious attempts to set the agenda and define the terms of public debate.

At least as important as the question of whether political actors can achieve their political goals by waging campaigns is the question of whether the increasing relevance of campaigning in the political process of modern democracies has ramifications for the very nature of democratic politics itself. If political actors were able to affect the course of governance in ways favourable to them by building up public support through campaigning, questions would arise over the quality of the democratic linkage between elites and citizens. Through successful campaigns political actors would become capable, at least to some degree, of defining the terms upon which they are evaluated by the citizens to whom they are accountable. Elite responsiveness could be reduced as political actors seek to shift public debate into more symbolic arenas of conflict, thereby distracting attention from problem areas where solutions are difficult to attain. As Bartels notes, '[p]erhaps the most important question is whether new patterns of electioneering have weakened or severed altogether the connection between elections and government' (1992: 270). In addition, there is the chance that, as campaigning resources replace arguments and political debate, resourceful actors may become unduly advantaged in political competition. Voter alienation and decreasing system legitimacy might be a consequence of such tendencies.

Campaign politics may thus have implications for political culture, but it may also change the political process in other important respects, including the nature of the political actors themselves. As Ruostetsaari and Mattila observe in Chapter 6 of this volume, the personalized style of campaigning encouraged by the Finnish open-list system affects the character of the parliamentary elite: traditional party politicians are increasingly being replaced by amateur, personality candidates who are publicly known for their non-political merits and who are capable of private fund raising. Declining memberships of parties and other organizations, and a shift towards 'medialities' instead of 'personalities' in leadership elections, are other trends that may be caused by the rising centrality of campaigning in contemporary democracies.

The study of campaign effects

Whether campaigns matter is certainly an under-researched question. None the less, over the years it has attracted the attention of a range of scholars. It is useful to review some of this literature so as to locate this volume in its wider context. In the space available, however, it is not possible to do justice to the literature there has been; all we can do is sketch out some of the main trends in the study of campaign effects. The great majority of publications in this area focus on election campaigns, applying an instrumental perspective, by concentrating on the intentional effects of campaigning, either on the micro or the macro level of analysis. These studies, in broad terms, break down into three main groupings.

First, there are those studies that are, properly speaking, not so much studies of campaigning but rather studies of what happens during campaign *periods*. They are often not particularly interested in any details of particular campaigns but basically treat time as a proxy for direct measurements of political actors' campaign activities. At the base of this approach is the notion that somewhere between time t_0, when the campaign period presumably started, and t_1, polling day, there are a range of factors which can influence the vote, prominent among which are the campaigns waged by the parties and the candidates. Therefore, the degree to which there is evidence of a change – in the vote, in the inclination to vote, in the degree of importance attached to particular issues, etc. – can be accounted for, at least in part, by the campaign (e.g. Stöss 1997; Campbell 2000). Lazarsfeld's seminal study of the US presidential election of 1940 is a classic example of this approach (Lazarsfeld *et al.* 1968 [1944]; see also Finkel 1993; Finkel and Schrott 1995).

Often, the research in this tradition breaks the campaign process down into key *stages*, or *events* – such as primaries, party conventions or television debates – assessing voter tendencies around the same time. The assumption here is that, since the campaign organizations are concentrating their resources on these events, they provide ideal campaign high points where it can be expected that voter reaction will be significant. Needless to say, the United States is the main focus of attention, reflecting trends in scholarship and the nature of the electoral process there. For instance, Bartels (1988) shows how attitudes and opinions are formed over the course of presidential primaries. Another set of studies have examined the party selection conventions, finding evidence of significant 'bumps' in level of support for the presidential candidate after the relevant convention (e.g. Holbrook 1996). There have also been a series of studies assessing the extent to which television debates can influence voters, whether by increasing their awareness of candidates (Katz and Feldman 1962; Chaffee and Dennis 1979; Sears and Chaffee 1979), or affecting their opinions on major campaign issues (Abramowitz 1978; Lanoue and Schrott 1989). Not all of this research has been on US campaigns; there have also been studies on television debates and their effects in Canada (Lanoue 1991; Johnston *et al.* 1992) and Germany (Schrott and Lanoue 1989). Although some of these studies do apply a more fine-grained lens, for instance by inspecting specific features of campaign events more closely (e.g. Shaw and Roberts 2000), the basic message of analyses in this strand of research is whether or not it pays to campaign at all. They are less interested in whether and how differences between campaigns become relevant for their effects. Yet it is exactly the many options concerning details with which political actors are preoccupied when they start to plan and conduct a campaign. They hardly spend a thought on whether to campaign or not; to decide about the *how* is what keeps their minds busy, always in the hope that they can raise sufficient resources and choose the right communication strategies.

Responding to this, a second stream of campaign effects research goes inside the black box of the campaign organization and its activities, usually zeroing in on one component of campaigning and measuring the influence this might have on voters. These studies are primarily interested in the relevance of differences in the *resources* political actors invest for campaign purposes. They seek to unravel whether variables like campaign expenditures (in general or for specific purposes) or activists' manpower make a difference to the success of campaigns. Much of the early literature in this tradition focused on the local campaign. More recently, and reflecting the sorts of campaign shifts outlined in Table 1.1, the focus has switched to features of the national campaign, with particular emphasis on campaign advertising. Studies on local campaign effects date back to Harold Gosnell's (1927) pioneering research of the 1920s. Indeed, it is the title of Gosnell's book, *Getting Out the Vote*, which summarizes much of the findings of this predominantly US research, i.e. that the efforts of local party organizations affect voter turnout, but not voter persuasion.

There have been two main research methods (thoroughly reviewed in Weir 1985). First a series of studies have sought to assess the effects of strong local party organizations on the vote. A prominent indicator of a party's organizational 'strength' is the amount of money it has to spend in the district. Given the relative ease of access to data on campaign finance, this has spawned a large literature in the United States and the United Kingdom on the effects of campaign spending on the vote, which has found clear evidence of an effect (Jacobson 1978, 1980; Copeland 1983; Seyd and Whiteley 1994; Johnston and Pattie 1995). Also very prominent have been the studies that specifically set out to explore the effects of local party canvassing (e.g. Clarke *et al.* 1979; Pattie *et al.* 1994; Huckfeldt and Sprague 1995; Denver and Hands 1997).

In the latter part of the 1970s, and reflecting the centralization of campaign practices, the academic community shifted its attention to national-level campaign activities and their effects, particularly television advertising and party election broadcasts. The pioneering research was by Patterson and McClure (1976), who demonstrated how television spots have clear cognitive effects, contributing to a general increase in levels of awareness of the candidates and their policies. It has also been shown that advertisements can affect voters' opinions on issues (Kaid 1981; Johnston *et al.* 1992), candidate images (Kaid and Holtz-Bacha 1995), and even election outcomes (Shaw 1999).

Campaign effects studies in this second stream share in common an interest in the hardware of campaigns – so far mostly with a focus on expenditure, local campaign effort or advertising, but recently also supplemented by new topics, like the contribution of hired consultants to the success of campaigns (Medvic 2002). A third stream of research, which has become more prominent only of late, has more interest in the software of campaigning, in features of the campaign *message* and how this may impact on the voter. Prominent here are the studies on negative campaigning and how, among other things, this may be responsible for depressing voter turnout (Ansolabehere and Iyengar 1995; Lau *et al.* 1999). A study of the 1997 British election suggests that it is important for parties to run a campaign that is thematically undistracted by other competitors or external events and that stays 'on message' (Norris *et al.* 1999). Another analysis indicates that in the 1983 German election the Christian Democrats' campaign positively influenced voters' perceptions of the party's ability to solve the problems highlighted in its campaign, thus arguably contributing to its election victory (Bowler *et al.* 1992a); similarly clear-cut findings could not be provided for other elections, however (Brunner 1999). Taking into account that campaigns usually focus not only on 'hard' issues but also on vaguer political symbols, studies from the United States and Germany demonstrate that such communication strategies may also be successful, both directly with regard to image building and indirectly regarding the vote itself (Sullivan *et al.* 1992; Schmitt-Beck 2002).

Towards a comparative study of campaign effects

In the previous section we saw how much of the research in this area has concentrated on election campaigns and has tended to focus on the United States, though there have been some studies on the United Kingdom and (more sporadically) some other countries. Clearly, there is a need to widen the scope of analysis to take account of other sorts of campaign contexts and campaign scenarios, and to consider also the latent dimension of campaign effects such as, for instance, on attitudes towards the political system.

One of the problems with the research on campaign effects is that it is located at the interface of various sub-disciplines of political science – among them electoral studies, political communications research and party sociology, to name a few of the obvious ones – but does not fit easily into any one of them. To do this subject justice requires a multi-disciplinary approach, which can pick up on the rich range of themes explored in these and other sub-disciplines, such as: partisan dealignment (which, as Chapter 2 reveals, has a direct bearing on 'late deciders'), the issue salience model (and the related theme of issue 'priming'), electoral sociology (candidates and voting decisions) and the study of campaign and party professionalization. Such a multi-disciplinary objective lies behind the idea of this book. In the chapters that follow, the authors examine: the campaign process in a series of different national contexts (including established and new democracies) and for different types of campaigns (both presidential and parliamentary elections, and referendums); different features of the campaign process; different forms of campaign effects (e.g. cognitive or persuasive, positive or negative, intended or unintended); and a wide range of conditions which facilitate or impede such effects.

In Chapter 2, Ian McAllister uses longitudinal national election study data from the United States, Britain and Australia to plot the growing prominence of voters who delay their decision until the campaign period. The growth of late deciders is related to social modernization, more specifically to increasing political interest and decreasing partisanship. The chapter finds evidence that a significant proportion of these late deciders are not irrational, floating voters but 'calculating' voters, paying close attention to the campaign and therefore susceptible to campaign influence, although more to its issue content than to the emotional gimmickry. In their study of the Swiss 1999 election, Romain Lachat and Pascal Sciarini (Chapter 3) also place stress on the significance of late deciders. Following John Zaller's (1992) model of opinion formation, they use cantonal panel data to assess the effects of campaigns on voting behaviour. They provide clear evidence of such campaign effects, depending on the intensity of campaigning, with this being most pronounced among more attentive late deciders.

In Chapter 4, Marina Popescu and Gábor Tóka focus on an opportunity structure for electioneering that is particular to many new democracies – the ability of governing parties to instrumentalize the state-controlled broadcast media as campaign tools. Their study of the 1994 and 1998 parliamentary elections in Hungary suggests that this seeming advantage for governing parties is actually a mixed blessing. Analyses of panel survey data indicate that biased television programmes may help government parties, but only to a certain extent. If their onesidedness becomes too blatant, it may easily backfire and turn voters off, causing a 'boomerang effect'. The focus of Chapter 5 is on 'priming' in recent Canadian elections. Elisabeth Gidengil and her colleagues use rolling cross-section data to explore the extent to which leadership and issue evaluations changed in importance for voters' electoral preferences during the campaigns. They find that the extent to which priming occurs is contingent, depending on the particular circumstances of the campaign, in particular concerning the prevailing thematic agenda of public debate.

In the next two chapters the focus shifts to campaigns at the local level, following the second main tradition of campaign effects studies that were outlined in the previous section. In Chapter 6, Ilkka Ruostetsarri and Mikko Mattila examine the campaign in a Finnish electoral district during the 1999 parliamentary election, based on a survey of successful and unsuccessful candidates. Finland provides a fascinating case for analysis because of its unusual electoral system, which is candidate-focused and therefore requires candidates to chase personal votes, placing a high premium on the individual campaigns of candidates and their support groups. In this study, and also in Denver and Hands's analysis of constituency campaigning in Britain in 1997 (Chapter 7) – another system which promotes emphasis on the local campaign – there is clear evidence that the local campaigns mattered, though in the latter case this is found to vary with the party: the Conservative campaign, if anything, had a depressing effect on its vote. In addition, Denver and Hands's survey of party agents suggests that targeted 'stage III'-style constituency campaigning so far has not surpassed more traditional modes of constituency campaigning in terms of effectiveness.

In Chapter 8, the attention shifts to macro-campaign effects, and in particular to the theme of the unintended consequences of campaigns. Pippa Norris uses US election studies data across five decades to assess the impact of party campaigns and media coverage of them on civic engagement in US politics. Contrary to the fashionable view that such effects tend to be negative – the 'media malaise' hypothesis – the evidence Norris uncovers, if anything, points to a 'virtuous circle' of civic engagement promoted by voter attention to campaigns and media coverage of them.

The final two chapters deal with campaign effects in the context of referendum campaigns. Chapter 9 sets the scene with a large-scale comparative analysis of the role of referendum campaigns. As Lawrence LeDuc points out, these are a classic case of voting based on low party identification and late decision making, which by their very nature are bound to involve a far higher level of voter volatility than in most election scenarios. Similar to the findings of Chapters 2 and 3, late decision making is found to be significant. As in Chapter 5, campaign effects are found to be contingent on the type of issue being fought over. In Chapter 10, Michael Bützer and Lionel Marquis examine the opinion formation process in thirty-two Swiss federal referendums, once again applying Zaller's model of opinion formation. Consistent with Zaller's theory, they find that campaign effects are influenced by the degree of conflict between the competing elite as well as by individual voters' political predisposition and level of political awareness.

Between them, these nine studies provide a rich range of different scenarios of political campaign effects based, among other things, on national contexts, methodological approaches, types of campaign, sets of actors, types of voter and aspects of the influence process. The last chapter of the book seeks to draw the threads together, to show how collectively these studies demonstrate some important steps forward in the literature on campaign effects, and to set out a stall for further possible research.

2 Calculating or capricious?

The new politics of late deciding voters

Ian McAllister

More than any time since democratization, modern election campaigns bring uncertain outcomes. This change is most visible in the growing proportion of voters who now delay their voting decision until the election campaign is under way. Where once the vast majority of voters entered an election campaign with fixed views about how they would vote, such voters have declined dramatically in numbers. A study of changes in the timing of the vote in twelve OECD democracies found that in all but one (Denmark), there was an increasing trend to delay the voting decision, and in three – Australia, Finland and Sweden – the trend was particularly marked (Dalton *et al.* 2000: 48; see also Gopoian 1994). In short, more voters than ever before are potentially available for conversion during the election campaign, with major consequences for how election campaigns are organized and conducted.

This new phenomenon of the late deciding voter is often traced to partisan dealignment; with fewer voters possessing affective loyalties to the major parties, they enter the election campaign undecided about their vote and therefore more susceptible to the issues, appeals and themes which emerge during the course of the campaign (Crewe 1983; Bowen 1994; Dalton 1996). Such behaviour has usually implied a superficial voting decision, with random events or political personalities subsuming a rational evaluation of the issues. But this change has also occurred at a time when voters are better educated, possess more cognitive skills and display more political interest than ever before (Neuman 1986; Bennett 1988; Nie *et al.* 1996). Does delayed voter decision making imply greater volatility and capriciousness in electoral outcomes, or a more calculating, issue-oriented electorate?

The political behaviour of late deciders has significant implications for the conduct of election campaigns. If late decision making is generally calculating, with voters evaluating party policies for the potential benefits to themselves or to other groups, then the campaign is likely to focus on economic issues. The character of the campaign will be serious and objective, and the parties will appeal to voters' pocketbooks. By contrast, if the voters who delay their decision are capricious, then the parties are more likely to emphasize a single message during the campaign, and to place more weight on subjective factors, such as the personalities of the leaders, a factor that has already assumed greater weight in campaigns (McAllister 1996). The campaign will be organized so as to avoid unpredictable events which might be highlighted by the mass media and compromise the party's central message (Norris *et al.* 1999).

The overwhelming impression conveyed by modern election campaigns is that the parties assume voters are capricious, easily converted and generally ill-informed about the issues (Butler and Ranney 1992; Kavanagh 1995; Swanson and Mancini 1996). This view has gained considerable currency as an interpretation of the electorate as a whole, ever since modern survey techniques were first applied to mass populations (see, for example, McCloskey 1964; Sullivan *et al.* 1982; but cf. Page and Shapiro 1992). But much less is known about the voters who delay their decision – and arguably who are crucial in deciding the election outcome. Are late deciders calculating political actors evaluating information and making an informed choice, or capricious voters prone to being influenced by trivia and superficiality? This chapter addresses this question by examining the timing of the voting decision and its political consequences in three established democracies: Australia, Britain and the United States.

The rise of the late decider

Electoral volatility has been measured in a variety of ways. It is most commonly measured by aggregate interelection changes in party vote shares, and studies have highlighted an increasing degree of volatility starting in the 1970s (Pedersen 1983; Dalton *et al.* 1984; Crewe and Denver 1985; but cf. Bartolini and Mair 1990). At the individual level, national election surveys have been used to show voters' disengagement from the main parties (dealignment); declining turnout and its roots in dissatisfaction with parties (demobilization); and the degree to which voters report doubt about their decision or change their preferences close to polling day (conversion). But it is perhaps the evidence about the increasing proportions who delay their voting decision until the election campaign is under way that is the most persuasive indicator of potential electoral volatility.

Although most national election studies include a question on the timing of the vote, overtime trend data are much harder to find. The United States has the longest time series, starting in 1948, and Figure 2.1 shows the results for voters in the presidential election years between 1948 and 2000.[1] The average proportion of voters in the first two presidential elections who said that they did not decide how to vote until the election campaign was under way is 30 per cent, compared with an average of 40 per cent for the last two elections in the series. However, the figures have varied considerably, from a low of 21 per cent in 1956 to 47 per cent in 1996. The inter-election fluctuations, particularly in the 1950s and 1960s, are caused by incumbency. In elections involving an incumbent President, voters are generally familiar with

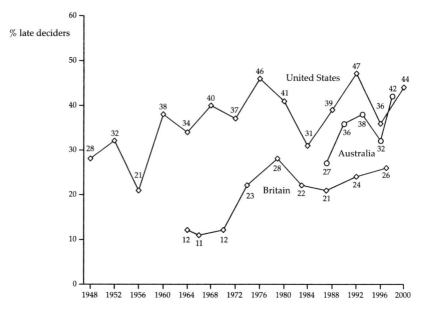

Figure 2.1 Voters deciding during the election campaign.

Sources: American National Election Studies, 1948–2000; Political Change in Britain, 1963–70; British Election Studies, February 1974–97; Australian Election Studies, 1987–98.

Notes
Estimates are the proportion of voters making their voting decision after the election campaign had commenced. In Britain the estimate for 1974 averages the February and October 1974 general elections.

policies and image and are therefore more likely to have made up their minds early. By contrast, the proportion of late deciders is greater when the contest involves non-incumbents.

The effects of an incumbent President seeking re-election are most obvious in the elections prior to 1980. In 1956, just 21 per cent of voters were late deciders, when the incumbent Dwight D. Eisenhower stood for re-election; in 1960, when two new candidates stood, John F. Kennedy and Richard Nixon, the figure climbed to 38 per cent. In the most recent elections the pattern has been less clear. The contest between Ronald Reagan and the incumbent Jimmy Carter in 1980 produced a large proportion of later deciders, but the subsequent re-election of Reagan conformed to the incumbency pattern by producing the second lowest proportion of late deciders in the post-war years. However, during the contest between Bill Clinton and the incumbent George Bush almost half of the electorate were undecided during the course of the campaign, the highest figure since the survey series commenced in 1948. The contest between George W. Bush and Al Gore in 2000 attracted 44 per cent of the electorate as late deciders.

The trend is similar in Britain, although the time series is shorter. Up until 1970, just one in eight voters delayed their decision until the election campaign was under way. However, that proportion almost doubled in 1974,[2] and increased again, to 28 per cent, in 1979. Following a decline in the early 1980s, the trend has once again been towards an increase; in the 1997 general election, just over one in four voters were late deciders. As in the United States, there is some evidence that parties with new leaders and reworked images which are unfamiliar to voters produce more indecision. The highest figure for late deciders occurs in 1979, when the Conservatives' new leader Margaret Thatcher led them to victory against Labour, and in 1997, when John Major and the Conservatives were defeated by New Labour, led by their recently elected leader, Tony Blair. The trend shows that British late deciders have been increasing by 1.9 per cent at each election.[3]

The Australian trend in Figure 2.1 is similar to the United States and Britain, albeit over a shorter period again. In 1987, the first election for which data are available, 27 per cent of voters were late deciders; by the 1998 federal election this had increased to 42 per cent.[4] The only exception to the steady upward trend occurs in the 1996 election, when a long period of Labor rule came to an end with the election of a Liberal-National government promising major economic reform. The inter-election trend suggests an increase in late deciders in Australia of 2.6 per cent.[5] To put this in context, if the observed trend were to continue, by the third federal election following 1998 (due around 2007), half of all voters would not have decided how to vote until the start of the election campaign.

The survey questions on which these trends are based indicate a considerable distribution of opinion. The most recent survey results in Table 2.1 show that the largest group in Australia and Britain is those who decided far in advance of the election campaign. This is a majority of the electorate in Britain, and more than one-third in Australia. In the United States the estimate is complicated by not knowing the identity of the challenger to Al Gore until the Republican Convention; if we combine those who made up their minds when the names of the candidates were known with those who 'knew all along', the total is 47 per cent, again the largest group in the United States. Among the voters in Australia and the United States who made up their minds during the campaign, about one in ten in Australia and one in twenty in the United States delayed their decision until election day itself.

One caveat to the foregoing concerns the validity of the survey responses in accurately measuring the timing of voter decision making. While we assume that the respondents know when they made their voting decision, it could also be argued that voters are often unaware of their own decision-making process, as Lazarsfeld suggested in *The People's Choice* (Lazarsfeld *et al.* 1968 [1944]). Do late deciders really decide late, or do they merely believe that they do so, while their decision is actually set long before the campaign? There are no objective data with which to prove or disprove this possibility,

Table 2.1 Timing of the voting decision in recent elections

Australia, 1998		Britain, 1997		United States, 2000	
Long time ago	35	Long time ago	57	Knew all along	13
Before election announced	14	Some time last year	8	When candidate announced	34
When election announced	9	Some time this year	9	During conventions	9
Total pre-campaign	*58*		*74*		*56*
First weeks of campaign	14	During campaign	26	Post-convention	22
Few days before election day	17			Last two weeks of campaign	17
Election day	11			Election day	5
Total campaign	*42*		*26*		*44*
Total	100		100		100
N	1,886		2,849		1,160

Sources: Australian Election Study, 1998; British Election Study, 1997; American National Election Study, 2000.

Note
The questions were: (Australia) 'When did you decide how you would definitely vote in this election?'; (Britain) 'How long ago did you decide that you would definitely vote the way you did?'; (United States) 'How long before the election did you decide that you were going to vote the way you did?'

since we are always dependent on what the voter reports about when they made the decision. Two factors tend to support the general reliability of these self-reports about late decision making. The trends show a clear increase in late decision making first over time and, second, across a wide range of advanced democracies. If the self-reports about the timing of the vote are unreliable, the factors making them unreliable have been replicated across time and space – a not impossible but highly unlikely scenario.

Interest and the timing of the vote

By any standards, there are increasingly large numbers of voters who are potentially available for conversion during the course of an election campaign. As noted earlier, this high level of apparent indecision could reflect apathy and disengagement, with particular implications for how election campaigns are organized. But indecision could equally well be a consequence of considered judgement, with voters evaluating the information that emerges during the course of the election campaign from the mass media and from their family, work and social networks. In short, the timing of the vote itself does not permit us to make any differentiation between possibly very different types of late deciders. The information that enables us to discriminate among late deciders is whether or not the voter cared about who won the election.

Ever since the early voting studies found that voters knew little about politics, there has been an on-going debate about the sophistication of the electorate, and about whether the trend is increasing or remaining static.[6] Philip Converse and *The American Voter* authors argued that it was static (Campbell *et al.* 1960; Converse 1964), an argument supported more recently by Smith (1989). Others have argued that rising educational attainments, by enhancing cognitive skills, should increase political sophistication and produced evidence to support their view (for reviews, see Abramson 1983; Page and Shapiro 1992). Although these studies have disagreed about the direction of the trend, they have generally agreed that caring about who won the election is a key indicator of political interest. We would predict that late deciders who cared about the election outcome would be accumulating information on which to make a calculated decision, while those who did not care would be more capricious in their choice.

In both Australia and Britain there is a clear trend in the direction of voters increasingly caring about who wins the election, with a slight decline in both countries in the most recent elections. Nevertheless, in each case the proportion is increasing by between one-quarter and one-third of 1 per cent per year over the observed period.[7] There is a different pattern in the United States, where interest remained stable during the late 1950s and 1960s, only to decline significantly through the 1970s in the wake of Watergate and defeat in the Vietnam War. It was this trend which led some to argue that this was the cause of declining turnout in presidential elections (Abramson

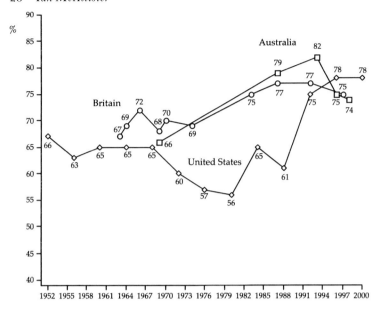

Figure 2.2 Voters caring who won the election.

Sources: American National Election Studies, 1952 2000; Australian National Political Attitudes Survey, 1969; Australian Election Studies, 1987 98; Political Change in Britain, 1963 70; British Election Studies, February 1974 97.

Note
The questions were: (Australia) 'Would you say you cared a good deal which party won the federal election or that you didn't care very much which party won?'; (Britain) (1963, 1969) 'Would you say that you usually care a good deal which party wins a general election or that you don't care very much which party wins?'; (1964, 1966, 1970 97) 'Would you say that you cared a good deal which party won the election or that you didn't care very much which party won?'; (United States) 'Generally speaking, would you say that you personally care a good deal which party [1992, 1996: who] wins the presidential election this fall, or that you don't care very much which party wins?'

1983: 294). Since its nadir in 1980, the trend has reversed (while the overall decline in turnout has continued); in 1996 and 2000 no less than 78 per cent of voters said that they cared who won.[8]

Whatever the nature and origins of these patterns, caring about the election outcome enables us to discriminate between our hypothesized calculating and capricious late deciders. In Australia, only 43 per cent of those who said that they decided on their vote on election day cared about the outcome, compared with no less than 87 per cent who made up their minds a long time before the election. The pattern is similar, though less dramatic, in Britain and the United States; for example, 75 per cent of election day deciders in the United States cared about the outcome, compared with 93 per cent deciding well in advance of the election.[9]

Using the timing of the voting decision and whether or not the voter cared about the election outcome enables us to identify four groups within the

Timing of the vote decision

Interest in election outcome	Before campaign		During campaign	
	Partisan		Calculating	
Cares	Australia	49	Australia	25
	Britain	64	Britain	18
	United States	51	United States	36
	Disengaged		Capricious	
Doesn't care	Australia	9	Australia	17
	Britain	10	Britain	8
	United States	5	United States	8

Figure 2.3 Types of voter and their distribution in the most recent election (%).

Sources: Australian Election Study, 1998; British Election Study, 1997; American National Election Study, 2000.

electorate. Figure 2.3 shows that the largest group of voters in each of the three countries, based on the most recent election, are *partisans*, who cared about the outcome and who made their decision before the election campaign had begun. Despite the process of dealignment, most voters remain loyal to a political party and decide on their vote well in advance of the campaign. Voters who are *disengaged* also decided before the campaign got under way, but display little interest in the outcome; they are the least numerous of the four groups, and in voluntary voting systems would probably swing from election to election between turning out to vote and abstention. Nevertheless, one in ten British voters fall into this category, and one in twenty in the United States.

The remaining two groups are the main focus of interest: they decide on their vote while the election campaign is under way, with major consequences for the conduct of the campaign. *Calculating* late deciders constitute one in every four voters in Australia, one in three in the United States, and just under one in five in Britain; they are interested in the election outcome and, we would hypothesize, carefully weigh the consequences of each party's policies on their individual economic situation. *Capricious* voters are most numerous in Australia, at 17 per cent – presumably because of the system of compulsory voting, which requires every citizen to vote under the threat of a court-imposed fine (Mackerras and McAllister 1999). By contrast, such voters make up about one in every five voters in Britain and the United States. We expect such voters to be swayed by random factors, since they have little interest in the outcome of the election.

Only the United States has over-time data with which to examine how the distribution of these four groups has changed within the electorate. Partisans, who care about the outcome and decide in advance of the election campaign, have remained consistently the largest group in the post-war years, as we would expect. They were least numerous during the 1970s, and constituted

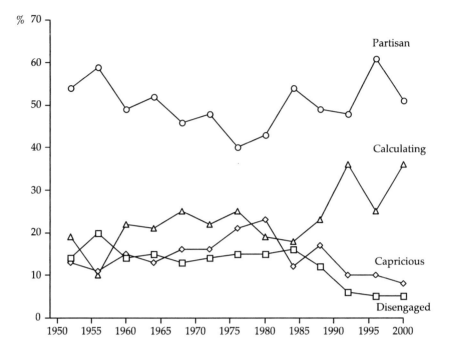

Figure 2.4 Types of voter in US elections, 1952–2000.

Source: American National Election Study, 1948 96, cumulative file; American National Election Study, 2000.

Note
Each of the four groups is defined by the timing of their voting decision and by whether or not they cared about the outcome of the election. See Figure 2.3 for details.

just 40 per cent of all voters in 1976, following Watergate. They peaked in 1956, when 59 per cent fell into the category, and again in 1996, when the figure was 61 per cent. Calculating late deciders have generally been the next largest group, reaching peaks of 36 per cent in 1992 and 2000. However, during the post-1952 period they have grown considerably in size, from an average of 17 per cent in the first three elections in the time series to an average of 32 per cent in the last three elections. Both capricious late deciders and disengaged voters have experienced declines, particularly since the mid-1980s.

Explaining late decision making

How do we explain the rise of the late deciding voter? More specifically, how do we explain the two divergent trends that appear to be under way, based on different levels of political interest in the election campaign? The most obvious explanation is partisan dealignment. Traditional party identification theories explain how most voters cast a ballot through their standing partisan predisposition; these predispositions are based on affective party ties or on group identities linked with parties. In the ideal partisanship model, election campaigns do not sway voting intentions, and most individuals ultimately cast a vote for their preferred party. Partisan dealignment implies that fewer voters begin the election cycle with such predispositions, making them more susceptible to the short-term issues and themes of the campaign. We might expect dealigned voters to be more capricious than calculating voters, since they will have less interest in the election outcome and lack the relevant party cues with which to structure their vote.[10]

The growth in the number of reasoned late deciders, at least in the United States, suggests that a second change in Western mass publics may be involved: social modernization. As educational levels have risen in virtually all Western democracies, there are reasons to expect that this has enhanced the political skills and abilities of contemporary publics, in turn stimulating political interest and knowledge (Teixeira 1992; Topf 1995; Inglehart 1997). The cross-national evidence suggests that there is a secular trend in increasing political interest generally, and interest in elections more specifically (Dalton *et al.* 2000). However, there are also significant variations within as well as between countries. The United States is the most distinctive, with interest declining following the peaks which occurred during the urban unrest and Vietnam War protest activity of the 1960s and 1970s.[11] In Australia, interest increased in a linear trend until the late 1990s, when it declined.

Some scholars have questioned the assumption that social modernization should stimulate political interest. Robert Putnam (1993) has identified the potentially atomizing influences of modernization on the accumulated social capital within a society. He argues that some of these same modernizing forces, such as television and changing employment patterns, have demobilized citizens, leading to decreasing involvement in social and political groups. The net effect is declining trust and, as a consequence, reduced economic development as the social cohesion necessary to ensure economic growth dissipates. We can measure social capital by the extent of the social networks that the individual possesses, here reflected in marriage, trade union membership and religiosity.[12] But we can also measure social capital by trust in government, which is arguably a consequence of free, competitive elections (Rahn *et al.* 1999).

These hypotheses are tested in Table 2.2, which presents logistic regression estimates predicting calculating versus capricious late deciders, and partisans versus the disengaged. The independent variables reflect the three main explanations discussed above, together with controls for gender and age. The results show a remarkable degree of consistency across the three countries. The major influence in differentiating both sets of voters is dealignment, with calculating and partisan late deciders displaying significantly more partisanship than either capricious or disengaged late deciders, net of other things. The effects of dealignment are particularly strong in the

Table 2.2 Explaining different types of decision making

Variable	Calculating v. capricious						Partisan v. disengaging					
	Australia		Britain		United States		Australia		Britain		United States	
	Est.	(SE)	Est.	(SE)	Est.	(SE)	Est.	(SE)	Est.	(SE)	Est.	(SE)
Dealignment												
No partisanship	−0.87	(0.43)	−1.97*	(0.29)	1.33	(0.61)	−1.33	(0.68)	−2.40*	(0.33)	−3.95*	(1.14)
Weak partisanship	−1.36*	(0.20)	−0.98*	(0.19)	−0.72	(0.55)	−1.30*	(0.22)	−1.32*	(0.14)	−2.90*	(1.02)
Social modernization												
Tertiary education	−0.19	(0.24)	−0.19	(0.24)	0.12	(0.41)	0.02	(0.28)	0.14	(0.27)	−0.32	(0.56)
Strong political interest	1.09*	(0.24)	1.25*	(0.23)	1.48*	(0.49)	1.24*	(0.27)	1.12*	(0.18)	0.93	(0.47)
Social capital												
Social networks	−0.16	(0.21)	0.21	(0.19)	0.47	(0.28)	−0.38	(0.23)	0.45*	(0.17)	0.04	(0.35)
Trust in government	−0.24	(0.21)	−0.18	(0.19)	−0.41	(0.26)	0.52	(0.24)	0.11	(0.15)	−0.19	(0.34)
Controls												
Gender (male)	−0.47*	(0.20)	−0.27	(0.18)	0.03	(0.27)	−0.28	(0.22)	−0.01	(0.14)	0.06	(0.01)
Age (years)	−0.01	(0.01)	−0.01	(0.01)	0.01	(0.01)	−0.01	(0.01)	−0.01	(0.01)	−0.01	(0.01)
Constant	1.29		2.05		1.13		1.29		−2.57		5.36	
Pseudo R^2	15.6		11.3		6.8		12.9		12.9		12.2	
N	559		736		421		844		2,090		469	

Sources: Australian Election Study, 1998; British Election Study, 1997; American National Election Study, 2000.

Notes

* Statistically significant at $p < 0.01$, two-tailed.

Weak partisanship is 'not very strong' party identification; social capital is having at least two of the following attributes: being married, being a trade union member and attending a church least once a month; strong political interest is 'good deal' of interest in politics. All variables are scored zero or one except for age, which is in single years.

United States, where dealignment has progressed furthest among the three countries in the past three decades.

The second consistently important influence is social modernization, reflected in political interest. In all three countries, interest is important in distinguishing between the two groups of later deciders. However, the other aspect of social modernization, tertiary education, has no direct impact on late decision making, confirming the finding that its major direct role is through enhancing political interest, rather than shaping political behaviour *per se* (Nie *et al.* 1996: 76–8). The results suggest no significant role for social capital, measured either by social networks or political trust; whatever its impact on other aspects of behaviour, it has no consequences for late decision making in any of the three countries. Similarly, the controls exert no significant effects. Overall, the two sets of late deciders are shaped first by dealignment, and by social modernization, via different levels of political interest.

The political consequences

In principle, the presence of large numbers of late deciders within an electorate should result in greater electoral volatility and increased uncertainty in outcomes. In practice, other things being equal, the greater the randomness in the factors that affect such voters, the less their impact on the outcome should be. However, the results have suggested that the largest group of late deciders (and the one which is growing at the fastest rate) is calculating voters. It is this group which should be crucial to electoral success or failure at the polls. But, prior to the vote itself, we need to consider how such voters behave in terms of their patterns of campaign participation and media attentiveness.

One potential consequence of the increase in late deciders is in the level of campaign participation. As levels of education and political interest increase across mass publics, we would expect greater involvement in election campaigns. Based on a survey of twenty-nine countries in the 1970s and 1980s, Powell (1982) argued that social modernization promoted strong links between parties and social groups, thereby increasing political participation. This prediction was largely supported by the data on campaign participation across the twenty-nine countries. The contrary view is that elections are primarily party affairs; parties organize and structure the activities that take place during elections. With continuing partisan dealignment, weakening social cleavages and a declining membership base, parties have fewer resources with which to mobilize voters. The most recent evidence suggests that it is the latter which is taking place. Wattenberg (2000) shows that across the twenty established democracies of the OECD, turnout has declined significantly in eighteen of them, and the declines have been most precipitous since the mid-1980s, after the publication of Powell's study.

Declining turnout is clearly associated with a long-term decrease in the proportion of disengaged voters in the United States, already observed in

Figure 2.2. As dealignment increases, disengaged voters are more likely to choose abstention, thereby leaving a smaller number of their counterparts among those who actually cast a ballot. There is some support for this proposition; the correlation between the proportion of disengaged voters and turnout in presidential elections since 1952 is 0.46. We would also assume that it is a factor in Britain, although it is impossible to test it empirically since sufficient over-time data are unavailable. In Australia, the system of compulsory voting ensures that all enrolled voters cast a ballot, and around 95 per cent comply at each federal election. However, when asked whether they would vote if participation was voluntary, just 69 per cent of disengaged voters in 1998 said that they would, compared with 95 per cent of partisans, 90 per cent of calculating late deciders and 64 per cent of capricious late deciders. Turnout is therefore a mechanism for reducing the number of disengaged voters who participate in an election, as well as reducing the number of capricious late deciders.

In addition to turnout, other aspects of electoral participation are influenced by late decision making. In both Australia and the United States (data for Britain are unavailable), partisans are most likely to say that they talked to others about how to vote; almost half said that they participated in this type of electoral activity. Disengaged voters in the United States are least likely to talk to others; just 17 per cent reported doing this in the 2000 presidential election. In Australia, about half of all calculating late deciders talked to others, compared with 38 per cent of their counterparts in the United States. Other forms of campaign participation that require more commitment – attending meetings, contributing money or working for a party or candidate – display much lower levels across the four groups. The most notable finding is that almost one in five partisans in the United States engaged in such activities. There is, then, a clear link between the four groups and the major forms of campaign participation.

A second area in which the rise of late deciders may have political consequences is in the conduct of election campaigns. To be sure, election campaigns have changed considerably over the past half-century; they are now highly professional affairs, involving public relations consultants and media specialists, and the party is less an entity with a history and an established platform than a political product that must be marketed to its best advantage (O'Shaughnessy 1990). The growth of the electronic media, particularly television, has made it easier to communicate events and issues through personalities, and voters themselves find it easier to hold an individual leader accountable than an institution such as a party (McAllister 1996). Overall, the modernization of political communications may have contributed to an increasing personalization of politics, regardless of whether the system is presidential or parliamentary (see above, pp. 30–3; Swanson and Mancini 1996).

There is little disagreement that these changes in mass communications have focused more popular attention than ever before on political leaders,

Table 2.3 Campaign participation

Per cent participated in:	Disengaged	Partisan	Capricious	Calculating
Talked to people about vote				
Australia	29 (167)	45 (916)	33 (321)	49 (467)
United States	17 (52)	47 (594)	23 (91)	38 (416)
Attended meeting, contributed money, worked for party				
Australia	1 (167)	6 (916)	3 (321)	3 (467)
United States	6 (52)	19 (594)	5 (91)	12 (416)

Sources: Australian Election Study, 1998; American National Election Study, 2000.

Notes
Numbers of cases in parentheses. The questions were: (Australia) 'During the election campaign did you do any of the following things . . . talk to people about why they should vote for or against one of the parties or candidates . . . go to any political meetings or rallies . . . continue money to a political party or election candidate . . . do any work for a party or election candidate?'; (United States) 'We would like to find out about some of the things people do to help a party or a candidate win an election. During the campaign, did you talk to any people and try to show them why they should vote for or against one of the parties or candidates? Did you go to any political meetings, rallies, speeches, dinners or things like that in support of a particular candidate? Did you do any (other) work for one of the parties or candidates? During an election year people are often asked to make a contribution to support campaigns. Did you give money to an individual candidate running for public office?'

largely through the coverage of politics on television. In turn, this has weakened the discussion of policy issues during election campaigns, and what discussion occurs in the media is often superficial and personalized (for a review, see Semetko 1996). Moreover, aware of the potentially large number of voters who are available for conversion, politicians and their advisers ensure that their popular appeal is encapsulated in little more than simple slogans ('sound bites') which are constantly repeated ('remaining on message') (Norris *et al.* 1999). They also go to extreme lengths to ensure that random events and accidents which might be televisual are avoided at all costs.[13] In Australia this is reflected in a greater propensity among calculating late deciders to use policy issues as a basis for their choice.[14]

In principle, calculating late deciders should display most media attentiveness during the campaign, since they are sufficiently interested in the outcome to seek the additional information required to make their decision. This is not confirmed by the results in Table 2.4, and in all three countries, partisans are at least as – and in some cases more – attentive than calculating late deciders. The level of television viewing of politics is particularly high in Australia (over 7 on the 0–10 scale, for the two groups), followed by the United States and last Britain. The frequency of following the election on radio and newspapers is also more common in Australia than in the United States or, in the case of newspapers only, Britain.

The final area in which the rise of the late deciders has changed political behaviour is in the vote choice itself. In principle, the presence of large

Table 2.4 Mass media attentiveness during campaigns

Medium	Disengaged	Partisan	Capricious	Calculating
Television				
Australia	5.5 (153)	7.2 (886)	5.3 (300)	7.4 (453)
Britain	2.8 (222)	4.6 (1,662)	2.8 (168)	4.3 (465)
United States	4.1 (52)	6.7 (593)	4.1 (91)	6.1 (416)
Radio				
Australia	3.6 (142)	5.1 (807)	3.6 (290)	5.4 (424)
Britain		—n.a.—		
United States	1.6 (52)	3.2 (594)	1.6 (90)	2.7 (415)
Newspapers				
Australia	4.7 (163)	6.2 (908)	4.5 (318)	6.3 (463)
Britain	2.4 (143)	4.3 (1,098)	2.4 (101)	4.0 (273)
United States	2.5 (40)	5.0 (472)	2.9 (63)	4.7 (335)

Sources: Australian Election Study, 1998; British Election Study, 1997; American National Election Study, 2000.

Notes
Mean scores, 0 to 10; numbers of cases in parentheses. The questions were: (Australia) 'How much attention did you pay to reports about the election campaign in the newspapers? Did you follow the election campaign news on the television? And did you follow the election campaign news on the radio?'; (Britain) 'People pay attention to different parts of [newspapers/television news] . . . how much attention do you pay to stories about politics?; (United States) 'Did you watch any programs about the campaign on television? Did you listen to any speeches or discussions about the campaign on the radio? How much attention did you pay to newspaper articles about the campaign for President?' In each case, coding is from 0 (least attention) to 10 (most attention).

numbers of voters within the electorate who remain undecided until the campaign is under way should increase volatility. There is considerable evidence that volatility has indeed increased, but to what extent is it attributable to the greater number of late deciders? At one level, shifts in voter support to minor parties and independent candidates represent one indicator of greater electoral volatility, particularly since it is now clear that such support is often a protest vote, and is rarely sustained past one or, at most, two elections (see, for example, Crewe and King 1995). But other indicators are also important. In a political system that allows voters the option, the likelihood of choosing competing parties for different levels of government is one indicator of volatility; another is whether the voter thought of changing his or her vote and whether, in the event, he or she actually does so. Table 2.5 shows the results for these four indicators, for each of the four voter groups.

Based on the evidence in Table 2.5, there is little doubt that late deciders are significantly more volatile in their political behaviour when compared with those who decided their vote before the election campaign commenced. Averaged over all of the measures, capricious late deciders are more than three times more likely to be volatile compared with partisans, while

Table 2.5 Electoral volatility (%)

Indicator	Disengaged	Partisan	Capricious	Calculating
Minor party vote				
Australia	21 (151)	9 (881)	30 (291)	20 (450)
Britain	32 (276)	17 (1,782)	41 (220)	40 (499)
United States	6 (52)	2 (594)	10 (91)	5 (416)
Split ticket				
Australia	13 (167)	12 (916)	27 (321)	26 (467)
United States	25 (36)	14 (455)	18 (60)	29 (317)
Considered changing vote				
Australia	23 (161)	17 (905)	45 (310)	45 (455)
Britain	23 (276)	19 (1,781)	52 (220)	66 (498)
United States		—n.a.—		
Actually changed vote				
Australia	30 (143)	16 (833)	54 (261)	63 (428)
Britain	18 (237)	12 (1,622)	57 (149)	44 (394)
United States	26 (39)	13 (542)	39 (61)	30 (338)

Sources: Australian Election Study, 1998; British Election Study, 1997; American National Election Study, 2000.

Notes
Numbers of cases in parentheses. Minor party is defined as other than Liberal-National or Labor in Australia, Conservative or Labour in Britain and Bush or Gore in the United States. A split ticket is defined in Australia as a different party vote for the House of Representatives and Senate, and a different party vote between the presidential and congressional elections in the United States. Actually changed vote is voted differently for the House of Representatives between the 1996 and 1998 Australian federal elections, between the 1992 and 1997 general elections in Britain and between the 1996 and 2000 presidential elections in the United States.

calculating late deciders are not far behind. Indeed, in the case of British late deciders considering changing their vote and their Australian counterparts actually doing so, calculating voters are actually more volatile than their capricious counterparts; almost two-thirds of Australian late deciders changed their vote between the 1996 and 1998 federal elections, representing almost 16 per cent of the electorate. Bearing in mind that just 0.6 per cent of the first preference vote separated Labor from the winning Liberal-National coalition in 1998, it would have required just one in twenty-five of these late deciders to change their vote in order to alter the election outcome.

Conclusion

Election campaigns have attracted, and continue to attract, considerable academic attention. The growth of modern opinion polling techniques and the extensive use of the mass media in elections gave rise in the 1950s and 1960s to systematic analyses of the impact of election campaigns, notably

Stanley Kelley's *Professional Public Relations and Political Power* (1956) in the United States and Richard Rose's *Influencing Voters* (1967) in Britain. The earliest voting studies devoted much attention to election campaigns, since voting was conceptualized in terms of consumer choice (Berelson *et al.* 1954; Lazarsfeld *et al.* 1968 [1944]). However, the publication of *The American Voter* in 1960 and the emergence of party identification as the dominant paradigm in voting behaviour research relegated the election campaign to a secondary role in shaping vote choice (Campbell *et al.* 1960).

In the past three decades, as discussed in Chapter 1, election campaigns have once again become a major focus of attention. There are several reasons for this change. First, political parties as institutions are in decline; with fewer members and activists, they frequently lack the resources, human and material, with which to maintain local-level campaigning, such as canvassing and mail drops.[15] Second, the growth of the electronic media, particularly television, has made it easier to communicate events and issues through personalities, and to make the leader rather than the party accountable for government performance. The increasing personalization of politics has occurred regardless of whether the system is presidential or parliamentary (Swanson and Mancini 1996).[16] Third, the constant use of public opinion polls ensures maximum voter acceptability for the final political product (Herbst 1993; Geer 1996).

While it is difficult to disentangle the causality in this complex process of change, it is apparent that large numbers of voters across many established democracies now delay their decision until the election campaign is under way. The two most recent elections in Australia, Britain and the United States show that between one-quarter and almost one-half of voters are late deciders. But late deciders are not all the same and they can be distinguished most easily by whether they care who wins the election. In all three countries voters who care about the outcome of the election have increased in recent years, to about three in every four voters. Using these measures, we have distinguished capricious later deciders from calculating later deciders, with the latter being more numerous in all three countries than the former; moreover, the US evidence suggests that there has been a consistent increase in the proportion of later deciders within the voting electorate, particularly over the 1990s.

How do we explain the rise of these late deciders? The results suggest that dealignment is important, as well as social modernization, channelled through political interest. There appears to be a complex longitudinal relationship between modernization and party-related factors which is altering the nature and outlook of democratic electorates. Late deciders also have a major impact on political behaviour; as predicted, calculating late deciders participate more actively and pay more attention to the media than their capricious counterparts. But perhaps more surprising is the generally greater volatility in the voting behaviour of calculating late deciders, notably in Australia.

What are the implications of these changes for the conduct of election campaigns, as well as for the future of parties more generally? The increasing numbers of late deciders suggest that election campaigns will attract at least as much attention in the future as they have in the past. But the growing number of calculating late deciders indicates that, paradoxically given the trend, a party strategy based on reasoned debate and utilizing detailed factual information is more likely to succeed than a superficial campaign based on slogans and sound bites. While possessing a popular leader will remain crucially important for parties, it may well be that leaders will be under greater pressure to associate themselves directly with policy stances. Overall, the message is that not all – indeed, a minority – of late deciders are whimsical. The conduct of modern election campaigns need to cater for this group to a greater extent than has hitherto been the case.

Notes

The 1998 Australian Election Study was collected by Clive Bean, David Gow and Ian McAllister; the 1997 British Election Study by the Centre for Research into Elections and Social Trends and Pippa Norris; and the 1996 American National Election Study by Steven J. Rosenstone, Donald R. Kinder and Warren E. Miller.

1 The estimates are for voters only in all three countries. In Britain and the United States this excludes a significant minority of the electorate who abstain from voting. In Australia, the compulsory voting system ensures that all but a negligible proportion of the electorate turnout to vote. In the United States, estimates exclude congressional election years.
2 The figure is an average of the February and October 1974 general elections, which was 22 per cent and 23 per cent, respectively.
3 The equation is $y = 1.87x + 10.56$, $r^2 = 0.62$.
4 In the November 1999 constitutional referendum on the republic, late deciders made up 39 per cent of all voters.
5 The equation is $y = 2.6x + 27.60$, $r^2 = 0.51$.
6 No one has suggested that political sophistication is declining; the argument is whether it is static or increasing.
7 The Australian equation is $y = .35x - 617.8$, $r^2 = 0.45$; the British equation is $y = 0.27x - 458.2$, $r^2 = 0.75$.
8 It may be, of course, that there is a selectivity taking place, so that as turnout declines and abstainers are least concerned about the outcome, those who remain have higher levels of interest. This would explain the post-1976 period, but not the preceding period.
9 The figures for Britain are 69 per cent caring about the outcome who decided during the campaign (the question does not permit discrimination between the stage in the election campaign when they decided) compared with 88 per cent who decided a long time ago.
10 Partisanship is obviously a major factor differentiating disengaged from partisan voters. In the 1998 Australian federal election, for example, 17 per cent of disengaged voters had no partisanship and 50 per cent had only weak partisanship, compared with 5 per cent and 15 per cent, respectively, of partisans. This is explored in greater detail in the next section.

11 In the 1976 presidential election, 38 per cent of voters said that they were interested in politics 'most of the time'; in the five elections since then, the same figure has fluctuated between just 21 per cent and 26 per cent. Interest in the election has shown a similar decline, with the exception of the 1992 election, when 39 per cent said that they were 'very interested'.

12 Social capital is more usually (and more accurately) measured by membership of voluntary social organizations, but this information was not available in all three of the surveys.

13 It is often the unexpected accidents which are televised that voters recall about a campaign, such as Jimmy Carter finishing a jog totally exhausted; Gerald Ford tripping while leaving an aircraft; or George Bush forgetting the name of the town he was delivering an election speech in.

14 The detailed results are shown in Table 2.6.

Table 2.6 Policy issues as a basis of choice in Australia (%)

Main voting consideration	Disengaged	Partisan	Capricious	Rational
Policy issues	52	66	56	79
Parties as a whole	30	20	23	13
Party leaders	10	10	10	4
Candidates in local area	8	4	11	4
Total	100	100	100	100
N	148	903	314	464

15 Not least, a smaller party membership reduces the number of potential candidates and has significant implications for the types of candidates that are selected, how they manage their campaigns, and for elite recruitment generally. This has given rise, it is argued, to the phenomenon of the 'career politician' (Riddell 1996; Norris 1997b).

16 In Britain, Butler and Stokes (1974: 367–8) trace the change to the 1960s, when they estimated that the party leaders had a significant impact on party fortunes. In the United States, the change is usually traced to the 1964 presidential election, when Johnson's victory over Barry Goldwater was attributed to his personal popularity (Nie *et al.* 1976: 307 ff.).

3 When do election campaigns matter, and to whom?

Results from the 1999 Swiss election panel study

Romain Lachat and Pascal Sciarini

The stability of voting behaviour was a central finding of the pioneering studies of the 1950s and 1960s (Berelson *et al.* 1954; Campbell *et al.* 1960; Lazarsfeld *et al.* 1968 [1944]). According to the classics, voting was to be explained on the basis of long-term factors, such as one's position in the social structure, or traditional loyalties acquired through socialization. In line with this, the electorate was said to be largely immune from the short-term influence of campaign activities, which could only contribute to a reinforcement of predetermined intentions.

This traditional view has not remained unchallenged, however, and the issue of campaign effects has attracted increased interest in the scholarly community. The main reasons for this renewed interest are twofold. First, the weakening of the traditional ties with parties that has occurred since the 1960s (see, for example, Dalton and Wattenberg 2000) has not only reduced the impact of party identification on electoral choice, but has also led citizens to rely more heavily on information delivered during the electoral campaigns when making up their minds. Second, the professionalization of campaign activities, together with the empowerment of the mass media, has created new opportunities for campaign influence (Flanagan and Dalton 1984; Mancini and Swanson 1996). As a result, individual voting choices are both less predictable and more prone to short-term changes.

Having said that, the issue of campaign effects remains, of course, hotly debated. Both the advocates of the 'minimal effects' model and those who claim that campaigns can have substantial effects on opinion formation have provided convincing evidence to support their view. In our opinion, this mixed picture – and the resulting controversy regarding campaign effects – is mainly due to two shortcomings of the literature in the field.

First, several studies are based on a homogeneous view of the electorate. Yet not all voters are likely to be influenced by campaign information, at least not to the same extent. A crucial difference regards whether a voter identifies with a party, or not. While traditional ties with parties have weakened over time, many voters still hold a party identification, and are likely to vote accordingly. Thus party identifiers are expected to be fairly immune from the influence of the electoral campaign. The same holds, more generally, for citizens who base their choice on other kinds of pre-campaign information.

Second, many studies fail to recognize that elections differ from one another with respect to campaign intensity. These variations are, however, of the utmost importance, since they provide voters with different opportunities and incentives to use campaign information. In that sense, the intensity of a contest affects the influence a campaign can have on voters' decisions. More specifically, we assume that an increase in campaign intensity encourages voters to reassess their traditional party preferences in the light of information delivered during the campaign.

To test these hypotheses, we need to spell out how variations in the characteristics of individuals and campaigns can affect the process of electoral choice. This is the purpose of the next section (pp. 42–4), where we develop our theoretical argument, present our model of electoral choice and specify our hypotheses. The operationalization of the variables, as well as the presentation of the data and of the model appear in the third section (pp. 45–9) and set the stage for the empirical part that we present in the fouth section (pp. 49–54). We test our hypotheses on data from the 1999 Swiss elections. The data were gathered in a three-wave panel study carried out in three cantons. In Switzerland, national elections are essentially a collection of cantonal elections. Therefore our data set allows a comparative analysis of campaign effects across contexts that are politically and institutionally similar, but that differ from each other with respect to campaign intensity.

A model of opinion formation during campaigns

Since the first voting studies of the 1940s, it has been repeatedly argued that citizens possess, at best, sketchy knowledge of the political system and of its actors. Similarly, research on opinion formation has shown that individuals tend to be 'cognitive misers' and do not process all available information when making their electoral choice. Rather, they rely on simplifying strategies, drawing inferences on candidates' qualities or political stances from a few salient pieces of information (Chaiken 1980; Petty and Cacioppo 1986; Popkin 1994). It is not the purpose of this chapter to discuss the wide range of cognitive strategies and related 'cues' or 'heuristics' available to voters. Instead, we focus on a basic distinction; we distinguish voters who are likely to use the information delivered during the campaign to make their electoral decision from those whose choice is likely to be based on pre-campaign information. We use two criteria to identify these two groups of voters: party identification and the timing of the voting choice.

In the first case, we know from the classical work of the 'Michigan school' that party identification is a powerful explanatory factor of electoral choice (Berelson *et al.* 1954; Campbell *et al.* 1960). It allows voters to avoid an extensive processing of information delivered during an electoral campaign while, at the same time, providing them with enough confidence in the quality of their electoral choice. In that sense, party identification has a sheltering effect, meaning that it protects citizens from the influence of the election campaign. This is not to say that party identifiers will not pay any attention to the campaign, but that their party identification will strongly bias the way they process new information.

Of course, party identification is not the only cue a voter may use to make her electoral choice. Other kinds of cues or pre-campaign information, such as parties' previous positions and performance, may also be at work. Trying to capture them all would be an extremely difficult endeavour. Hence the indirect strategy that we have chosen: we use the timing of the voters' decision as a general proxy for the reliance – or not – on pre-campaign information.[1] More specifically, we believe that an electoral choice made well before – or at the beginning of – the election campaign is a sign that the choice was based on pre-campaign information. Among the corresponding group of voters, therefore, we do not expect any campaign effects. Only voters who make their electoral choice during the campaign and who hold no party identification will be influenced by it.

Furthermore, we argue that voters' reliance on pre-campaign information is also affected by the context of an election and, more especially, by the intensity of an election campaign. For a long time, almost all models of electoral choice were premised on the simplistic assumption that the rules voters employ to make their decisions are non-responsive to variations in the election campaign. This was so because most studies focused on US presidential races or general elections in other countries, which were hard-fought contests. More recent works have tried to address this shortcoming, and have begun to examine the impact of the campaign context on voters' evaluations and opinion formation. Thus Kahn and Kenney (1999) have shown that differences in the intensity of US Senate elections have far-reaching consequences for the cognitive strategies used by voters (see also Westlye 1991; Krasno 1994). In essence, they argue that an increase in campaign intensity matters not only with respect to the quantity of information delivered to voters, but also with respect to the incentives it produces among voters. An intense election campaign leads voters to deem their choice more important, and to make more sophisticated decisions. In such a setting, voters are likely to update their traditional loyalties with new information in order to reach a higher level of confidence in their voting choice.[2] In other words, we assume that the sheltering effect of party identification is lower when campaign intensity is high. Accordingly, party identifiers are expected to rely as much as non-party identifiers on campaign information.[3] In contrast, when campaign intensity is low, information about the election is scarce and voters have little incentive to make complicated judgements.

In sum, we argue that these two fundamental distinctions (regarding reliance on campaign information and campaign intensity) help highlight for whom, and when, campaigns matter. Now, we still have to describe how these distinctions can be identified empirically, that is, how we shall measure the existence or absence of campaign effects. More precisely, we need a model of opinion formation that enables us to anticipate how voters will process the information they receive during the election campaign. To this end, we .use a general model of opinion formation that is rooted in some basic arguments found in the literature. Thus, in line with several scholars (see, for example, McGuire 1969; Ottati and Wyer 1990; Zaller 1992; Luskin 1994), we argue that political sophistication and ideological orientation regulate jointly the reception and acceptance of political messages:[1] the higher individuals' level of sophistication, the greater their exposure to political communications, but also the higher their ability to scrutinize and evaluate these communications in the light of their ideological orientation. As a result, more sophisticated people are likely to display opinions or to make decisions that correspond closely to their political values, beliefs and interests, whereas citizens with a lower level of sophistication are prone to decide according to the dominant messages delivered in the public space. According to this model, the likelihood of voting for a party of the left, for example, is expected to increase as a function of political sophistication among voters with left ideological orientation, but to decrease with political sophistication among voters with right-wing political preferences.

We argue that party identification or reliance on pre-campaign information has disruptive effects on this standard model of opinion formation. More specifically, we assume that among party identifiers and 'early deciders' the relation between electoral choice and ideological orientation does not vary as a function of political sophistication. Party identification, as well as other sources of pre-campaign information, will strongly bias the way in which new information delivered during the electoral campaign is processed. We can now summarize our hypotheses.

1   The electoral campaign has an influence only among voters who use campaign information as a central impetus in their electoral decision, that is, among voters who take their decision during the election campaign *and* hold no party identification; for this specific category of voters, the higher the political sophistication, the higher the support for the party closest to their ideological orientation. Among the other groups of voters, the link between ideological preferences and electoral choice does not vary as a function of political sophistication.
2   In a very intense contest, even campaign deciders with a party identification are likely to use the information delivered during the campaign to update their preferences. Conversely, an election campaign of low intensity has little effect, even among non-party identifiers who make their electoral choice during the campaign.

Data and model

Data

Our data come from a three-wave panel survey carried out in three cantons (Geneva, Lucerne, Zurich) in the context of the 1999 Swiss national elections. The three waves were conducted in June, in September, and immediately after polling day (24 October). In each canton, of the 850 citizens who were interviewed in June, about 600 participated in all three waves.[5]

In the Swiss federal system, national elections are essentially a collection of cantonal elections (Kerr 1987). Data from various cantons thus provide ideal grounds for a comparative analysis of the effects of election campaigns across different contexts. While the three selected cantons differ with respect to the cleavages and party systems,[6] they nevertheless represent very similar political and institutional contexts. Furthermore, and of particular interest for the present study, these cantons differ heavily with respect to the intensity of election campaigns: electoral contests are usually heated in Zurich but of very low intensity in Geneva, Lucerne being an in-between case. This variation is mainly due to two sets of factors. First, as a result of differences in size (number of inhabitants) and, therefore, of the number of seats each canton holds in the National Council – the lower chamber of the Swiss parliament – electoral competition is much higher in Zurich (thirty-four seats), than in Geneva (eleven seats) or Lucerne (ten seats). Second, it has been shown that federal election campaigns are more intense in the German-speaking cantons than in the French-speaking ones (Kriesi 1998b).[7] Thus our three cantons display three distinct levels of campaign intensity, with Zurich ranking first, Lucerne second and Geneva third. This ranking is confirmed by data generated from a study of newspaper advertisements, which included all party ads published in all major daily newspapers and magazines during the six months prior to the election, in the cantons under consideration.[8]

The results reported in Table 3.1 highlight the huge spending that characterized the election campaign in Zurich: parties spent roughly ten times

Table 3.1 Intensity of the electoral campaign in the three cantons: cost of advertisements (Swiss francs)

	Lucerne	*Geneva*	*Zurich*
Left parties	45,356	94,752	358,053
Centre parties			308,204
Right parties	329,292	188,772	3,177,618
Total cost	374,648	283,524	3,843,875
Cost per citizen	1.62	1.36	4.93

Source: Swiss Election Study, 1999.

more on newspaper ads in Zurich than in Lucerne, and fourteen times more than in Geneva. Even if we divide those figures by the number of registered electors, the differences are still considerable: spending was more than three times higher in Zurich than in Lucerne, and almost four times higher in Zurich than in Geneva. Lastly, the distribution of newspaper ads by political camps suggests that the election campaign was dominated overall by parties on the right.

Operationalization

Our dependent variable is *electoral choice*. Given the large number of parties in competition and the relatively small size of our samples, we refrain from studying electoral choice for each single party. Instead, we group parties according to their ideological proximity. To this end, we use the average position of each electorate in each canton on the left–right scale. Based on this, we can distinguish two groups of parties in Geneva and Lucerne (left and right), and three groups in Zurich (left, centre and right).[9]

Our indicator of citizens' level of political sophistication is based on a set of items measuring their general knowledge of Swiss politics and specific information about elections. Three questions regarding the political system were used during the first wave of the panel: respondents were asked to provide the number of parties represented in the federal government, the name of the current President of the federal government, and the number of signatures required to launch a popular initiative at the federal level. Questions measuring specific knowledge about the 1999 election were asked in waves two and three: respondents had to provide names of State Council (the upper chamber of parliament) candidates in their canton, the number of seats their canton holds in the National Council, and the party affiliation of three prominent National Council candidates in their canton. Adding these variables, we obtain a fifteen-point scale (Cronbach's alpha = 0.71) that we have centred around its mean. The resulting scale ranges from −6 (lowest level of sophistication) to +8 (highest level of sophistication).[10]

As an indicator of a citizen's *ideological orientation*, we use self-placement on an eleven-point left–right scale, ranging from −5 (left) to +5 (right).[11] *Party identification* is a dichotomous variable that is coded 1 for voters who say they feel close to a party and 0 otherwise. Party identification, like left–right self-placement, was asked during the first wave of the panel.

To identify the timing of the voting decision, we rely on the stability of voting intentions across panel waves. Voters who held a stable voting intention from the first wave on are coded as 'early deciders'. All other voters, that is, those who switched party and those who were undecided during the first wave, are classified as 'campaign deciders'.[12] The resulting dummy variable takes the value 0 for early deciders and 1 for campaign deciders.

Model specification

Our dependent variable is dichotomous in two cantons (Geneva and Lucerne) and takes three possible values in the third (Zurich). Our model will hence be estimated using a logistic regression in Geneva and Lucerne and a multinomial logistic regression in Zurich.[13]

Remember that we are interested in the relationship between ideology and electoral choice and, more precisely, in the mediating role played by political sophistication in this relationship. Accordingly, we model voters' choices as a function of both the separate and the joint impact of their position on the left–right scale and level of political sophistication. Further, we multiply the interaction term between ideological position and political sophistication by the dummy variables measuring the timing of the voting decision and/or party identification. This allows the campaign effect to vary between the corresponding groups – i.e. between citizens holding different levels of political sophistication, making their decision before or during the electoral campaign, and being close to a party or not – and, therefore, enables us to test our corresponding hypothesis.

The model which we test is, thus, as follows:

$$Z_j = \beta_{0j} + \beta_{1j} \cdot \text{left–right position} + \beta_{2j} \cdot \text{sophistication}$$

$$+ \beta_{3j} \cdot \text{party identification} + \beta_{4j} \cdot \text{time of voting choice}$$

$$+ \beta_{5j} \cdot \text{left–right position} \cdot \text{sophistication}$$

$$+ \beta_{6j} \cdot \text{left–right position} \cdot \text{sophistication} \cdot \text{time of voting choice}$$

$$+ \beta_{7j} \cdot \text{left–right position} \cdot \text{sophistication} \cdot \text{party identification}$$

$$+ \beta_{8j} \cdot \text{left–right position} \cdot \text{sophistication} \cdot \text{time of voting choice}$$

$$\cdot \text{party identification} + \beta_{9j} \cdot \text{income} + \beta_{10j} \cdot \text{education (1)}$$

$$+ \ldots + \beta_{13j} \cdot \text{education (4)} + \varepsilon_j \tag{1}$$

with

$$Z_j = \ln\left[\frac{P(y=j)}{P(y=1)}\right] \tag{2}$$

being the natural logarithm of the ratio of the probability of voting for the party j to the probability of voting for the party chosen as the reference category.[14] It should be added that we do not expect any direct effect of political sophistication on the level of support for a given group of parties. Yet several authors have shown that levels of political sophistication are correlated with other individual characteristics like education or income, whose influence on electoral choice is equally well documented in the literature (see, for example, Neuman 1986). In order to avoid a possible specification bias, therefore, we include income and education as control variables in

Table 3.2 Estimated coefficients for model of voting choice

	Lucerne		Geneva		Zurich			
					Centre parties		Right parties	
	Est.	SE	Est.	SE	Est.	SE	Est.	SE
Left–right position	1.59***	0.20	1.01***	0.13	0.63***	0.14	1.14***	0.13
Political sophistication	−0.04	0.07	−0.02	0.05	0.07	0.06	−0.05	0.05
Partisan identification	0.55	0.40	−0.63	0.33	0.30	0.44	−0.49	0.34
Time of the voting decision	0.31	0.38	−0.19	0.33	0.47	0.43	−0.01	0.33
L–R pos.*pol. soph.	−0.03	0.11	0.05	0.10	−0.08	0.08	−0.05	0.07
L–R pos.*pol. soph.*time	0.30*	0.14	0.05	0.11	−0.02	0.12	0.09	0.10
L–R pos.*pol. soph.*part. id.	0.06	0.13	−0.07	0.11	0.08	0.10	0.14	0.09
L–R pos.*pol. soph.*part. id.*time	−0.37*	0.18	−0.06	0.14	−0.06	0.15	−0.10	0.14
Income	0.05	0.07	0.05	0.05	0.08	0.08	0.12*	0.06
Compulsory education	−0.10	0.66	−0.48	0.53	−1.40	1.23	0.34	0.64
Diploma/high school	−0.51	0.51	−0.46	0.48	−0.88	0.56	−0.62	0.43
High vocational education	−1.15*	0.46	−0.63	0.47	−1.24*	0.56	−1.25**	0.43
University	−1.15	0.71	−0.45	0.44	−0.65	0.66	−0.32	0.56
Constant	2.14***	0.40	0.53	0.39	−0.76	0.45	0.96**	0.33
N	416		327		378			
Log likelihood	−110.73		−133.38		−248.26			
Likelihood ratio chi-square (df)	194.31*** (13)		181.40*** (13)		223.62*** (26)			
Likelihood ratio index	0.47		0.40		0.31			

Notes
* $p < 0.05$; ** $p < 0.01$; *** $p < 0.001$ (two-tailed tests).

our estimations.[15] We do not expect to find a relationship between party choice and either party identification or the timing of the voting choice.

The most crucial tests regarding our hypotheses are provided by the parameters of the interaction terms. They show how the impact of ideology varies as a function of political expertise, party identification and the timing of the voting decision. However, the most interesting quantities are given by the *sums* of these parameters. Among early deciders who identify with a party, for example, a change in the impact of ideology linked with a variation in political expertise is indicated by the sum of two parameters, namely those of the two-way interaction between ideology and sophistication (β_5) and of the three-way interaction between ideology, sophistication and party identification (β_7). To simplify the presentation of these results, we define four γ parameters that correspond to the sums of parameters among different groups of voters: $\gamma_1 = \beta_5$, $\gamma_2 = \beta_5 + \beta_7$, $\gamma_3 = \beta_5 + \beta_6$, $\gamma_4 = \beta_5 + \beta_6 + \beta_7 + \beta_8$. These γ parameters show how the impact of ideology varies with political sophistication among the following categories of voters: early deciders without (γ_1) or with (γ_2) a party identification, and campaign deciders without (γ_3) or with (γ_4) a party identification. Thus, if our model of opinion formation is correct, γ_3 should be the largest of these four coefficients, but it should become smaller if campaign intensity is particularly low. As far as the three other coefficients are concerned, we expect them to be close to zero. γ_4, however, should become larger if the campaign is particularly intense.

Empirical analysis

The results of the model's estimations appear in Table 3.2. Their interpretation is not straightforward, notably due to the inclusion of several interaction terms. Therefore, we shall discuss the coefficients briefly and then turn to the graphical presentations of the predicted probabilities.

Let us start with the canton that constitutes an in-between case with respect to campaign intensity, namely Lucerne. We can see from Table 3.2 that the coefficient of the left–right position is positive and strong. This means that the probability of voting for a party on the right increases with a move to the right on the ideological scale. More important for the test of our assumptions are the values of the γ parameters, which inform us about the parameters of the interaction terms. The results provide strong support for our hypotheses. The impact of ideology on electoral choice varies significantly as a function of political expertise among campaign deciders without a party identification $(\gamma_3 = 0.27, p < 0.001)$.[16] All other γ parameters are close to zero and not significant $(p > 0.71)$, which suggests that voters who rely on easily accessible information are not influenced by the election campaign.

Our results are even clearer when we use the coefficients to calculate predicted probabilities. As an illustration, we present the probabilities of voting for a party of the right among early deciders (Figure 3.1) and among campaign deciders (Figure 3.2). We do so for voters with two different positions on the left–right scale, with and without party identification, and with various levels of political sophistication. The two positions on the left–right scale that we have chosen correspond with the average positions held by voters of left parties (−1.8) and of right parties (0.9), respectively.

The differences between the various groups of voters are only too evident. We see from Figure 3.2 that the probability of voting for a party of the right decreases dramatically with political sophistication among voters with a left ideological orientation, but only if they do not feel close to a party. Among other groups of voters (Figures 3.1 and 3.2), by contrast, the probability of voting for the right does not vary much with political sophistication. The very high probability of voting for the right displayed by voters not close to a party and with a low degree of sophistication should not come as a surprise. It is mainly a result of the relative intensity of the electoral campaign that, as was suggested by the distribution of newspaper ads (see Table 3.1), was strongly biased in favour of parties on the right.

In sum, results obtained in the case of Lucerne provide strong support for our hypothesis that the campaign has a strong influence only among the specific group of voters who make their choice during the campaign and who hold no party identification.

We now turn to the case of Geneva, a canton where the campaign was of low intensity (Table 3.2, middle group of columns). We can see, first, that ideological position once again has a strong impact on the vote. In stark contrast to Lucerne, however, the magnitude of the parameters of the interaction terms is very small. This result suggests that, within all groups of voters, the impact of ideology on electoral choice is not influenced much by political expertise. Again, these findings are more explicit if we look at the

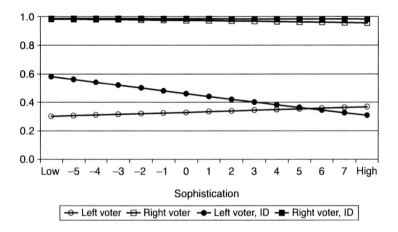

Figure 3.1 Probability of voting for a right-wing party among early deciders, Lucerne.

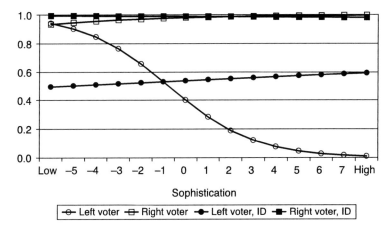

Figure 3.2 Probability of voting for a right-wing party among campaign deciders, Lucerne.

γ parameters. In line with our hypothesis, only γ_3 is statistically significant, but its value is much smaller than in the case of Lucerne ($\gamma_3 = 0.10$, $p < 0.02$). Among other groups of voters, political sophistication has no significant influence on the link between ideology and the vote (apart from γ_3, the coefficient with the highest value regarding early deciders without a party identification; $\gamma_1 = 0.05, p > 0.58$).

Once again, graphs offer a clearer picture of these relationships. As with the case of Lucerne, Figures 3.3 and 3.4 display the probability of voting for the right.[17] Among early deciders or party identifiers, voting for the right varies little as a function of political sophistication. By contrast, among

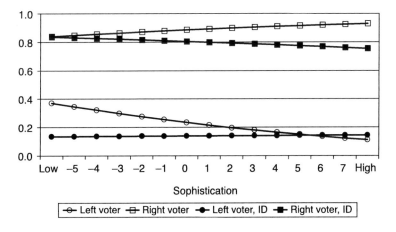

Figure 3.3 Probability of voting for a right-wing party among early deciders, Geneva.

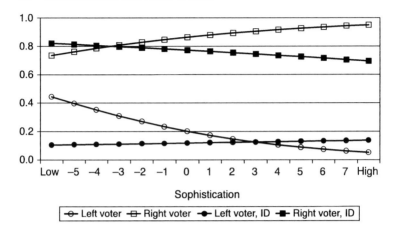

Figure 3.4 Probability of voting for a right-wing party among campaign deciders, Geneva.

campaign deciders without a party identification (Figure 3.4), some sort of polarization effect between right and left voters is at work, but it is less pronounced than in the canton of Lucerne.

Last of all, we apply our model to the case of Zurich (Table 3.2, last group of columns). Remember that this canton was characterized by the most intense election campaign. In addition, given that we have divided political parties into three groups, we obtain two sets of estimates.

The results obtained for the group of early deciders are in accordance with our hypotheses. None of the γ parameters reaches statistical significance, which once again shows that, within this group, the relationship between ideology and voting is hardly influenced by the level of political sophistication. As an illustration, we plot the predicted probabilities that early deciders will vote for a left party (Figure 3.5).[18]

At first glance, however, the results are less clear-cut with respect to campaign deciders. None of the γ parameters is significant, which runs counter to our assumption that, owing to a heated electoral contest, strong campaign effects were likely to occur in Zurich. Furthermore, we also unexpectedly observe that the γ coefficients for the group of centre parties are negative. While they are not very strong (the largest is $\gamma_3 = -0.10, p > 0.24$), this is nevertheless a surprising result, which suggests that, among voters on the left, political sophistication is negatively related to the probability of voting for left parties. However, given that the estimations are now based on three groups of parties, the resulting voting probabilities are pretty hard to grasp without graphical help. We have thus computed the probabilities of voting for each of the three groups of parties (Figures 3.6–8).

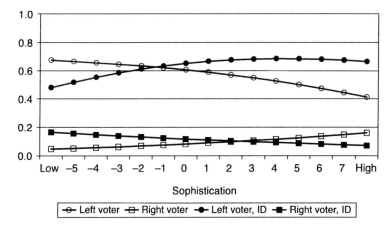

Figure 3.5 Probability of voting for a left-wing party among early deciders, Zurich.

Figures 3.6 and 3.7 show how the negative values of the γ coefficients affect voting probabilities. Among voters on the left, an increase in political sophistication makes a vote for centre parties more likely, at the expense of left parties. This is presumably due to strategic voting among leftist voters and, more especially, among those who are most sophisticated.[19]

Apart from this finding, Figures 3.6–8 show some polarization effect, even if this effect is not as strong as expected. Still, on the positive side, campaign effects hardly differ among party identifiers and among voters who do not feel close to a party. This tends to support our hypothesis that, when the campaign is intense, party identifiers are less immune to campaign influence.

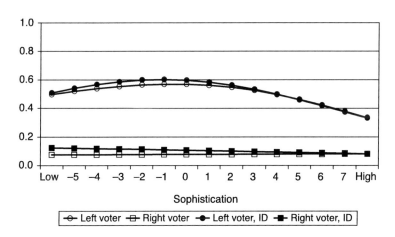

Figure 3.6 Probability of voting for a left-wing party among campaign deciders, Zurich.

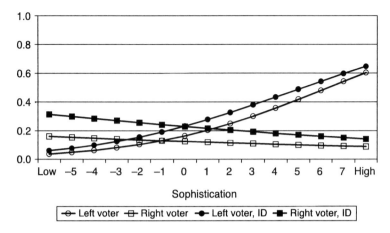

Figure 3.7 Probability of voting for a centre party among campaign deciders, Zurich.

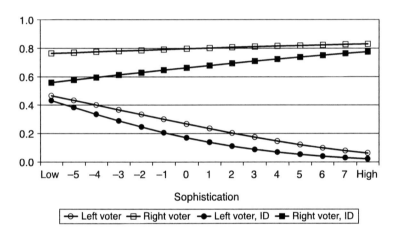

Figure 3.8 Probability of voting for a right-wing party among campaign deciders, Zurich.

Conclusion

In this chapter we have applied a model of electoral choice to the case of the 1999 Swiss national elections. Panel data from three different cantonal contexts have helped us to highlight when, and to whom, election campaigns matter. At the theoretical level, we have elaborated on how reliance on cues, as opposed to campaign information, reduces the influence of the election campaign. More specifically, we have assumed that voters who identify with a party or use any kind of pre-campaign information are likely to be sheltered from the political messages diffused during an election campaign;

only voters who do not use such cues will be influenced by it. We have also hypothesized about how an increase in the intensity of the election campaign might lead voters to reassess their traditional party preferences in the light of the new information delivered during the campaign, this in order to reach a higher level of confidence in their electoral choice.

To test these hypotheses, we used a general model that sees opinion formation as the product of the interaction between political messages, on the one hand, and voters' characteristics (political sophistication and ideological orientation), on the other. The crux of these empirical tests lies in the mediating role played (or not played) by political sophistication in the relationship between ideological orientation and electoral choice.

Our empirical tests, overall, provide considerable support for our hypotheses, at least in two of the three cantons we have studied. First, campaign effects turn out to be very small at best among voters who feel close to a party and/or who make their decision early. This result does not necessarily mean that party identifiers and early deciders do not pay attention to the election campaign but, rather, that they base their choice on factors other than those provided by the campaign. As a result, and as expected, the link between ideological orientation and electoral choice does not vary as a function of political expertise.

Second, we found strong campaign effects among voters who hold no party identification and who make their choice during the campaign. Within this group, the process of opinion formation reflects the expected interaction effects between political sophistication and ideological orientation: for example, support for a party of the right increases as a function of political sophistication among voters with a right-wing ideological orientation; conversely, support for the right decreases as a function of political sophistication among voters with a left ideology. In the case of Zurich, however, the polarization effect was not as marked as we would have expected, given a very intense campaign.

Third, we found that the patterns of opinion formation vary with campaign intensity. When it is very low, as in Geneva, voters who identify with a party, and who decide during the campaign, have neither opportunities nor incentives to make sophisticated judgements. Consequently, they are affected little by the campaign. On the other hand, results in Zurich suggest that the very intense campaign prompted even party identifiers to use new information to reassess their partisan preferences.

Notes

This chapter presents results of a research project on the 1999 Swiss elections. We thank the Swiss Science Foundation for its financial support (subsidy 5004-056086). Romain Lachat is grateful to the Social Science Research Centre, Berlin, which hosted him while he did part of the research.

1 Similar to Ian McAllister (see Chapter 2), we consider campaign deciders as 'potentially available for conversion'. However, we add the further restriction that they must also have no party identification.

2 See Maheswaran and Chaiken (1991) for a description of this process in the more general case of attitude formation.

3 As far as the timing of the voting decision – our second indicator of the use of campaign information – is concerned, we would expect an increase in campaign intensity to be linked with a larger proportion of the electorate postponing their voting decision until the campaign is under way. However, we cannot test this idea here, as we would need intensity to vary over several elections *in the same context*.

4 'Political sophistication' refers to individuals' levels of interest in, attentiveness to, and knowledge about, politics. Ideological orientation is grounded on stable traits, such as political values or belief systems, and hence is not likely to be influenced by political discourse, at least in the short run.

5 The number of cases available for our analyses is, however, smaller (between 320 and 420). This is mainly due to non-voting (in our sample, between 69 per cent and 81 per cent) and to respondents not answering the income question (about 15 per cent of the cases).

6 These cantons reflect the three political contexts that exist in Switzerland (Kriesi 1998a; Klöti 1998): the Catholic cantons (Lucerne), the German-speaking and religiously mixed cantons (Zurich) and the French-speaking, religiously mixed, cantons (Geneva).

7 One reason for this lies in the emphasis parties in the French-speaking cantons put on cantonal elections at the expense of national elections.

8 This data set includes fourteen daily newspapers, three Sunday papers, four weekly newspapers and two weekly magazines.

9 In each canton, the left comprises the Social Democrats, the Greens and far left parties. In Zurich the group of centre parties includes the Christian Democrats, the Alliance of Independents, the Protestant People's Party and the Christian Social Party, whilst the right parties consist of the Radicals, the Swiss People's Party and far right parties. In Lucerne and Geneva, these two last groups of parties make up the right parties. The Liberals, present only in Geneva, are also among the parties of the right. It should be noted that some small parties are not present in all three cantons.

10 Each correct answer adds one point, except for the question on the number of cantonal seats (two points for a correct answer, and one point for figures up to 20 per cent higher or lower than the correct answer). The question about the name of State Council candidates was asked twice – i.e. in the second and third wave – and up to three correct answers were coded.

11 Several studies have shown that the opposition between left and right is the most salient in Swiss politics, among both the political elite and the public (see, for example, Kriesi 1980; Kerr 1987; Finger and Sciarini 1991).

12 The operationalization differs in Geneva: here we consider as early deciders voters who had a stable voting intention from the second wave on, and not from the first wave. This is because the election campaign started much later in Geneva, as a cantonal popular ballot was held at the end of September, on which most political debates were focused until then.

13 See Liao (1994: 48-59) or Long (1997: 148 ff.) for an introduction to multinomial logistic regression. The restrictive assumptions of this model may render it inappropriate in some cases (Alvarez and Nagler 1998). We have performed Hausman specification tests (Long 1997: 183-4) and did not find any disconfirming evidence, at the usual 0.05 level of significance.

14 In all three cantons, the group of left parties will be used as the reference category.
15 Income was measured in categories and has been coded as the middle value of the corresponding income category (in thousands of Swiss francs). The lowest category has been coded to its upper bound and the highest category to its lower bound. Furthermore, the variable has then been centred on the middle value of its mean category. Education takes the form of four dummy variables: compulsory education, diploma or high school, high vocational education, and university. The reference category is vocational education. Both income and education have been measured during the first wave of the panel.
16 The standard errors of the γ parameters were calculated using the variances and covariances of the β parameters, according to the following formula (adapted from Gujarati 1995: 108):

$$s\left(\sum_i \beta_i\right) = \sqrt{\sum_i \mathrm{var}(\beta_i) + 2\sum_i\sum_j \mathrm{cov}(\beta_i, \beta_j)}, \; i \neq j$$

17 The curves labelled 'left' and 'right voter' correspond again to the average position on the left–right scale of left parties' voters (-1.7) and of right parties' voters (1.5).
18 The average left–right positions of left parties' and right parties' voters are -1.5 and 1.2, respectively.
19 There was in fact a fear that the main centre party in Zurich (the Independents) would not gain enough votes to be represented in the Swiss parliament. This presumably prompted the most sophisticated leftist voters to switch to the centre.

4 Campaign effects and media monopoly

The 1994 and 1998 parliamentary elections in Hungary

Marina Popescu and Gábor Tóka

This chapter explores some interactions between campaign resources, campaign style and campaign impact in a new democracy. The variable of interest is the campaigners' use of a peculiar opportunity structure that authoritarian legacies create. The 1994 and 1998 Hungarian elections showed much similarity in relevant aspects of this opportunity structure. Hence they can be treated as a natural laboratory to study variance in campaign impact while keeping a host of cultural, social and political variables constant.

Some features of these campaigns were typical for a large number of late democratizing countries. First, new democracies often show a dearth of necessary resources for the deployment of most pre- and post-Fordist – or 'pre- and postmodern', 'stage I' and 'stage III' – campaign technologies, in the case of everything from personal canvassing to direct mail.[1] In the absence of long-established party loyalties, it may be extremely hard to tell supporters, swing voters and committed opponents apart. Therefore, get-out-the-vote campaigns may easily backfire. As party organizations are often inchoate, personal contact with the voters is difficult to establish, and rallies rarely attract substantial audiences. Parties are often many and their ideologies shifting, hence it is unusually hard to calculate vote-maximizing party locations on the relevant issues.

Second, in many post-authoritarian democracies public television is easily available for partisan use. Given various legacies of authoritarian rule, there is often monopolistic control of television broadcasts. New democracies are middle- or low-income countries, hence government-controlled electronic media may be the only mass media many citizens are exposed to. Spreading partisan propaganda as supposedly non-partisan information programmes on a large and publicly financed provider of political information often turns into a major political issue, with intriguing implications for campaigns.

Third, the weakness of party loyalties leaves a lot of space for campaign influence. Defeat may mean the total disappearance of a party from electoral competition, and victory seems to be within reach for quite a few competitors. Consequently, party leaders are pushed to make full use of whatever tools of campaigning they can rely on.

We claim neither that the journalists in control of public television programmes are always behaving like committed partisans of the governing
parties, nor that they follow some master plan conceived in party offices.
But conventional wisdom suggests that partisan motivation significantly
shapes public media in many new democracies. The chief government party's
influence is variable, just like the means via which this influence is exercised.
Direct instruction and briefing of news editors may be unusual, but indirect
means seem perfectly capable of achieving a situation where key journalists
act like party delegates.[2]

These means include the appointment of trusted partisans to head public
service media, and providing loyal journalists with attractive career opportunities – plus a safe haven when the next government promptly fires them.
They can often take it for granted that they will keep or lose their job depending on the electoral success of a party – a situation not unlike that of ordinary
campaign personnel.

In this chapter we, first, provide supportive evidence about the centrality
and partisanship of public television in the two Hungarian elections. On
further particulars of these elections, the reader is referred to Fowler (1998)
and Tóka and Enyedi (1999). Here we merely treat them as illustrative
examples that are particularly well suited to exploring a more general issue.
We, then, develop our hypotheses about campaign impact and anchor them
in scholarly theories about political communication. Finally, we offer empirical tests of the propositions and discuss their implications.

Public television and election campaigns

It is hard to overestimate the importance of electronic media for campaign
communication in Hungary. In both the 1994 and the 1998 elections the
major contenders relied mostly on paid advertisements and centrally produced billboards, posters and leaflets, randomly bombarding voters across
the country. However, modest campaign budgets curtailed these efforts: the
fattest party coffer in either year contained roughly one US dollar per eligible
citizen. Although rallies had a significant place in the campaign of some
smaller parties, and mass telephone canvassing made a nebulous debut in
1998, their overall role in the campaigns was secondary to that of mediated
messages.

Following the requirements of the election law, the public broadcast
media provided equal subsidized air time for the competitors' election
appeals, and aired debates between representatives of over ten parties, i.e.
about twice the number of parties (six in both years) that win seats. These
debates had a rigid format that perfectly protected the media from any
charge of favouritism – the space for each party representative to speak on
the predetermined topics was timed to the second – but excluded any element
of interaction, probably turning most attention to the alarm clock constantly running on the screen.[3] Commentaries unequivocally considered the

'debates' uninformative and painfully boring. The exceptional head-on confrontation between the leaders of the front runners before the second round of the 1998 elections was unrelated to these officially scheduled rituals.[1]

In this context, the regular news and information programmes assumed a particularly important role in campaign communications. Television had a pre-eminent role: in a Median poll of eligible voters carried out in the middle of the 1994 campaign, 65 per cent said that television was their main source of information about the election, compared with just 14 per cent and 11 per cent for the newspapers and radio respectively.[5] In the post-election surveys, analysed below, 69 per cent of the 1994 respondents reported watching television every day, whereas 49 per cent read a newspaper with political coverage, and 67 per cent listened to radio news. The respective figures in the 1998 survey were 84 per cent, 41 per cent and 69 per cent – a further increase in favour of television.

Prior to 1997 public television was practically in a monopoly position. By the time of the 1998 election, however, private television broadcasts could be received by 90 per cent of the population, and provided extensive political coverage. But the key reason for our analysis of the electoral impact of public television is not just its importance and that it was partisan in tone (like most newspapers), but that it was subject to governmental influence. Indeed, literally all the media personnel who controlled political coverage on public television lost (or pre-emptively quit) their job shortly after the opposition victories of 1994 and 1998; for that matter, they had little reason to expect that they could keep it in such an eventuality. Thus they were arguably in the position of being more campaigners than public service journalists.

Ironically, the government lost both elections. But this only raises the question whether they would have done better, or worse, if public television broadcasts had not been designed to serve the electoral interests of the main government party, which in 1994 comprised the centre-right Hungarian Democratic Forum (MDF) and in 1998 was the ex-communist Hungarian Socialist Party (MSZP). For the bias did seem to be there. The Democratic Forum (MDF) alone had 64 per cent of the time the first public channel allotted to politics during the 1994 campaign, all featuring neutral or positive coverage. The main challenger, the Socialist Party (MSZP), received only 11 per cent of coverage, a significant part of which was negative. On the satellite-transmitted public channel, Duna TV, the Democratic Forum had 83 per cent of the time slots – a stunning figure compared with their 12 per cent share of the vote in that year's election (Lange 1994).

Although we do not have directly comparable data on coverage in 1998, the direction of the bias was similar (this time giving at least two, if not more, bites of the cherry to MSZP), but its extent less pronounced. Indeed, in the surveys that we shall analyse below, 42 per cent of the respondents after the first round of voting in 1998 said that public television was 'always' fair and balanced in its coverage of the parties; this contrasts with an equivalent figure of 13 per cent in 1994.[6] In 1994, 45 per cent of respondents said that the MDF was favoured in public television coverage, compared with just 9 per cent who felt the main challenger party, the MSZP, was favoured. Four years later, 22 per cent said the main government party, MSZP, was the one favoured by public television, and 7 per cent attributed this status to Fidesz-MPP, the chief challenger in 1998.[7]

Given the strong presence of the private channels, fewer people watched public television in 1998 than in 1994, and political coverage also seemed less one-sided. Therefore the electoral impact of public television exposure could have been bigger in 1994 than in 1998. There was a factor that probably acted in the opposite direction, however. The 1994 campaign took place in the context of a long controversy over governmental control of public broadcasting. This so-called 'media war' regularly filled headlines and editorials between 1991 and 1994, featuring unusual presidential vetoes, Constitutional Court rulings, parliamentary hearings, street demonstrations and spectacular confrontations between government and the – eventually removed – presidents of public television and radio. There was little chance of not noticing the many critiques of political coverage on public television as strongly biased in favour of the main government party.

None of the above occurred in the 1994–98 period. The right-wing parliamentary opposition of the time was certainly not happy with the political coverage of public television, but did little to undermine its credibility. In December 1995 a media law was passed by an overwhelming super-majority composed of both government and opposition deputies. This created the legal framework for private terrestrial broadcasting. The law took the public broadcast media out of direct government control and placed them under the supervision of boards elected by parliament in which opposition and government representatives were to have parity. As far as we can tell, the political coverage on public television was still positively biased towards the incumbents during the 1998 election, but its tone was not overtly propagandistic, and it certainly did not stir as much controversy as in 1994. Moreover, dissatisfied viewers could simply switch to the private channels. The lack of such viewers' exposure to public television may even have reduced the chances of its pro-government bias resulting in an unintended boomerang effect of the kind discussed below. Hence, the two Hungarian elections offer a natural setting to explore how different uses of public television promote the electoral interests of the main government party, while holding a number of contextual factors largely constant.

Hypotheses

Our postulates about campaign effects are informed by intuitively appealing scholarly theories that may have parallels in the thinking of real-life campaigners. We assume that politicians seek re-election and see, like Zaller (1996), ample room for information effects in elections. If they have more or less monopolistic control over the media, they will ensure that the general tone of coverage is favourable to them. We expect to find some evidence of positive returns on this effort, namely that attitudes towards the main government party and economic evaluations become more positive as exposure to public television increases (hypothesis 1).

We expect message impact not to be determined by the sender's intent alone. For instance, a recent study has argued that the British audience is so accustomed to overtly negative coverage of parties that it discounts much of it. This would explain why positive news coverage consistently increases support for a party more than negative coverage decreases it (Norris *et al.* 1999: 142). In a similar vein, the Hungarian public may be accustomed to pro-governmental bias on public television and might therefore ignore it.

Indeed, the impact of any new information is proportional to how credible the source is in a particular information domain for a particular audience (cf. Lupia and McCubbins 1998). Thus enduring opposition criticism of biased coverage on government-controlled media may shape message impact, preparing voters to see all the niceness about the government and the dirt about the opposition in the television news programmes as mere confirmation of the government's abuse of power. Indeed, many Hungarian commentators speculated that in the 1994 campaign the biased coverage of public television had an unintended boomerang effect among viewers, reducing support for the main government party (hypothesis 2).

Hypothesis 3 expects partisan actors to also try to increase tactical voting where that may benefit them, and to sometimes succeed. These efforts must be particularly strong when uncertainty about the likely election outcome is high, and, due to monopolistic control of significant and supposedly non-partisan media, the contenders are unequally equipped to shape the voters' perception of who may win. Thus government-controlled television will affect voters' perception of the race in ways that are conducive to prompting a tactical bandwagon towards the incumbents.

Finally, we expect partisan actors to share the intuition of salience theory, which holds that strategic self-positioning on issues is not the typical form of electoral competition. Rather, election campaigns merely influence the salience of different considerations for voters. Campaigners avoid, as much as possible, the topics where their rivals are believed to have a more attractive position; they seek to direct voters' attention to considerations that put the sender at an advantage in the electoral arena (Budge and Farlie 1983).

This resonates well with the theory of accessibility bias, which holds that more easily retrievable information 'tends to dominate judgements, opinions and decisions', especially 'in the weights individuals assign to various considerations when expressing attitudes or making choices' (Iyengar 1990: 2). Clearly, election campaigns often try to achieve exactly this kind of priming effects (see Chapter 5 in this volume). Given the degree of governmental influence on public television in Hungary, we expect to find evidence of such pro-government priming effects by public television (hypothesis 4).

Data and models

The analysis below relies on panel survey data collected at the time of the two elections by the Political Science Department of the Central European University. Technical information about the surveys and the variables in the analysis are included in the appendix to this chapter. For the sake of brevity, we discuss the operationalization of the above hypotheses together with the findings.

Four linear regression equations were run for each year (see Tables 4.1–4, respectively). The first three assessed the impact of public television on campaign-affected determinants of the vote: short-term changes in general party sympathy, short-term changes in economic evaluations, and voters' perception of who may win the election. The fourth equation explored direct influences on vote choice, with the dependent variables of the first three equations becoming independent variables together with an indicator of those issue attitudes that the main contenders were trying to prime voters on in these elections.

It is likely that voters' general sympathy (or antipathy) towards parties may be linked with all other determinants of vote choice – i.e. economic evaluations, perceptions of the expected winner and issue attitudes – via reciprocal causation. But, in the absence of better data, the equations only control for what are presumably the strongest of these reciprocal effects, namely the impact of early-campaign party sympathy on perceptions of the likely winner and within-campaign changes in economic evaluations. Because of this limitation we may slightly underestimate the total effect of the latter variables on vote choice. But, unfortunately, we have no data to estimate television's impact on within-campaign changes of issue attitudes, and thus must ignore a possible type of campaign effect.

Economic evaluations and public television exposure were measured identically in both elections, but the choice of issue variables and the way we coded the perception of the likely winner were determined according to the particular context of each election (see below). The coding of vote choice reflects the likely calculus of the people who designed the pro-governmental coverage on public television. We presume that these people wished to see the government re-elected. Given Hungary's electoral and party system, this vastly simplified the determination of the utility of a vote (or non-vote) for them.[8] To capture this calculus, we coded the dependent variable 1 for respondents who voted for the main government party, 0 for voters of the main challenger party and 0.5 for all other respondents. The construction of the party sympathy variable followed the same logic. To derive early-campaign party sympathy, the respondents' ratings of the main challenger party in the pre-election poll were subtracted from their ratings of the main government party. Then a parallel measure was created from their post-election ratings of the two parties, and the within-campaign change of sympathy towards parties was calculated as the difference between early-campaign and post-campaign measurements.

Findings

Our simplest test is shown in Table 4.1. Campaigners' are naturally concerned with overall party sympathies, and they see them as a major influence on the vote – rightly so, as Table 4.4 confirms. Hypothesis 1 expects exposure to public television to lead to a more positive evaluation of the main government party, and/or a more negative evaluation of the main opposition party, during both election campaigns. In contrast, hypothesis 2 expects a boomerang effect, at least in 1994: because of the blatant pro-government bias of public television, exposure to public television should have reduced sympathy for the incumbents and increased liking for the opposition. Hence the dependent variable is within-campaign change of party sympathy, and the independent variable of interest is exposure to public television broadcasts.

We control for early-campaign party sympathy, since the starting value powerfully limits how one's response to the questions on party sympathy could change during the campaign. People who had a maximum score to begin with could not become any more positive during the campaign. Similarly, after a maximally negative initial score, within-campaign change – if any was observed – had to be in the positive direction. In recognition of this methodological artefact, the equation controls for the sizeable, but theoretically irrelevant, negative effect of early-campaign evaluation.

As Table 4.1 reveals, exposure to public television did significantly increase sympathy for the main government party and/or reduced sympathy for the main challenger during the 1998 campaign. In 1994, however, we see a negative effect, i.e. the opposite of what was intended. Despite the pro-MDF tone of the programmes, the more one watched public television during the campaign, the more one's sympathy shifted towards the challenger. Hence hypothesis 1 is supported by the 1998 data but not by the 1994 data, thus lending credence to hypothesis 2 instead.

Table 4.1 The net impact of public television exposure on changes in party sympathy during the 1994 and 1998 campaigns (standardized regression coefficients)

	1994	*1998*
Public television exposure	−0.10**	0.07**
Early-campaign party sympathy	−0.45***	−0.36***
Adjusted R^2	0.21	0.13
N	627	1,330

Notes
*** $p < 0.001$; ** $p < 0.01$; * $p < 0.05$.

Table 4.2 The net impact of public television exposure on changes in retrospective economic evaluations during the 1994 and 1998 campaigns (standardized regression coefficients)

	1994	1998
Public television exposure	−0.13***	0.02
Early-campaign party sympathy	0.14***	0.13***
Early-campaign economic evaluations	−0.60***	−0.64***
Adjusted R^2	0.35	0.38
N	629	1,324

Notes
*** $p < 0.001$; ** $p < 0.01$; * $p < 0.05$.

A replica of the test is offered in Table 4.2. The incumbents in both 1994 and 1998 saw their chief electoral liability in the pains of post-communist economic transformation. Indeed, just before the 1994 and 1998 elections, respectively 64 per cent and 40 per cent of respondents thought that economic conditions in the country had become worse in the previous twelve months, while only 16 and 27 per cent thought that things had improved.[9] Even these figures, however, showed that popular evaluations of the economy were already turning more optimistic compared with the dramatic lows of 1992 and 1996. No surprise, then, that a prime concern of pro-government propaganda in both campaigns was to convey good news about the economy. According to the spirit of hypothesis 1, therefore, exposure to public television must have made viewers' evaluation of the state of the economy more favourable during both campaigns. Hypothesis 2, again, suggests the opposite, i.e. that a boomerang effect occurred. As above, the large but theoretically uninteresting negative effect of the early-campaign evaluation is controlled for in the analysis of within-campaign changes.

The 1994 results once again support hypothesis 2: no matter how citizens felt about the economy at the beginning of the campaign, the more they watched public television, the less their economic evaluations became optimistic in the course of the campaign. In the 1998 data, exposure to public television shows a positive but statistically non-significant effect on within-campaign changes of economic evaluations. Again, the findings suggest that the less blatant 1998 campaign on public television did less damage to the government's chances of re-election than its 1994 counterpart.

It might be speculated that all these seeming effects of public television broadcasts were merely spurious. Indeed, they could have been caused not so much by public television itself as either by the real world events that it willy-nilly covered or by some peculiar aspect of audience composition. However, when we added a host of socio-demographic and media exposure variables to the two equations, the impact of public television remained unchanged, and the respondents' frequency of reading newspapers failed to register a significant effect (data not shown).[10] We conclude that it was the coverage of the public television (or the opposition's reaction to it), rather than the composition of the audience or the real-world events covered by public television and newspapers alike, that accounts for the apparent boom-erang effect of public television broadcasts on short-term attitude change.

Ultimately, several explanations remain for the spectacular difference in campaign impact between the two elections. Since it differed in direction, and not just magnitude, the 1991–94 media war probably offers a more plausible explanation than the mere difference of degree in how blatant the public television's bias was in 1994 compared with 1998. A plausible alterna-tive is that viewers who could be offended by the overtly propagandistic coverage of public television had little choice but to watch it in 1994, while in 1998 they could simply switch to the private channels, thus reducing the backlash against public television coverage. Whichever explanation is best, they all find the reason for the boomerang effect in the extraordinary visib-ility of the underlying intent and bias in public television coverage. Where they disagree is over whether the extraordinary visibility was caused by the coverage itself, or by the media war, or by the lack of private television. Our next equation is designed to test hypothesis 3. Did exposure to public tele-vision make viewers more likely to perceive the state of the election contests in ways conducive to a tactical swing away from the opposition and/or a shift to the main government party? Support for hypothesis 3 would be pro-vided by a positive impact of public television exposure on perceptions that might have prompted a tactical bandwagon towards the main government party.[11]

In both elections, arguably the best chance for a tactical bandwagon to the main government party was created by a mistaken, but not unusual, percep-tion of the relative standing of those parties that were actually trailing in the polls behind the MSZP – the biggest vote-getter in both years despite its defeat in 1998. In 1994, pro-government strategists presumably pondered the idea that some liberal voters might move their way if they believed that only the MDF could prevent the left-wing MSZP winning the election. Consequently, our dependent variable was coded 1 for everyone who named the MDF as the likely winner of the election, and −1 for everyone who named one of the liberal parties.[12] Similarly, it made good sense only if the 1998 MSZP campaign had portrayed the widely resented FKGP as the main challenger, rather than the far more popular Fidesz-MPP.[13] In reality, the latter was closing the gap in the polls with the main government party, but prior to the election many citizens still deemed the FKGP more likely to win than Fidesz-MPP. Given the majoritarian aspects of the Hungarian electoral system, this misperception could no doubt benefit the government parties, and therefore our dependent variable for 1998 was coded 1 for every-one who named the FKGP as the party most likely to win the election, and −1 for everyone who named Fidesz-MPP.

Public television broadcast no polling information in either election, despite its ready availability. The polls reported in the press revealed, in both elections, a fairly widespread misperception among the public – exactly along the above lines – about the standing of the second and the third most popular parties. Thus the withholding of polling information – though probably not the only means used to this effect – can be read as *prima facie* evidence that public television deliberately tried to confuse people about where the major competition to the MSZP came from.

Its success in manipulating popular perceptions can be judged from Table 4.3. The impact of public television exposure on the perception of the likely winner was in the expected direction in both years, and reached statistical significance in 1998. The explanation for the non-significance of the effect in 1994 might be that the pro-government campaign tried to spread a visibly self-serving message in that year, i.e. that the main government party was ahead of either of the two liberal parties. In comparison, the 1998 pro-government message was more sophisticated, merely misrepresenting which was the strongest opposition force.

Hypothesis 4 attributes a pro-governmental priming effect to public television broadcasts. This proposition is assessed with the help of the two *interaction terms* included in the fourth equation (see Table 4.4). The equation takes vote choice as the dependent variable, and controls for exposure to public television, perception of the likely winner, relevant issue attitudes, and early-campaign party sympathy and economic evaluations as well as their change during the campaign. Note that the sum of the 'Early-campaign economic evaluations' and the 'Change in economic evaluations' variables equals the 'Post-campaign economic evaluations', i.e. the variable that, multiplied by 'Public television exposure', forms one of the two interaction terms focused on in the analysis.

If, after controlling for the direct effect of its component parts, the interaction term registers a positive effect on vote choice, then the impact of post-campaign economic evaluations on the vote was bigger among frequent

Table 4.3 The net impact of public television exposure on perceptions of the likely winner during the 1994 and 1998 campaigns (standardized regression coefficients)

	1994	*1998*
Public television exposure	0.03	0.06*
Early-campaign party sympathy	0.18***	0.18***
Adjusted R^2	0.03	0.04
N	652	1,392

Notes
*** $p < 0.001$; ** $p < 0.01$; * $p < 0.05$.

viewers of public television than among other voters. A negative effect of the same interaction term would imply the opposite: namely that among frequent viewers voting support for the main government party was less dependent on positive economic evaluations than among other citizens, and voting support for the main challenger was less dependent on negative economic evaluations. Both effects would constitute evidence of priming vote choices on particular kinds of considerations by public television, although the negative effect of the interaction term may be better described as 'de-priming' on the economy, i.e. a reduction of the weight of economic evaluations in the vote function.

However, the mere statistical significance of priming effects would support hypothesis 4 only if the direction of priming had been consistent with the intentions of pro-government campaigners. We can only infer intent indirectly. The 1994 MDF campaign had a compelling reason to reduce the dependence of voting decisions on retrospective economic judgements: the latter, as we saw, were overwhelmingly negative. Indeed, the pro-government campaign on public television – arguably even more than the party's own campaign – tried to prime voters' decisions on another consideration: the perils and sins that could be associated with the communist past. While it was much debated by commentators whether priming in this direction could possibly have benefited the MDF in 1994, the inference that the intention and the attempt were present in the campaign was widely accepted.

This helps to operationalize hypothesis 4: in 1994, exposure to public television had to decrease the impact of economic evaluations on the vote, and increase the impact of anti-communist attitudes. Anti-communist attitudes

Table 4.4 Effects on the vote during the 1994 and 1998 campaigns (standardized regression coefficients)

	1994	1998
Public television exposure	−0.07*	−0.03
Early-campaign party sympathy	0.73***	0.68***
Change in party sympathy	0.39***	0.36***
Perception of the likely winner	−0.01	0.10***
Early-campaign economic evaluations	0.25*	−0.10
Change in economic evaluations	0.36*	−0.11
Issue position	−0.29*	0.14*
Post-campaign economic evaluations* public television exposure	−0.26*	0.13†
Issue position* public television exposure	0.36**	−0.13†
Adjusted R^2	0.46	0.46
N	610	1,265

Notes
*** $p < 0.001$; ** $p < 0.01$; * $p < 0.05$; † $p < 0.10$.

are measured by the issue attitude variable in the 1994 data. To assess the priming of voters by public television on this issue domain, the issues-with-exposure interaction term was entered into the equation. Note that the issue variable, and its interaction with exposure, will refer to an entirely different issue domain in the analysis of the 1998 data, reflecting a different campaign agenda.

The positive impact of the issues-with-exposure interaction term in 1994 signals that the more people watched television, the more likely anti-communists voted for the main government party – or at least not for MSZP – and the more likely pro-communist voters did the reverse.[14] The direct impact of economic evaluations on the vote appears to have been weak anyway – of course, they may have had a large indirect influence on the vote via party sympathy – but the effect further decreased in proportion to public television exposure, as shown by the negative effect of the interaction term in Table 4.4. Thus the results suggest that, in 1994, pro-governmental priming of the vote on anti-communism rather than economics worked very much as intended, despite the boomerang effect of public television on other attitudes in the same year.

Regarding 1998, it is not entirely clear whether government propagandists aimed at priming voters on economic performance or not. Popular evaluations of the economy were still predominantly negative (see above). Nevertheless, the MSZP seemed confident that the state of the economy was good enough to enable it to win the election. At any rate, its lacklustre 1998 campaign lacked clear issue content, apart from claiming success and competence in economic management. This emphasis may have primed voting decisions on the state of the economy.

However, the main challenger did run an issue-oriented campaign in 1998. This may have reflected the greater opportunities than in 1994 to put across relatively complex opposition messages, via the new and non-partisan private television channels, but probably also on public television. In 1998, the opposition front runner, Fidesz-MPP, called for higher welfare spending in particular areas, and for a stronger state more resolutely fighting corruption and promoting law and order (see Fowler 1998: 258–9). Two prominent issues covered by our data were the abolition of tuition fees in higher education and means-testing eligibility for child-care allowance – i.e. to repeal two prominent innovations in the 1995 austerity package that did more than anything else to define the legacy of the 1994–98 socialist-liberal government.

Our data (not shown) reveal that on both issues an overwhelming majority of the public favoured the position of Fidesz-MPP over that of the government. Yet the opposition campaign still faced an uphill battle. It had to explain that Fidesz – previously a strongly monetarist liberal party – had become a stauncher advocate than the MSZP of the cherished welfare provisions of the former communist regime. The dull way the campaign debates were organized on the public channels, and the relatively modest coverage of the opposition in the news programmes were certainly obstacles to this effort. Thus public television served the main government party by hampering the communication of the opposition messages on these welfare state issues.

Accordingly we operationalize hypothesis 4 in the 1998 context in the following way: exposure to the pro-government public television primed vote choices on the state of the economy, and reduced the impact of the two welfare state issues on voting support for the MSZP versus the Fidesz-MPP. The issue attitudes variable, therefore, measures the respondents' support for the unpopular governmental policies on child-care allowances and tuition fees.

As Table 4.4 shows, public television primed vote choices largely as expected by the hypothesis. The main effect of the issue attitudes variable in 1998 was positive – i.e. the more voters agreed with the government's line, the more likely they were to vote for the MSZP, and the less likely to vote for the main challenger advocating the repeal of these policies. This was only good news for the opposition, since the government's position was very unpopular. Hence only the MSZP benefited from the fact that the issue-with-exposure interaction negatively influenced the vote: that is, the more people watched television, the less their votes were moved by the issues of child-care allowances and university tuition fees. The impact of the other interaction term (economic evaluations with exposure) was positive, suggesting that the more one watched public television, the more likely one's vote choice was directly influenced by economic evaluations. The significance level of the effect of the two interaction terms may seem less than impressive, but further checks suggest that the reported findings are robust.[15]

As in the case of all previous equations, we experimented with controlling for socio-demographic and further media exposure variables, and also with a change in the coding of the dependent variable.[16] The relevant results remained the same (data not shown). Hence we are reasonably confident that hypothesis 4 is supported by the 1994 and 1998 data, with regard to both economic evaluations and issue attitudes: public television primed voters on issues as the pro-government campaign desired.

A brief look at the effects of the remaining variables in Table 4.4 completes our analysis. Naturally, party sympathy had the greatest direct effect on vote in both elections. Its change during the campaign had a sizeable effect too, so public television's impact on it (see Table 4.1) indirectly influenced vote choices too. The perception of the likely winner only affected vote choice in 1998, but not in 1994.[17] It seems, then, that even if public television shaped these perceptions more strongly, this would not have benefited the main government party in 1994. In 1998, however, the effect worked as expected. In the case of two voters with otherwise identical values on all independent variables, the one who thought that the widely resented FKGP would win became more likely to vote for the main government party and less likely to vote for Fidesz-MPP than the one who thought that the latter would win. Hence public television's impact on perceptions (see Table 4.3) yielded electoral pay-offs for the MSZP in 1998.

Our most interesting finding concerns the direct impact of public television exposure on the vote – reaching statistical significance in 1994 only.[18] This negative effect signals that in 1994, among otherwise identical voters in terms of party sympathy and so forth, those who watched more public television became less likely than others to vote for the main government party, and more likely to vote for the main challenger. Our theory explains this neatly. The media themselves became an issue directly bearing on the vote, either because dissatisfied viewers could not switch to private channels, or because of the tone of the coverage itself, or because of the media war. The more one watched public television, the more plausible and salient became the charges about governmental abuse of the media, and the more likely a defection from MDF was to follow. Hence the direct effect of exposure to public television on the vote.

Conclusion

In this chapter, we have argued that public television is likely to be a very central weapon in election campaigning in many new democracies. A relatively poor supply of campaign resources for parties and weak party loyalties in the electorate on the one hand, and likely governmental control of an unusually important channel of political communication on the other, make the partisan use and abuse of the media both highly likely and potentially a major political issue in itself. We outlined plausible reasons why imprudently blatant use of this campaign device may actually hurt the re-election bid of incumbents.

We offered some empirical tests of the proposition in the context of Hungarian elections and found some evidence for such boomerang effects. We also showed that these are not inevitable. In some contexts public television coverage did seem to help the pro-government campaign by increasing sympathy for the main government party and/or reducing sympathy for the main challenger, by priming vote choices on particular considerations as pro-government campaigners apparently wished, and by promoting such perceptions of the likely winner of the elections as could induce a tactical bandwagon to the incumbents in some sections of the electorate. Moreover, our theory seemed to offer sensible explanations of where, when and in what respect the pro-government coverage of public television helps the incumbent's campaign, and where it hurts it.

Our preferred explanation for the contradictory effects of public television is that blatant propaganda backfires (probably through the reactions of the competitors that it triggers), while subtle messages may work. These are, of course, just hypotheses, distilled from a single case study. But they are anchored in our findings: boomerang effects of public television coverage occurred in the 1994 campaign, but not in 1998; even the generally unsuccessful 1994 campaign on public television achieved its intended priming effects; even the relatively subtle 1998 pro-government coverage failed to persuade voters about the rosy state of the economy; public television could impact on citizens' perceptions of the likely winner when the pro-government message was more sophisticated, but not in 1994, when it was more obviously self-serving.

At a more general level, our reasoning implies that the fit between campaign resources on the one hand, and the chosen targets and methods on the other, influences campaign impact. Campaigners make choices with an eye on their resources, but some assets may facilitate counterproductive choices. Pursuing the matter still further, counterproductive choices may be attributed to the force of circumstances. After all, why was the pro-government bias of public television so unwisely blatant in 1994? Lack of experience, or the absence of the checks and balances provided by competing channels may have been part of the story. But, then, why did the post-1998 centre-right government return to the high-handed interventionism of the 1990–94 governments? An often-heard justification of the media policies of the centre right gives a plausible account. It argues that the (self-)selection processes to elite positions under state socialism were such that most journalists of the immediate post-communist era are natural partisans of the centre left and the liberals. Consensual and *laissez-faire* policies would only sustain an imbalance that has to be combated by the right to improve one's lot. In this light, the apparently counterproductive pro-government campaign on public television in 1994 could be seen as either the result of pursuing the long-term goal of transforming the media system at the expense of short-term vote maximization, or as a structurally induced misperception of strategic opportunities. In either case, the choices were just shifting shadows of slow-moving constraints. But they had their own effects.

APPENDIX

Data sets and variables

Data sets

The data used in the chapter are made available via the Hungarian data archive, TARKI. Random route samples of the adult population (1,200 respondents at a time) were interviewed with standardized questionnaires in April 1994 (about three weeks before the first round of the 1994 election), March 1998 and April 1998. The last two data sets (collected approximately six and three weeks before the first round of the 1998 election, respectively) are merged in the data analysis below. Between the first and second round of balloting, as many of the respondents in the pre-election interviews as could be reached were contacted again, with 719 and 1525 of them successfully re-interviewed in May 1994 and May 1998, respectively. Only these respondents were included in the analyses reported here. The data were weighted so that in both years the weighted proportion of forty non-overlapping demographic groups (defined in terms of gender, age, urban versus rural place of residence and education), and of the overlapping group of Budapest residents, corresponded to the findings of the 1996 micro-census by the Central Statistical Office.

Variables:

Public television exposure: frequency of watching the first channel of public television measured on a six- (in 1994 five-) point scale running from $0 = $ never to $1 = $ every day.

Early-campaign party sympathy: the difference between the respondent's pre-election rating of the main government party (MDF in 1994, MSZP in 1998) and the main challenger party (MSZP in 1994, Fidesz-MPP in 1998) on a seven-point feeling thermometer. Positive values stand for more positive evaluation of the main government party than the main challenger.

Change in party sympathy: the difference between respondent's early-campaign party sympathy and a parallel measured derived from the post-election data. Positive values indicate that over time the difference became more favourable (or less unfavourable) for the incumbents.

Early-campaign economic evaluations: pre-election responses to 'Do you think that in the last twelve months the economic situation (1) has got much worse, (2) has got somewhat worse, (3) has stayed the same, (4) has got somewhat better, or (5) has got much better?'

Change in economic evaluations: the difference between the pre- and post-election retrospective economic evaluations (measured as described above), with positive values standing for change towards more favourable retrospective assessments.

Post-campaign economic evaluations in interaction with public television exposure: the product of the two variables.

Issue position: respondents' position on selected issues, with high values indicating more agreement with government than opposition. For 1994, the issue variable is the respondents' rating of the importance of 'removing former communists from positions of influence' in the pre-election survey. For 1998, the issue scale runs from -10 to $+10$, and sums the original post-election responses, recorded on eleven-point scales, to self-administered questions about respondents' preferences between tuition-free higher education versus cost-based tuition at universities, and universal versus means-tested eligibility for child-care allowance.

Issue position in interaction with public television exposure: the product of the two variables.

Perception of the likely winner: the respondents' pre-election response to a question about which party is going to win the election. In 1994, the responses were coded as: $1 = $ MDF, $-1 = $ SZDSZ or FIDESZ, $0 = $ all else. In 1998, the responses were coded as: $1 = $ FKGP, $-1 = $ Fidesz-MPP, $0 = $ all else.

Vote choice: the respondents' post-election recalls of which party list they voted for. To reflect the utility of the vote for pro-government campaigners, the 1994 responses were coded as: $1 = $ MDF, $0 = $ MSZP, $0.5 = $ all else. In 1998, the responses were coded as: $1 = $ MSZP, $0 = $ Fidesz-MPP, $0.5 = $ all else.

Notes

1 On these terms, see Chapters 7, 8 and 1, respectively.
2 Part of the explanation is the understandable lack in many new democracies of a culture of public service journalism, and the dominance of a 'political advocate' rather than 'watchdog' and 'information provider' role definition among journalists.
3 The topics were apparently selected with the consensus of the parties, and only included major policy areas, broadly corresponding to the jurisdiction of cabinet ministries.
4 We shall not deal with this event because it was in no way the initiative or under the control of the media personnel who staged the pro-government campaign on public television. At any rate, the debate took place ten days after the first round of the election, and one day after the last interviews were done for the post-election wave of the 1998 survey.
5 Other information sources were mentioned by just 7 per cent of the respondents. These data were made available to us by the Median Public Opinion and Market Research Institute, and refer to a random route sample $(n = 1,200)$, weighted to match the demographic composition of the adult population.
6 In both years, 15–16 per cent could not answer, while the rest saw more or less bias in television coverage. The sources are the post-election waves of the studies described in the appendix.
7 Most of the remaining respondents either could not positively answer these questions, or thought that the coverage was always fair and balanced. Ten per cent in 1994, and 3 per cent in 1998, mentioned other parties as most favoured by the coverage.
8 Hungary has a mixed electoral system and the coalition alternatives, at least for informed actors, are exclusive and fairly clear in advance. The fate of the government is decided mainly in the single-member constituencies, in multi-candidate yet essentially two-way races. In both 1994 and 1998, each party in the government coalition had its own candidates in all constituencies, but the MDF in 1994 and the MSZP in 1998 were rightly expected to be the main vote-winners among the incumbents nearly everywhere. The erstwhile voters for the smaller parties were believed to have a relatively weak propensity to rally strategically behind the strongest candidate of their side in the second round. Thus, for someone interested in the survival of the government, votes for the main government party had the highest positive value, and votes for the main challenger party the most negative value.
9 The remaining respondents saw no change or did not know. The sources are the pre-election waves of the studies described in the appendix.
10 We used the following socio-demographic controls: gender, age, age squared, education, employment status, place of residence, log of family income, frequency of church attendance and former Communist Party membership. The additional involvement variables were frequency of reading any newspaper with some political coverage, frequency of listening to radio news, interest in politics and – in 1998 – frequency of watching any of the three main private television channels.
11 We have no data on within-campaign changes in the perception of the likely winner. Therefore early-campaign perceptions define the dependent variable.
12 This coding reflects the complexity of the strategic context. In some of the last polls, and in the election, the SZDSZ came second and the MDF third, but in most polls published in the months before the election FIDESZ – then SZDSZ's chief partner in the liberal electoral alliance formed for the 1994 election – was in second place and the MDF in third or fourth.

13 This idea was so much in the air that foundations sympathizing with the Fidesz-MPP even sponsored media polls to counter the mistaken impression.

14 The estimated impact of the issues-with-exposure interaction is inflated by the obvious collinearity with the issue attitude variable, but when we removed the latter variable from the equation, the impact of the interaction term still remained positive and statistically significant (data not shown).

15 Given the inevitable multicollinearity between the interaction terms and their component parts, we re-estimated the equation by excluding three variables from the analysis: early-campaign economic evaluations, change of economic evaluations during the campaign and issue attitudes on their own. Furthermore, the issues-with-exposure interaction term was altered to reflect that a drop, not an increase, is expected in the welfare state issues' impact on the vote as public television exposure decreases. The new formula multiplied the issue attitudes variable by (1 − public television exposure), rather than by public television exposure. In the results so obtained (not shown), both with and without controls for socio-demographic variables and further media exposure variables, the two interaction terms registered the same effects as in Table 4.4 but with $p < 0.05$.

16 The alternative coding assumed that, for partisans of the main government party, votes for allies were slightly better, and votes for smaller opposition parties slightly worse, than abstention. Accordingly, voters of possible allies were coded 0.75, and voters of the possible allies of the main challenger as 0.25.

17 Maybe there were simply too few voters who could have been persuaded to vote for the incumbents just for a fear of an MSZP victory.

18 The non-significant effect in 1998 is hardly a surprise: we would not expect mere watching of the programme to prompt a vote for the government. Rather, it should be through the impact of exposure on party sympathy, perceptions, issue concerns and so forth that we would expect pro-government coverage to boost behavioural support for the government.

5 Priming and campaign context

Evidence from recent Canadian elections

Elisabeth Gidengil, André Blais, Neil Nevitte and Richard Nadeau

The most obvious place to look for the effects of election campaigns is in the realm of persuasion. After all, this is what election campaigns are about: the strategic efforts of parties and candidates to gain votes by persuading as many voters as possible to vote for their party's candidates. We typically think of persuasion as getting voters to change their opinions of the parties, the leaders or the issues of the day, but this is too narrow a conception. In this chapter we focus on a more subtle but none the less important form of persuasion: getting voters to change the bases on which they decide their vote.

This is precisely what motivates the parties' struggle to control the election agenda. Parties seek to emphasize considerations that will help them – be it a popular leader or an issue on which they possess a recognized expertise – and to downplay those that will hurt (Budge and Farlie 1983; Petrocik 1996; Nadeau *et al.* 2000a). From the parties' perspective, then, election campaigns can be conceptualized as a competition for control of the agenda. Political parties, however, are not the only players in this agenda-setting competition. The media are also potentially critical players (Semetko 1996; Norris *et al.* 1999). Political parties rely on the media for communicating their core messages to voters, but the media do not serve simply as a neutral transmission belt between the parties and the voters. In a very literal sense, they mediate the campaign communication flows, highlighting some messages and downplaying others. This is the essence of the media's power to prime (Iyengar and Kinder 1987).

Priming can be thought of as 'an extension of agenda-setting' (Ansolabehere *et al.* 1991: 127; Semetko 1996: 275). Indeed, Miller and Krosnick (2000) have argued that priming occurs *via* agenda setting.[1] Agenda setting refers to the media's power to influence the public agenda (McCombs and Shaw 1972). In the context of elections, the basic proposition is that the more attention the media pay to an issue, the greater will be its perceived electoral importance. Priming occurs when extensive media coverage leads voters to attach more importance to a given consideration in deciding their vote. Priming can lead people to change their minds, not because they have changed their opinions of the leaders, the issues or the parties themselves, but because the relative weight of those opinions in their decision has changed. As Johnston and his colleagues (1992: 212) aptly put it, 'Priming is the electoral manifestation of the elite struggle for control of the agenda.'

Analyses of priming have emphasized the contingent nature of priming effects. The focus, though, has been on individual-level conditioning factors like political interest and knowledge about politics (Krosnick and Kinder 1990; Weaver 1991). What has been overlooked is the conditioning effect of the election campaign itself. In this chapter, we develop some propositions about the contingent conditions of priming during election campaigns. These propositions are then assessed using data from recent Canadian election studies. The rolling cross-section design of these studies is particularly well suited to detecting campaign effects. The analysis is restricted to the official campaign that begins with the dropping of the election writs. This is the period when the strategic efforts of parties to win votes are most intense and when media coverage is most extensive.

What gets primed and when?

Our first proposition relates to the priming of issues. We hypothesize that issue priming will occur only by exception. The conditionality of issue priming effects is implicit in Norris and her colleagues' (1999: 182–3) work on agenda setting in the 1997 British election. The British public apparently 'followed its own agenda' (p. 128), an agenda that was driven by social and economic concerns. Reflecting as they do the preoccupations of day-to-day living, issues like health care and education and jobs will typically be on the public agenda long before the election campaign actually begins. It follows that the scope for agenda setting – and, by extension, priming – during the election campaign itself will be correspondingly diminished. For issue priming to occur, the election campaign has to revolve around an issue that is 'dramatically new' (Norris *et al.* 1999: 129). An example is the 1988 Canadian election campaign. That election amounted to almost a referendum on the issue of ratifying the Canada–US Free Trade Agreement, and Mendelsohn (1996a) has shown that the campaign did indeed prime the issue. When classic valence issues predominate or when multi-issue agendas prevail, issue priming is much less likely to occur.

What *is* likely to occur more routinely is the priming of leadership. In fact, Mendelsohn's (1996a) central proposition was that the personalized nature of media coverage serves to prime leadership considerations. He links this priming effect with Iyengar's (1991) arguments about the predominance of episodic framing in news reports. By failing to situate political issues in some broader context, news reports encourage the public to attribute undue responsibility to individual political actors (as opposed to political parties or larger societal forces). Mendelsohn also points to the large body of research that has demonstrated the media's propensity to personalize issues, downplay political parties, and encourage 'the rise of candidate-centered politics' (Wattenberg 1991) in the United States.

As a presidential system, the United States may be particularly prone to the personalization of politics, but there is evidence that leadership has a significant independent effect on the vote (though not necessarily on election outcomes) in Westminster-style parliamentary systems like Australia, Britain, Canada and New Zealand as well (Graetz and McAllister 1987; Bean and Mughan 1989; Clarke *et al.* 1991; Stewart and Clarke 1992; Bean 1993; Crewe and King 1994; Nevitte *et al.* 2000). Whether leadership has become *more* important to the vote in parliamentary systems remains an open question (Gidengil *et al.* 2000), but the presumption is that the changing nature of the mass media has played an important role in focusing attention on the party leaders (McAllister 1996), and so have changes in campaign strategy. Such is the personalized nature of media coverage in Canada that a party will typically receive little or no coverage on the nightly news if the leader takes the day off from campaigning (Mendelsohn 1993). There are good reasons, then, to expect that election campaigns will generally tend to prime leadership, *unless* a dramatically new issue dominates the agenda, and that the extent to which leadership is primed in any given campaign will be a function of the degree to which the campaign is 'personalized' (as the result of a deliberate strategy on the part of campaign managers and/or the media's personalizing style of reporting).

One likely corollary of personalized coverage is the muting of partisanship (see Mendelsohn 1996a). Indeed, we predict that the more leadership gets primed over the course of an election campaign, the more muted partisanship will become. This is consistent with the role of party identification in the original Michigan model. Partisan ties may have weakened,[2] but there are still many voters who have long-term affective ties with a particular party that predispose them to vote for that party. Short-term forces, though, may intervene to sway their vote. Figuring prominently among those short-term forces are evaluations of the leaders. If short-term forces do induce temporary defections, then partisanship *should* become decreasingly important as the election campaign progresses. This muting of partisanship will be contingent on the pull of the short-term forces: the stronger the priming of leadership, the less important party identification will become to the vote. Both effects will be heightened by media exposure (see Mendelsohn 1996a).

Our final proposition relates to the effects of interpersonal communication. Drawing on the work of Huckfeldt and Sprague (1987) and MacKuen and Brown (1987), Mendelsohn hypothesizes that interpersonal communications will serve to prime issues. The logic here is that conversations about politics are likely to focus on aspects of the election that are particularly salient in people's every day lives and that means the issues that affect them. Moreover, political discussion is a much less passive way of acquiring information (Lenart 1994) and so, presumably, the objects of discussion are likely to weigh more heavily in the voting decision. This leads Mendelsohn (1996a) to predict that political discussion will provide a possible offsetting influence to the media. Indeed, he found that the priming of the free trade issue in the 1988 Canadian election was due to the effect of interpersonal communication rather than media exposure.

Again, though, we would argue that this happens only by exception. As Mendelsohn (1996a: 121) himself cautions, the counterbalancing effects of interpersonal communications may be much less evident 'under more typical campaign conditions' when no single issue dominates. When the issue agenda is more varied and the issues themselves reflect voters' on-going priorities, political discussion appears unlikely to offset the media's emphasis on the leaders. Indeed, in the absence of a novel and divisive issue, political discussion may, if anything, serve to reinforce media messages.[3] To the extent that leaders dominate the election campaign, they are also likely to dominate discussions *about* the election campaign. This is especially likely when the issues at stake are valence issues (like inflation and unemployment) that focus attention on who will do the best job of dealing with them. Accordingly, we predict that it takes a dramatic new issue for interpersonal communication to offset the media's priming of leadership.

Variations in campaign context

Recent Canadian election campaigns illustrate just how much campaign contexts can vary.[4] The 1988 Canadian election brought to the fore exactly the sort of 'dramatically new' (Norris *et al.* 1999: 129) issue that could reshape the public agenda in the relatively short time span of an election campaign.[5] The election campaign was dominated, to a degree unusual in Canadian elections, by a single issue, the Canada–US Free Trade Agreement (see Johnston *et al.* 1992). When asked which issue was most important to them personally, 62 per cent of respondents in the 1988 Canadian Election Study mentioned free trade (see Figure 5.1). There is reason to believe, then, that the 1988 election campaign was particularly likely to see issue priming.

Notwithstanding the dominance of the free trade issue, the 1988 election campaign also kept the spotlight on the party leaders. The two opposition parties pursued a very deliberate strategy of personalizing the free trade issue as the 'Mulroney trade deal' and there is every indication that this rhetorical ploy was effective (Johnston *et al.* 1992). Moreover, the campaign featured a particularly acrimonious televised debate among the party leaders during which the Liberal leader, John Turner, accused his Conservative counterpart of selling out the country. However, account also has to be taken of the offsetting role of interpersonal communication. It is likely that the free trade issue dominated discussions about the election campaign. Seventy-one per cent of those who reported discussing politics with others over the previous week named free trade as the most important issue to

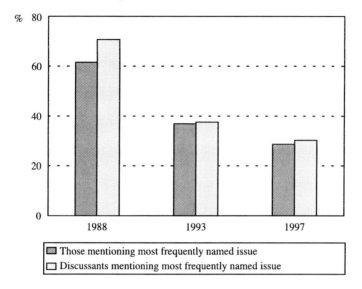

Figure 5.1 Single-issue dominance, by election.

them personally (see Figure 5.1). Given the dominance of the issue, it is plausible that interpersonal communication served to counterbalance media priming of leadership.

The Conservatives won the 1988 election. Five years later, though, the party had become massively unpopular in the wake of failed attempts to resolve the constitutional *impasse*, the introduction of a controversial Goods and Services Tax, and chronically high unemployment. In the hope of restoring their party's fortunes, the Conservatives chose Kim Campbell to become their new leader and, briefly, Canada's first female Prime Minister. It was not to be. The 1993 election proved to be an 'electoral earthquake', shattering Canada's traditional two-plus-one party system. The Conservative Party, long one of Canada's two major parties, was reduced to a mere two seats in Parliament, and two new political parties broke through – the Bloc Quebecois in Quebec and the Reform Party in western Canada. 1993 was the first election as party leader for all five leaders. The election was won by the Liberal Party, Canada's dominant party for much of the post-war period.

No single issue emerged to dominate the electoral agenda. When respondents in the Canadian Election Study were asked to name the most important issue to them personally, the modal response – jobs – received only 37 per cent of mentions, followed by government spending and programmes at 27 per cent (Figure 5.1). Not only was the issue agenda varied, but unemployment was a classic valence issue. Kim Campbell misstepped on the jobs issue on the opening day of the campaign, and within days she was also being accused of having a 'hidden agenda' to cut spending on social programmes.

In the absence of a dramatically new issue, the 1993 election was unlikely to prime issues. And the priming of leadership was unlikely to be offset by interpersonal communication. Only 38 per cent of respondents who reported discussing politics over the previous week mentioned jobs as the most important issue to them personally and they were scarcely more likely to name this issue than respondents who had not discussed politics in the previous week. In other words, the topics of political discussion are likely to have been more varied than in 1988 and less focused on a single issue.

The 1997 election campaign was also an unlikely setting for issue priming. The Liberal Party campaigned on its record and the opposition parties responded by attacking that record. Again, no single issue dominated the agenda. The most frequently named issue in the 1997 Canadian Election Study was again jobs, but now it was mentioned by only 29 per cent of respondents, followed by government spending and programmes at 24 per cent. The figures were scarcely higher among those who reported having discussed politics over the past few days.

With three new leaders contesting the election, and opposition parties portraying the Liberal leader as 'yesterday's man', leadership was very much on the agenda in the 1997 campaign. The Conservative Party was led by an attractive new leader who can take much of the credit for rescuing his party from electoral oblivion (Nevitte *et al.* 2000). Given this electoral context, we should expect to find strong evidence of leadership priming during the 1997 election campaign.

Data and methods

In order to assess our hypotheses about the nature and extent of priming, we analyse data from the 1988, 1993 and 1997 Canadian Election Studies. The surveys were Canada-wide and were conducted using computer-assisted telephone interviewing.[6] All three studies used a rolling cross-section design for the campaign-wave survey. This design is particularly well suited to testing hypotheses about priming. For each survey, respondents were interviewed throughout the campaign, beginning the day the election writs were issued and ending on the final day of the campaign. The overall samples were broken down into replicates, one for each day of the campaign, with the date of interview constituting a random event. Because each daily replicate is as similar to the others as random sampling variation permits, all that distinguishes the replicates (within the range of sampling error) is the date of interview. This makes for an extremely powerful design for assessing campaign dynamics and media effects.

The leader variable is a comparative evaluation derived from 100-point leader rating scales.[7] There is growing evidence that voters do not evaluate leaders discretely, but make these evaluations on a comparative basis (Miller and Wattenberg 1985; Mishler *et al.* 1989; Nadeau *et al.* 1996). As Nadeau and his colleagues note, 'This is perhaps so because elections themselves are by their very nature comparative; two or more candidates vie for a post, and only one secures office' (1996: 248). They also point out that the 'point–counterpoint' (Ansolabehere *et al.* 1993) nature of media coverage encourages leaders to be seen in relation to one another rather than separately. Finally, and crucially, leader evaluations are likely to matter to vote choice only to the extent that one leader is judged better than another (Mishler *et al.* 1989: 230–1). Accordingly, our leader variable is the difference between the voter's ratings of the leader of the winning party and the highest rated of the other party leaders, re-scaled to run from -1 to $+1$. Respondents who said they knew nothing about a leader were not asked to rate that leader.

For the 1988 election, the issue position variable was represented by opinion about the Canada–US Free Trade Agreement.[8] The choice of issue variable was complicated for the 1993 and 1997 elections by the lack of a single dominant issue. As we saw above, jobs were the modal response in both elections when respondents were asked to name the most important issue to them personally, followed quite closely by government spending and programmes. We have chosen jobs as the issue for 1997, but for 1993 we have opted for spending cuts.[9] The decision to go with spending cuts rather than jobs for 1993 was an empirical one. Spending cuts (unlike jobs) were mentioned much more frequently by those who discussed politics than by those who did not. This was similar to the pattern for free trade in 1988. Moreover, views on spending cuts had a more robust initial relationship with vote intention than did views about unemployment. This is not surprising given the tenor of the 1993 campaign. The Liberal Party attacked the Conservative and Reform Party proposals for eliminating the federal budget deficit within five and three years, respectively, arguing that both parties had a hidden plan to cut social programmes. The Conservatives' supposed secret agenda was the subject of a good deal of media speculation and may well have been the key to the party's collapse in the 1993 election (Johnston *et al.* 1994). In 1997, by contrast, jobs were clearly the most salient issue. When respondents were asked to rate the personal importance of a series of issues in the 1997 campaign, many more rated 'creating jobs' as 'very important' (83 per cent) than was the case for 'protecting social programmes' (59 per cent) or its flip side 'reducing the deficit' (59 per cent). And it is clear that negative perceptions about unemployment hurt the incumbent Liberals on election day, despite their efforts to campaign on a record of deficit reduction (Nadeau *et al.* 2000b). Because creating employment is a classic valence issue, we used evaluations of the incumbent's performance on the jobs front as the issue variable.[10]

The choice of media variable is complicated by differences in the questions asked in the three election studies. While the 1988 survey asked about media exposure and attention to the media, the 1993 survey only included questions about media exposure and the 1997 survey only inquired about attention to news about the election on television or in the newspapers.[11] This raises the question of whether comparisons across the three elections are confounded by differences in the media variable. There is reason to believe that media consumption is better captured by attention measures (Chaffee and Schleuder 1986; Mutz 1992; Joslyn and Ceccoli 1996). In particular, exposure measures are likely to understate the impact of television news because they imply a lower cognitive engagement than attention measures (Chaffee and Schleuder 1986). Clearly, then, exposure and attention should be viewed as distinct variables whose effects may potentially be different (Krosnick and Brannon 1993). Whether they are, in fact, different is an empirical question. Fortunately, the inclusion of both exposure and attention measures in the 1988 study allows their effects to be compared empirically. It turns out that the basic conclusions are not affected by the choice of media variable.[12] Since the interaction terms involving media attention produced severe multicollinearity problems in 1988 (see note 14), we have opted to present the results for media exposure only.

The analysis proceeds in stages, adding first-order and then second-order interactive terms to the initial estimation. The key independent variables are comparative leader ratings, issue position and party identification.[13] The first-order interactives are obtained by multiplying each of the three original independent variables by day of the campaign. Their effects indicate how the relative weight of each of the independent variables changed as the campaign progressed. There are two sets of second-order interactives. The first set is generated by multiplying the independent variables by day of the campaign and the level of media consumption, while the second set is obtained by multiplying the independent variables by day of the campaign and political discussion.[14] These terms indicate how the relative weight of the independent variables changed as the campaign progressed and as media consumption and political discussion, respectively, increased. All estimation is performed using logistic regression, with vote intention as the dependent variable. The dependent variable is coded 1 for a vote for the winning party (the Conservative Party in 1988 and the Liberal Party in 1993 and 1997) and 0 for a vote for another party. Minor-party voters and those with no stated vote intention are excluded from the analyses. In order to ensure that the observed effects were not simply due to differences in political sophistication, we include controls for interest and education.[15]

Findings

Table 5.1 presents the initial estimation. We can see that each of the three independent variables is significantly related to vote intentions. This is the case for all three elections. As predicted, the effects of comparative leader evaluations were stronger in the two later elections. Leadership seems to have been an especially important factor in 1993, the year of Canada's

Table 5.1 The impact of leaders, issues and party identification on vote intentions

Variable	1988	1993	1997
Constant	−0.89 (0.43)**	0.47 (0.30)	−0.66 (0.35)*
Leaders	4.78 (0.46)****	7.52 (0.45)****	5.60 (0.41)****
Party identification	1.86 (0.16)****	1.63 (0.11)****	2.17 (0.12)****
Issue position	1.24 (0.11)****	1.16 (0.38)***	0.64 (0.15)****
Media consumption	−0.16 (0.34)	0.20 (0.23)	0.03 (0.36)
Date of interview	−0.42 (0.35)	−0.08 (0.23)	−0.08 (0.27)
Interest in the election	0.02 (0.41)	−0.22 (0.26)	0.79 (0.39)**
Education	1.08 (0.47)**	0.09 (0.33)	0.55 (0.37)
Discussed politics	0.41 (0.22)*	−0.16 (0.16)	−0.22 (0.21)
% correctly predicted	90.0	87.6	88.4
2 × log likelihood	766.81	1,464.42	1,121.81
	(df = 1,540)	(df = 2,248)	(df = 1,904)
Chi-square	1,359.11	1,556.39	1,434.39
	(df = 11)	(df = 11)	(df = 11)
N	1,552	2,260	1,916

Notes

Maximum likelihood estimate coefficients; standard errors in parentheses. **** $p < 0.001$; *** $p < 0.01$; ** $p < 0.05$; * $p < 0.10$.

'electoral earthquake'. Not surprisingly, party identification had its weakest impact in the same election. The issue variables are not directly comparable across elections because of differences in measurement, but we can see that the issue effect was a little less robust in 1993.

Not only was leadership a more important factor in both 1993 and 1997, but it was only in these two elections that the election campaign primed leadership. As Table 5.2 shows, the predictive power of leadership evaluations significantly increased as the election campaign evolved. As the vote drew closer, voters became more likely to base their vote choice on their relative evaluations of the party leaders. The 1988 campaign turns out to be the exception. Indeed, the interactive term has the wrong sign, though the effect is not robust enough to infer that the election campaign actually muted leadership.[16]

What does get primed in 1988 is clearly the free trade issue. The effect is robust. As the election campaign progressed, opinions about the Canada– US Free Trade Agreement loomed larger in people's vote choice. This is hardly surprising. After all, the 1988 election amounted to a virtual referendum on the agreement. As predicted, campaigns do not routinely prime issues. There is no hint of a priming effect in either 1993 or 1997. In both years, the effects are no larger than their standard errors and, in any case, have the wrong signs. Clearly, the 1988 election was indeed an exceptional case, dominated as it was by a single issue and aptly dubbed 'the free trade election'.

Table 5.2 The priming of leaders, issues and party identification

Variable	1988	1993	1997
Constant	−0.79 (0.44)*	0.49 (0.32)	−0.65 (0.35)*
Leaders	5.78 (0.96)****	5.83 (0.87)****	3.94 (0.78)****
Party identification	2.18 (0.33)****	1.91 (0.23)****	2.66 (0.28)****
Issue position	0.74 (0.24)***	1.83 (0.84)**	0.87 (0.30)***
Leader × date	−1.99 (1.56)	3.36 (1.53)**	3.37 (1.41)**
Party identity × date	−0.64 (0.57)	−0.54 (0.38)	−0.86 (0.43)**
Issue × date	1.02 (0.42)**	−1.32 (1.36)	−0.44 (0.50)
Media consumption	−0.07 (0.34)	0.22 (0.23)	−0.02 (0.36)
Date of interview	−0.76 (0.39)**	−0.17 (0.34)	−0.14 (0.28)
Interest in the election	−0.05 (0.41)	−0.21 (0.26)	0.84 (0.39)**
Education	1.20 (0.47)***	0.10 (0.33)	0.59 (0.37)
Discussed politics	0.43 (0.23)*	−0.16 (0.16)	−0.21 (0.21)
% correctly predicted	90.8	88.1	88.8
2 × log likelihood	758.87 (df = 1,537)	1,457.08 (df = 2,245)	1,110.70 (df = 1,901)
Chi-square	1,367.05 (df = 14)	1,563.73 (df = 14)	1,445.50 (df =14)
N	1,552	2,260	1,916

Notes
Maximum likelihood estimate coefficients; standard errors in parentheses. **** $p < 0.001$; *** $p < 0.01$; ** $p < 0.05$; * $p < 0.10$.

The final prediction was that the priming of leadership would mute partisanship. In all three elections, the interaction term has the correct sign, though the coefficient is robust only in 1997. As the 1997 election campaign unfolded, partisanship came to matter less and less to the vote, just as leader evaluations came to matter more. The 1997 campaign clearly primed leadership to the detriment of partisanship.

Table 5.3 addresses the role of the media. The results show that the media did prime the free trade issue during the 1988 election campaign. As media consumption increased and as election day drew closer, opinion about the free trade agreement became more important to the vote. But Table 5.3 also confirms that issue priming occurs only by exception: in both 1993 and 1997 the issue interaction term was not only non-significant but had the wrong sign. In both 1993 and 1997 it was clearly leadership that got primed. As the campaign progressed and as media consumption went up, voters came to rely more on their relative evaluations of the leaders and less on their partisan cues. As predicted, the muting of partisanship appears to be related to the priming of leadership. Leadership was not as strongly primed in 1993 as in 1997, and we can see that the interaction term involving party identification approaches statistical significance only in that year. In 1997, on the other hand, the party identification interaction term indicates a robust effect.

Table 5.3 Media consumption and priming

Variable	1988	1993	1997
Constant	−0.77 (0.44)*	0.41 (0.33)	−0.63 (0.35)*
Leaders	4.64 (0.77)****	5.94 (0.68)****	3.86 (0.57)****
Party identification	2.08 (0.28)****	1.84 (0.18)****	2.60 (0.21)****
Issue position	0.95 (0.20)****	1.41 (0.56)***	0.69 (0.23)***
Leader × media × date	0.29 (1.81)	5.64 (1.98)***	8.38 (2.21)****
Party identification × media × date	−0.65 (0.63)	−0.70 (0.44)	−1.42 (0.57)***
Issue × media × date	0.84 (0.46)*	−1.18 (1.45)	−0.26 (0.67)
Media consumption	−0.22 (0.34)	0.19 (0.27)	0.01 (0.38)
Date of interview	−0.59 (0.36)*	−0.07 (0.27)	−0.04 (0.28)
Interest in the election	−0.02 (0.41)	−0.21 (0.26)	0.88 (0.39)**
Education	1.16 (0.47)***	0.13 (0.33)	0.58 (0.37)
Discussed politics	0.42 (0.22)*	−0.16 (0.16)	−0.30 (0.22)
% correctly predicted	90.2	88.2	88.5
2 × log likelihood	762.36 (df = 1,537)	1,454.06 (df = 2,245)	1,096.52 (df = 1,901)
Chi-square	1,363.56 (df = 14)	1,566.76 (df = 14)	1,459.68 (df =14)
N	1,552	2,260	1,916

Notes
Maximum likelihood estimate coefficients; standard errors in parentheses. **** $p < 0.001$; *** $p < 0.01$; ** $p < 0.05$; * $p < 0.10$.

This leaves the role of political discussion. Mendelsohn (1996a) hypothesizes that interpersonal communications will serve as a buffer against media messages: while media consumption primes leadership, talking about politics will make issues more salient. For 1988 his prediction is neatly confirmed (see Table 5.4). Comparative leader evaluations became more important as the campaign unfolded and as media consumption went up. Conversely, as the propensity to talk about politics increased over the course of the campaign, the free trade issue grew in significance *and* the impact of leadership declined. There is clear evidence, then, for the proposition that the media and interpersonal communications pull voters in opposite directions when it comes to what matters to their vote. As predicted, though, this pattern is peculiar to 1988. There is not even a hint of a similar pattern in either 1993 or 1997.[17] In fact, if anything, political discussion enhanced the importance of leadership in 1993, suggesting that interpersonal communications may actually have reinforced media messages. It appears, again, that the 1988 election was a special case where a single issue dominated political discussion to an unusual degree. While we do not have any direct evidence on the content of people's conversations about politics, the data on the most important issue (see above) strongly suggest that the issue content of political discussion was more varied in both 1993 and 1997.

Table 5.4 Media consumption, interpersonal communication and priming

Variable	1988	1993	1997
Constant	−0.63 (0.45)	0.38 (0.34)	−0.62 (0.36)*
Leaders	5.04 (0.82)****	5.63 (0.71)****	3.86 (0.65)****
Party identification	2.08 (0.28)****	1.81 (0.19)****	2.66 (0.24)****
Issue position	0.80 (0.20)****	1.38 (0.60)**	0.78 (0.25)***
Leader × media × date	5.11 (2.42)**	3.68 (2.41)	8.16 (2.72)***
Party identification × media × date	−0.63 (0.90)	−0.90 (0.56)	−1.13 (0.75)
Issue × media × date	−0.84 (0.61)	−1.26 (1.64)	0.21 (0.86)
Leader × discussed × date	−5.17 (1.75)***	2.25 (1.61)	0.14 (1.54)
Party identification × discussed × date	0.11 (0.69)	0.24 (0.41)	−0.29 (0.51)
Issue × discussed × date	1.91 (0.45)****	0.13 (1.16)	−0.49 (0.55)
Media consumption	0.12 (0.36)	0.17 (0.28)	0.02 (0.38)
Date of interview	−0.68 (0.37)*	−0.04 (0.28)	−0.07 (0.28)
Interest in the election	0.03 (0.42)	−0.21 (0.26)	0.89 (0.40)**
Education	1.08 (0.49)**	0.13 (0.33)	0.57 (0.37)
Discussed politics	0.07 (0.24)	−0.12 (0.20)	−0.32 (0.22)
% correctly predicted	90.9	88.4	88.7
2 × log likelihood	737.19 (df = 1,534)	1,451.64 (df = 2,242)	1,095.50 (df = 1,898)
Chi-square	1,388.73 (df = 17)	1,569.17 (df = 17)	1,460.70 (df =17)
N	1,552	2,260	1,916

Notes

Maximum likelihood estimate coefficients; standard errors in parentheses. **** $p < 0.001$; *** $p < 0.01$; ** $p < 0.05$; * $p < 0.10$.

Discussion

Clearly election campaigns can affect the bases on which people decide their vote. As the weeks pass, some considerations will grow in importance while others become less salient. This is the essence of priming. Our findings contribute to the understanding of priming by demonstrating the conditioning effect of the election campaign itself. Election campaigns, even within a single political system, are not all of a piece. It seems that the 1988 Canadian election was unusual in the degree to which a single issue dominated the campaign. The priming effect of the election campaign was clear: as the weeks passed, the free trade issue became increasingly important to people's vote choice. As predicted, no such effect was detectable in either of the two subsequent elections. In neither election did a single issue or set of issues dominate the public agenda, and the issues that were uppermost in voters' minds – social spending and jobs – were not the sorts of issues that are susceptible to priming. These issues were neither novel nor dramatic in the way that free trade was in 1988. Instead, they reflected on-going concerns that were likely to have been salient to voters even before the official election campaign began. The scope for issue priming, via the media or personal discussion, was correspondingly limited. Since new and dramatic issues do not, by their very nature, appear routinely on the public agenda, we can conclude that issue priming may be the exception rather than the norm.

What may well be more normal is the priming of leadership. This effect was apparent in both 1993 and 1997. As predicted, leadership became more salient over the course of both election campaigns, and media consumption clearly played a role in priming leadership. As the election campaign progressed and as media consumption increased, relative evaluations of the leaders became more important to the vote. In 1988, though, this priming effect appears only when the dynamic effects of political discussion are incorporated into the model (and it was completely offset by the pull of political discussion in the opposite direction).[18]

As predicted, the muting of partisanship is inversely related to the priming of leadership. A comparison of the results for the 1993 and 1997 election campaigns lends weight to the notion that the priming of leadership and the downplaying of partisanship are related: the more leadership is primed (as media consumption goes up and the campaign unfolds), the less important party identification becomes to the vote.

There is very little support for Mendelsohn's (1996a) prediction about the priming effects of interpersonal communication. As he suspected, the 1988 election campaign was probably exceptional in the degree to which a single issue dominated political discussion. When the issue agenda is more varied and the issues themselves reflect voters' on-going priorities, political discussion appears unlikely to serve as a counterbalance to the media's emphasis on the leaders. Indeed, it is possible that political discussion actually reinforces media messages. Clearly, we need to know more about the content of political discussion. We cannot assume that political discussion will revolve around the issues of the day. It is quite possible that interpersonal communication, like media coverage, focuses on the leaders.

The rolling cross-section design of the Canadian election studies provides a powerful means of examining campaign effects. While we were unable to incorporate measures of media content into our models, the inference that the effects of media consumption mirror patterns of media coverage is certainly plausible. There is ample evidence in Canada, as elsewhere, that media coverage is typically preoccupied with the leaders (Mendelsohn 1993, 1996b; National Media Archive 1993). And it should be noted that the media priming hypothesis does not require the media to focus increasing attention on leadership for priming to occur. As Fan (1988) argues, what really matters is the cumulative effect of repeated patterns of coverage.

In this study, we have emphasized the contingent nature of priming and we have tested some propositions about the conditioning effects of campaigns.

Our study, though, has only compared campaigns within a single political system. What differences might we expect across political systems? The most obvious distinction to make is between presidential and parliamentary systems. McAllister (1996) has argued persuasively that leadership effects should be strongest in presidential systems and the fact that 'candidate-centered politics' (Wattenberg 1991) first became visible in the United States lends weight to his argument. Candidate-centred politics are, of course, particularly conducive to the priming of leadeship. Semetko (1996) has also pointed to the possible importance of the electoral system, the argument being that politics will be more party-centred in systems with proportional representation. It follows that there will be less scope for priming leadership. Another contextual variable that needs to be taken into consideration is the nature of the party system. Semetko (1996) suggests that stronger party systems (like Britain's) afford party elites more discretion in setting the campaign agenda. To the extent that the media's power to prime presupposes their power to set the campaign agenda, priming effects will be weaker.[19]

This discussion of context raises the question of how we should characterize the institutional setting, and hence the potential for priming, in the case of Canada. On a continuum of parliamentary systems, Canada would rank toward the 'presidentialized' pole. Indeed, even back in the 1970s there was a good deal of speculation about the presidentialization of Canadian politics and the dominance of the executive (Smith 1977; Savoie 1999). More interesting than the phenomenon of presidentialization, perhaps, is the fact that Canada has a party system in flux. In the unfamiliar terrain of multipartyism under Westminster-style rules, comparative leader evaluations may serve as a particularly valuable guide to vote choice.

Notes

The authors gratefully acknowledge the financial support of the Social Sciences and Humanities Research Council of Canada under its Major Collaborative Research Initiatives Programme.

1 This is at odds with conventional wisdom, which assumes that priming is mediated via accessibility. In other words, the more attention the media pay to an issue, the more likely that issue is to come to mind and thus influence people's political judgements.
2 Bartels (2000) represents a fundamental challenge to the partisan decline thesis in the United States.
3 Mendelsohn (1996a) did recognize this possibility.
4 An election was also held in November 2000, but the election study data were not available at the time of writing.
5 Debate about the Canada–US Free Trade Agreement was cast very much in terms of competing claims about jobs and social programmes (which may also help to explain its capacity to dominate the campaign agenda), but the issue itself was clearly new to the public.
6 The campaign-wave sample sizes were 3,609 in 1988, 3,775 in 1993 and 3,949 in 1997. The response rates were 57 per cent, 64 per cent and 59 per cent,

respectively. The principal investigators were Richard Johnston, André Blais, Henry E. Brady, and Jean Crête for the 1988 Canadian Election Study, Richard Johnston, André Blais, Henry E. Brady, Elisabeth Gidengil and Neil Nevitte for the 1993 Canadian Election Study, and André Blais, Elisabeth Gidengil, Richard Nadeau and Neil Nevitte for the 1997 Canadian Election Study. The fieldwork for all three studies was conducted by the Institute for Social Research at York University and all three studies were funded by the Social Sciences and Humanities Research Council of Canada. Technical documentation is available from the Institute for Social Research and the data are also archived at the ICPSR.

7 Mendelsohn (1996a) used comparative trustworthiness ratings to represent leader evaluations in 1988. We prefer to use overall evaluations because different campaigns and different personalities can bring different traits to the fore.

8 'Oppose' was coded -1, 'neither support nor oppose' and 'don't know' were coded 0, and 'support' was coded 1.

9 Respondents were asked whether they would cut spending for pensions and old age security, health care, unemployment insurance and education, respectively, 'a lot' (coded 0), 'some' (coded 0.5) or 'not at all' (coded 1). A simple additive scale was created, rescaled to run from 0 to 1, with 1 indicating no cuts in any of the four areas.

10 Responses have been rescaled to run from -1, 'not good at all', to 1, 'very good', with 'don't know' coded 0.

11 Media exposure is represented by the total number of days the respondent said he or she had watched the news on television or read a newspaper in the previous week. Media attention is represented by the amount of attention the respondent reported paying to news about the election on television and in the newspaper over the previous few days. Both measures were rescaled to run from 0 to 1. It was not feasible to examine the effects of each medium separately. There is evidence, though, of media priming, whether the respondent relies on television or on print (Mendelsohn 1994).

12 The same is true of differences in the measurement of political interest. While the 1988 and 1997 surveys measured both interest in politics generally and interest in the election, the 1993 survey measured only interest in the election. Whether general political interest or interest in the election is used in 1988 and 1997, the results are the same. Accordingly, for the sake of consistency across elections, we present the results using interest in the election.

13 Those who identified very strongly or fairly strongly with the winning party are coded 1, while those who identified very strongly or fairly strongly with another party were coded -1. Weak identifiers, leaners and non-identifiers are coded 0. Weak identifiers are not counted as partisans because they seem to lack the sort of psychological attachment to their party that the concept of party identification implies. When asked whether they think of themselves as close to any particular political party, weak identifiers are no more likely than leaners to answer in the affirmative (Blais *et al.* 1999).

14 The political discussion variable is a binary variable, coded 1 for respondents who reported having discussed politics with other people over the past week (1988/93) or in the last few days (1997). The inclusion of higher-order interactives necessarily creates problems with multicollinearity. This makes for inefficiency which shows up in the form of inflated standard errors. The practical effect is to provide a more conservative test. The one instance where multicollinearity appears to be a fatal problem is in 1988, when media attention is used to represent media consumption. Adding the political discussion terms to the model causes the second-order interactive term for media consumption and issue position to change sign,

even while remaining statistically significant. Accordingly, we have chosen to use media exposure instead for the 1988 estimations. This does not materially affect the results in any other respect.

15 The eleven levels of education were rescaled to run from 0 to 1. Following Mendelsohn (1996a), controls were also included for region, using a series of dummy variables for Atlantic Canada, Quebec and the West. Region is the single most important electoral cleavage in Canada. To simplify the presentation of results, the regional coefficients are not shown in the tables, which focus on the substantively important results.

16 It is consistent, though, with detailed analyses of campaign dynamics which show that ratings of Mulroney had less impact on the Conservative vote following the televised leaders' debates (Johnston *et al.* 1992: chapter 8).

17 Given the multicollinearity problems entailed in the use of second-order interactives, the models were re-estimated without the media terms. The results were even less favourable to the proposition about the priming effects of political discussion. They suggested that, just like the media, political discussion primed leadership and, at least in 1997, muted partisanship.

18 Mendelsohn (1994: 119) himself found that the priming effect of media consumption was not very robust (the statistical significance was 'underwhelming') until the political discussion terms were added to the model.

19 Other, more idiosyncratic, factors to bear in mind are the legal context and the length of election campaigns. Norris and her colleagues (1999: 115–16), for example, suggest that the legal regulations governing political broadcasting, and especially the requirement of 'political balance', may limit the media's agenda-setting role. As for campaign length, it is plausible that longer election campaigns are more conducive to priming effects. It is worth noting, though, that the 1997 Canadian election campaign (at thirty-six days) was almost two weeks shorter than the previous election campaign and yet media priming of leadership (and the muting of partisanship) was even more in evidence.

6 Candidate-centred campaigns and their effects in an open list system

The case of Finland

Ilkka Ruostetsaari and Mikko Mattila

The purpose of this chapter is to examine the factors that influenced the electoral success of candidates in the Finnish parliamentary elections of 21 March 1999. The Finnish electoral system uses open lists, where a candidate's election is determined on the basis of a personal vote (a preferential system). In other words, the party organizations cannot prioritize the rank order of candidates; the voters alone decide their fate (e.g. Gallagher *et al.* 2001: 314). Thus the system emphasizes candidates' personal qualities, available resources and campaigning efforts. In fact, the open list system combined with the d'Hondt method of allocating the seats means that the most serious competitor for a candidate may well be from the same party, not from other parties. Compared with systems with closed lists, the Finnish system encourages individual candidates to invest much more time, effort and money in their election campaigns to secure their success. This is why Finnish election campaigns can be called candidate-centred as opposed to party-centred campaigns.

The main research question in this chapter is how much do campaigns matter in candidate-centred elections? We use survey data from an electoral district in the Tampere region of Finland collected during the 1999 election campaign. We analyse factors influencing the votes for individual candidates. Three rival models of possible influence on a candidate's personal vote are tested, two of which place stress on the candidates' campaigns. The first model emphasizes the candidates' prior *political experience* in determining their electoral success. Political experience is based on such things as candidates' status as incumbent MPs, or municipal councillors, or their participation in previous elections. The remaining two models focus on candidates' campaigns. While the second model concentrates on *organizational* aspects of the campaign, the third model's focus is on the candidates' access to *advertising resources*. We investigate how candidates' advertising expenditure in newspapers, on television and on radio are related to their election result.

We start with a discussion about the Finnish electoral system. Then we introduce our three models and evaluate their merits based on descriptive univariate and bivariate analysis. In the final part of the chapter we use multiple regression analysis to test the models in a multivariate setting to see which model performs best in terms of its explanatory power.

The Finnish electoral system and the recruitment of MPs

The opportunities to become a legislator in Finland are heavily influenced by the electoral system and the legal regulations surrounding the recruitment process. The 200 members of the unicameral Finnish parliament (Eduskunta) are elected for a four-year term on the basis of proportional representation. For electoral purposes, the country is divided into fifteen constituencies. Fourteen multi-member constituencies vary in size from seven to thirty-one members, with the exception of the single-member self-governing province of Åland. This means that in practice an electoral threshold exists in the smallest constituencies, even though there are no formal national or constituency thresholds (Helander 1997b: 57).

Usually, in Scandinavian elections the parties nominate the candidates and decide their rank order. The voters' task is to determine the distribution of mandates, while the parties determine which candidates are to be elected. In Finland open lists are used: the candidates are not ranked, and so the voters have decision-making power over both functions. Under the Finnish system electors vote for individual candidates. Every candidate is assigned a number and voters cast their ballot for an individual candidate by writing down the number of the candidate on the ballot. The seats are allocated to parties, based on the total vote for all the party's candidates, using the d'Hondt method (Kuusela 1995: 24–30). Given that the order of the names on the party list does not have any effect on the final result, candidates find themselves competing for the mandate both with candidates from their own party and with candidates from other parties. In this sense, the Finnish system clearly focuses more on the individual candidate than the more commonly used closed list electoral systems.

This stress on the role of individual candidates gives room for both financial and personnel resources to be used not only by parties but also by individual candidates. Indeed, Finland has seen a shift from a collective, party-based style of campaigning to individual candidate-centred campaigning, even on the political left (Helander 1997a: 65). While the probability of a candidate being elected is not directly dependent on the support of their party, it is worth while for the candidate to invest in the election campaign. This is not the case, for instance, in Sweden and Norway, where candidates' rank order on the party list determines *de facto* who will be elected, and personal campaigns have no influence (Pesonen *et al.* 1993: 295).

The Finnish Electoral Act lays down certain general principles about the process of candidate selection. These include provision for managing candidate nomination. Every local party branch, which is based on personal membership, is entitled to nominate people for the party primary. Legally all parties must hold a primary in order to select their candidates (unless no more than the number of candidates assigned to the constituency have been nominated). If the party has no internal rules for candidate selection the Electoral Act provides the framework, although the law does not regulate such practical issues as joining an electoral alliance, the timetable of a party primary, or the number of aspirants for which a party member may vote. Most parties have drawn up model rules in line with the provisions of the Electoral Act for organizing candidate selection at the constituency level. These include such matters as the way in which the party branches or individual party members can make proposals for the nomination process, whether a party member is entitled to vote for one or more aspirants and whether the voting may be completed by postal ballot or in some other way (Helander 1997b: 59; see also Sundberg 1995).

The Electoral Act further provides that persons supported by at least fifteen members of one party branch, or thirty members of separate party branches in the same constituency, must be put on the list for the party primary. The procedure also secures the right to participate for persons who have been rejected by the branch leadership (Helander 1997b: 59).

Overall, then, in terms of international comparisons, the Finnish electoral system is heavily focused on individual candidates. It opens up a pathway to candidacy for individuals outside parties, i.e. voters' associations and electoral alliances of voters' associations. The system is also very decentralized, stressing intra-party democracy. In contrast to most European counterparts, the Finnish electoral system also calls for active co-operation of party members as far as the nomination of candidates is concerned (Gallagher *et al.* 2001). The opportunities for national parties to influence district party organizations are rather limited; they can normally interfere in the activities of party district organizations only in order to settle conflicts. Similarly, the opportunities for party district organizations to manipulate the local party branches' supply of candidates and the results of party primaries are also limited. The district party leadership can, however, change a quarter of the results of the party primary – excluding the top of the list – in order, for instance, to balance the party list of candidates (Helander and Kuitunen 1997: 17–18).

Research task, method and data

The purpose of this chapter is to analyse the role of candidates' personal features in influencing their vote, and, in particular, those aspects of their campaigns which affect their electoral success. As the study focuses on a single electoral district – the district of Pirkanmaa – we cannot generalize our findings to all electoral districts. It is evident, however, that the study is of heuristic value because it can generate hypotheses concerning the whole country.

As far as the number of MPs elected from constituencies is concerned, the constituency of Pirkanmaa is the fourth largest in the country (sixteen). The largest constituency is Uusimaa (thirty) and the smallest North Karelia (seven). Voter turnout in Pirkanmaa in 1999 (68.9 per cent) was only a little higher than the national average (68.3 per cent). An industrial heartland, with rather big estates, Pirkanmaa has been dominated by the political left and the Conservatives, while the political support of the Agrarians (nowadays the Centre Party) has been essentially lower than in the country at large. Support for the parties changed quite significantly in the constituency in 1999, although changes at the individual level were even greater.[1] The Conservatives won five seats (+1), the Social Democrats four (−2), the Left Alliance three (+1), the Centre Party two (±0), the Green League one (±0) and the Christian League one (+1). Three of the MPs elected in Pirkanmaa in the 1995 election did not stand for re-election, whereas five others were not elected.

This study uses data from two sources. Most information was obtained by means of a postal survey of all 172 candidates nominated in Pirkanmaa, conducted between 18 February and 21 March 1999. The response rate was 76 per cent. Of the sixteen successful candidates elected to parliament, ten participated in the survey. In addition, information was collected about the candidates' media advertising. All newspapers, party papers, local papers and free distribution papers which were published or distributed in the electoral district between 25 January and 21 March were analysed to determine the amount of advertising in the press. The space, i.e. the size of each advertisement, was multiplied by the price of an advertisement's location in the paper, in order to determine the cost of the advertisement. An advertisement was interpreted as a candidate advertisement if no more than five candidates were mentioned.[2] In this case the same advertisement was coded for all the candidates involved. In all other cases the advertisement was interpreted as a party advertisement and excluded from the analysis. The cost of television and radio advertising was obtained directly from these media after the elections. As the candidates' electoral code numbers were asked in the questionnaire, information on election advertising could be combined with the survey data.[3]

Our empirical study starts with descriptive analyses in which successful candidates are compared with all candidates to see how they differ from the 'average'. This is followed by regression analysis in which the number of votes cast for candidates is used as a dependent variable. Three rival models are used to explain electoral success, and the relative explanatory power of these models is tested. The first model – political experience – includes a candidate's status as perhaps an incumbent MP, and previous participation in different types of elections at local and national level. Experience can further a candidate's electoral success in a number of ways. Incumbent MPs are likely to receive more free media exposure in newspapers and on television. Candidates who have taken part in elections before have more experience in running campaigns and they usually have their support groups ready to start campaigning. The second and third models are based on the assumption that, all else being equal, campaigning can enhance a candidate's electoral prospects. The second model – campaign organization – takes account of the number of election rallies which were organized, the range of municipalities which were campaigned in, and the utilization of a campaign office and a support group. The third model – resources – comprises variables measuring the extent of electoral advertising in the press, on television and on radio.

Political experience

The first of our three models hypothesizes that political experience is the key to understanding the electoral success of candidates. Obviously, having served previously gives incumbents a clear advantage. Their work as outgoing MPs guarantees them free media attention throughout the whole four-year electoral period, and most of the voters recognize their names even before the campaigns start. The 'incumbency effect' was strong in Pirkanmaa in 1999. Over 60 per cent (eight out of thirteen) of the MPs elected in 1995 were re-elected. Three MPs did not stand for re-election.

Candidates' previous participation in various elections is analysed in Table 6.1. A quarter of all candidates and a fifth of successful candidates had no prior electoral experience before the 1999 election. The most common form of experience among candidates was participation in municipal elections. Almost a third of all candidates had prior experience in parliamentary elections, while the figure for the successful candidates was 70 per cent. Table 6.1 suggests that electoral experience matters; the successful candidates have more experience with all kinds of elections than the average candidate.

In Finland, as in other European countries, politicians have traditionally been trained as legislators in lower elective offices, or through election to internal party bodies. Table 6.2 shows that more than half the candidates

Table 6.1 Candidates' prior electoral experience (%)

Type of election	All candidates	Elected candidates
Co-operatives	24	60
Parish	19	20
Municipal	68	80
Parliament	28	70
Electoral college	10	30
European Parliament	5	10
None of the above	25	20
N	130	10

Table 6.2 Candidates' prior experience as members of political institutions and organizations (%)

Member of	All candidates	Elected candidates
Municipal board	55	70
Municipal council or executive committee	43	80
Party organization	39	80
National party organization	26	30
None of the above	31	20
N	105	10

nominated in Pirkanmaa had previously been members of municipal boards or committees, while two-fifths had been members of municipal councils or municipal executive committees. Two-fifths had been leaders at the national, regional or local level of the party organization, with a quarter holding a leadership position at the national level (party executive committee or party council). A third of all candidates and a fifth of the successful candidates had no such prior experience. As before, Table 6.2 leads to the conclusion that successful candidates had more experience than those candidates who failed to be elected. More of them had already stood for office before, and more of them had actually held electoral office both in public institutions and in party organizations.

Having inspected candidates' political 'histories', the next two sections examine their campaigns.

Campaign organization

Our second model posits that candidates' campaign organizations and campaigning efforts help to explain their electoral success. In this section we consider as parts of a candidate's campaign organization such factors as the number of election rallies, the size of the candidate's support group, and the range of different municipalities campaigned in.

On the whole, the candidates' election campaigning was traditional in the sense that the most commonly used modes were newspaper advertising and participation in election rallies organized by the party or their own support group. Three-quarters of candidates in Pirkanmaa estimated that they used both modes during their campaign. Two-thirds of candidates distributed election material in the street. About half of them reported sending letters or cards to target groups, appearing in the party's mobile campaign unit, advertising on free poster spaces or appearing on radio (e.g. panel discussions). Use of the internet is a recent innovation in Finnish parliamentary elections. As many as half the candidates in the 1996 European Parliament election reported using it (Ahopelto-Marjamäki 1999: 62). In Pirkanmaa in the 1999 general election the internet (home page, e-mail address or own material on the internet) was the fourth most common mode of campaigning.

The increased role of individual candidates in Finnish campaigns was already evident in the early 1990s, at least partly as a result of the weakening of party organizations (Pesonen *et al*. 1993: 295–6). In the case of Pirkanmaa we can analyse the organization, and scope, of the candidates' campaigns by inspecting the number of election rallies held by candidates in the district's thirty municipalities, and by the number of municipalities that were covered by these activities.

Also of interest is whether candidates had support groups and what size these were. Candidate support groups have increased in importance in Finnish election campaigns over the last two decades. Their role includes fund raising, organizing campaigning activities and attracting publicity for the candidate. Furthermore, given that they include in their ranks individuals who are not party members, support groups function as a means of recruiting new party members (Pesonen *et al*. 1993; Venho 1999: 55).

In Table 6.3 we see how successful candidates were more likely to have support groups in the first place, and that their support groups had, on average, more members than those of unsuccessful candidates. The average size of support groups for all candidates was twenty-two members while elected candidates' support groups consisted of more than seventy members on average. Table 6.3 also shows how successful candidates had more election rallies in more municipalities than the average. Of all candidates, 33 per cent reported attending fewer than six election rallies, while at the other extreme about 7 per cent attended 100 or more rallies. As far as the regional distribution of election rallies is concerned, 11 per cent of candidates attended rallies in only one municipality, whereas the plurality (40 per cent) reported attending rallies in two to five municipalities. Both the number of rallies and the range of municipalities was greatest among the candidates of the major parties, i.e. the Social Democrats, the Conservatives, the Centre Party and the Left Alliance.

Table 6.3 Candidates' campaigning organizations and activities

Variable	All candidates	Elected candidates
Existence of support group (%)	61.0	80.0
Size of support group (mean number of members)	22.0	73.0
Number of election rallies held (means)	13.0	31.0
Number of municipalities campaigned (means)	4.0	16.0
Diversity of campaigning activities (means)	7.2	8.2
N_{min}	123.0	10.0

Earlier studies (e.g. Sundberg 1996: 46–59) have shown how, in contrast to the national campaigns of political parties, the planning and implementation of candidates' campaigns in Finnish parliamentary elections are mostly conducted by political amateurs. This study confirms this trend. Only one-tenth of candidates reported utilizing an election office or headquarters, a more permanent way to run the campaign compared with relying on a support group.

Election campaigns can be conducted in a number of different ways. Some candidates concentrate their resources on only one or two campaign tactics (such as newspaper advertising or personal web pages), while others invest time and resources in a wide variety of different campaign tactics. We measure the use of various different forms of campaigning with a variable called 'diversity of campaigning'. This variable is an additive scale calculated from questions in our survey. The respondents were shown a list of twenty-four different forms of campaigning and were asked to check every one they had used.[1] Accordingly, the scale can vary from 0 to 24. There is a difference, in Table 6.3, in the number of campaign forms used between all candidates and successful candidates. The average number was about seven for all candidates and about eight for the successful candidates. Successful candidates, therefore, relied on a somewhat more varied repertoire of campaign techniques.

Advertising resources

The previous section focused on the organizational pathways candidates rely on to communicate to the electorate. This section looks at mediated communication, and more particularly at candidate advertising. The extent to which candidates can make use of this channel of campaign communication is highly dependent on their financial resources. Our third model, therefore, assumes that resources available for advertising in newspapers, and on television and radio, are a major factor in explaining a candidate's success.

Since the 1970s, candidates' share of total expenditure on election advertising in Finnish general elections has averaged about two-thirds of the total, with the parties making up the remainder (Pesonen *et al.* 1993: 430). Our calculations suggest that expenditure on press and broadcasting advertisements by candidates in Pirkanmaa was FIM 3.4 million (equivalent to €0.57 million). Indeed, the total cost is likely to be greater, as the calculations do not include, for instance, advertising in periodicals, street advertisements, brochures, direct mail or advertising production costs.

Advertising expenditure trends are shown in Table 6.4.[5] Expenditure on press advertising accounts for almost 80 per cent of total candidate advertising, while the share of television advertising is 16 per cent and radio just 4 per cent. If we compare the cost of press advertising in 1999 (FIM 2.6 million) with that in 1991 (FIM 1.8 million, see Pesonen *et al.* 1993: 310), we can conclude that expenditure increased by a fourth, even if the

Table 6.4 Candidates' mean expenditure on advertising in various media (FIM)

Medium	All candidates	Elected candidates
Press	12,034	46,828
Radio	683	1,220
Television	2,360	18,158
Total	15,077	66,206
N	131	10

Note
FIM 5.95 = €1.

number of newspapers studied was smaller in 1991 than in 1999. Over the period, the share of advertising on radio has decreased in favour of television advertising.[6]

Table 6.4 shows how the resources spent on advertising differ significantly between successful and unsuccessful candidates. The advertising budget of the candidates who were elected was more than four times larger than the average. The difference is even more notable in the case of television advertising: a successful candidate used almost eight times more money on television commercials than an average candidate. According to Venho (1999: 25), financial resources for campaigning varied greatly between candidates in the 1999 parliamentary elections. The amount of money that was at a candidate's disposal was affected markedly by prior experience of candidacy, prior experience as an MP and the gender of the candidate. Typically, more experienced and established male candidates of major parties who stood for election in southern or western Finland had the largest budgets.

The introduction of political advertising on television in the 1990s has changed remarkably the modes of advertising used by candidates. While in the 1991 general election 76 per cent of candidates in Pirkanmaa advertised in the press (Pesonen *et al.* 1993: 309), in 1999 the figure dropped to 62 per cent. All candidates of the four major parties included newspapers in their electoral advertising. Radio advertisements were used by 11 per cent and television by 12 per cent of the candidates.

With regard to campaign finance in Pirkanmaa, the most important sources of funding included the candidates' own assets, the local party branch and the support group or other campaigning organization. For instance, a quarter of candidates reported that their own assets covered 91–100 per cent of total campaign costs. According to Venho (1999: 27–8), candidate campaigns in the 1999 Finnish election were financed by the following sources: own assets 30 per cent, local party branch 14 per cent, firms 11 per cent, selling of campaign material and revenue from fund raising 10 per cent, revenue from electoral publications 10 per cent, interest groups 7 per cent, private donations 5 per cent, personal loans 4 per cent and other associations 2 per cent. The small share of party finance highlights the individualistic, or candidate-centred, nature of Finnish election campaigning.

Factors explaining electoral success: regression analysis

The bivariate analyses reported in the previous sections provide tentative support for each of our three models. This section deploys regression analysis, first to study the explanatory power of the three models individually, and then of all the models simultaneously. This procedure enables the evaluation of the relative merits of each individual model and the total explanatory power of all the included variables.

The dependent variable in the analysis is the natural logarithm of the number of votes a candidate received in the polls. Taking a logarithm of the number of votes means that we assume constant proportional marginal returns from electoral inputs (such as money spent on advertising or number of electoral rallies).[7] This means, for instance, that increasing advertising expenditure from FIM 0 to FIM 1,000 leads to exactly the same increase in votes measured in percentage terms as it would if expenditure increased from FIM 10,000 to FIM 11,000. (This is different from the more common linear model specification; see Gujarati 1995: 169–71.)

In addition to the models we have been discussing so far, there are other factors that may contribute to the success of individual candidates. For instance, in the United Kingdom socio-demographic factors have been seen to influence the candidate recruitment process (Norris and Lovenduski 1997: 168). So far we have neglected these factors. For example, in Pirkanmaa the share of female candidates was 37 per cent but in the case of elected MPs it was closer to a half. To account for socio-demographic factors we include an additional regression model in Table 6.5, conveniently labelled the 'socio-demographic model', which incorporates measures of candidates' gender and levels of formal education. Table 6.5 includes five different regression models. The first four models are the socio-demographic model and the models discussed in the previous section. These can be used to evaluate their relative explanatory power individually. The last regression model (full model) includes all the variables together, providing a decisive test of the included variables.

Most of the models have a good fit. The full model explains 72 per cent of the variance in the dependent variable, while the explanatory power of the individual models varies between 8 per cent and 50 per cent. The socio-demographic model performs worst, while the three models of central interest each have adjusted R^2 values of around 45–50 per cent. In terms of the R^2 statistic the best model is the resources model.

While the socio-demographic model performs worst in terms of model fit, its results are nevertheless quite interesting. First, a candidate's education has a statistically significant impact on the number of votes received.

Table 6.5 The impact of socio-demographic factors, political experience and campaigning on electoral success

Variable	Socio-demographic model	Experience model	Campaign organization model	Resources model	Full model
Constant	5.17**	4.80**	3.14**	5.10**	3.50**
	(0.25)	(0.23)	(0.29)	(0.12)	(0.32)
Gender (1 = female)	0.30	—	—	—	0.43*
	(0.37)				(0.19)
Education: university degree	1.15**	—	—	—	0.50*
	(0.34)				(0.24)
Education: secondary degree	0.34	—	—	—	−0.17
	(0.37)				(0.26)
Incumbent MP	—	2.43**	—	—	2.02**
		(0.52)			(0.43)
Incumbent municipal council member	—	1.53**	—	—	0.26
		(0.32)			(0.26)
Previous participation in national elections	—	−0.24	—	—	−0.43
		(0.32)			(0.23)
Previous participation in municipal elections	—	0.51	—	—	0.51*
		(0.32)			(0.24)

Number of electoral rallies	—	—	0.41* (0.17)	—	0.17 (0.15)
Number of municipalities campaigned	—	—	0.44* (0.16)	—	0.16 (0.14)
Size of support group (number of participants)	—	—	0.00 (0.01)	—	−0.00 (0.00)
Diversity of campaigning	—	—	0.04 (0.04)	—	0.08* (0.04)
Expenditure on advertising in press (FIM '000)	—	—	—	0.06* (0.01)	0.04** (0.01)
Expenditure on advertising on radio (FIM '000)	—	—	—	−0.00 (0.45)	0.00 (0.04)
Expenditure on advertising on TV (FIM '000)	—	—	—	0.01 (0.01)	−0.00 (0.01)
Adjusted R^2	0.08	0.45	0.49	0.50	0.72
N	131	104	123	131	97

Notes
Unstandardized regression coefficients; standard errors in parentheses. * $p < 0.05$; ** $p < 0.01$.

Candidates with university degrees perform better than average, this observation reflecting the elitism of the recruitment process (Ruostetsaari 2000). The second observation from the socio-demographic model is rather surprising. The gender variable is statistically significant in the full model, suggesting that female candidates can attract more votes than their male counterparts. The value of the this coefficient (0.43 in the full model) means that female candidates receive, all things being equal, over 50 per cent more votes than male candidates ($e^{0.43} = 1.54$), a very substantial gain in vote count. Females' underrepresentation among candidates (37 per cent) was offset by their good success in the polls. Half the elected MPs in Pirkanmaa were women.

The experience model explains 45 per cent of the variance. The incumbency effect is statistically significant both in the experience and full models. In the full model, the coefficient of the incumbency variable is 2.02. This translates to a very large gain in votes: an incumbent candidate receives, all things being equal, over seven times ($e^{2.02} = 7.54$) more votes than other candidates. Thus it is clear that the most important factor explaining the success of candidates is their experience as an incumbent MP.

Participation in previous national elections[8] and being an incumbent municipal council member do not have statistically significant effects on votes in the full model. However, the variable measuring previous participation in municipal elections is statistically significant. Contesting local elections can improve candidates' 'name recognition' among the electorate and help them to gain more votes in future elections. It is interesting that candidate victory in local elections is not important (the municipal council incumbency variable is not significant); it is taking part in the local elections that counts.

The effect of local politics is not surprising. According to several previous studies (e.g. Noponen 1989), municipal politics has traditionally functioned as a stepping stone to the national parliament in Finland. However, the role of municipal politics as a training ground for politicians started to decline in the early 1970s, to the extent that a polarization in the training of MPs has occurred. On the one hand, there was an increase in the number of representatives who had no political background at all, prior to recruitment to parliament. On the other hand, the number of MPs with several types of political background also increased. This indicates the growth in Finland, not only of political professionals, but also of a new type of politician – the expert representative. This is a highly educated professional; increasingly a woman; and someone working in the public sector as a civil servant rather than having worked in political parties or labour unions. Interestingly, neither the candidates nor the electorate in Pirkanmaa see a lengthy party career (the background of the professional politician) as an important characteristic of a candidate (*Vaalikysely* 1998).

The main research question of this chapter is how campaign activities may have affected electoral trends. In the campaign organization model, the variables measuring the number of election rallies and the range of municipalities campaigned in are statistically significant. However, these variables fail to reach statistical significance in the full model. Furthermore, the size of the support group is not a significant factor in explaining a candidate's vote. By contrast, the variable measuring the diversity of campaign forms is significant in the full model. This means that candidates who invest in several different kinds of campaign tactics gain more votes than candidates who concentrate only on one or two tactics.

In the case of the resource model, the only significant predictor of the vote is the amount of resources spent on press advertising. This reflects the strong position of newspapers in Finnish political advertising. The results in Table 6.5 show that every additional FIM 1,000 invested in press advertising increased the number of votes by 4 per cent. Since the amount of resources spent on press advertising varied between FIM 0 and FIM 8,000 in our sample of candidates, this suggests a major role for press advertising in determining a candidate's vote. Those with ample resources to invest in press advertising can count on a substantial increase in their vote share compared with candidates with fewer resources. By contrast, expenditure on television or radio advertising does not affect a candidate's vote, an unexpected observation given that the amount spent on television and radio advertising has increased over the last decade.

Conclusion

This chapter has analysed the determinants of electoral success for candidates in Finnish parliamentary elections. The use of open lists emphasizes the role of individual candidates and their campaign efforts. Candidates compete not merely against competitors from other parties, but also against candidates from their own party. This means that co-operation between candidates from the same party is increasingly replaced by individual candidate campaigns. Such a development is revealed by the decline in the parties' share of the funding of candidates' election budgets.

Political experience is a major factor contributing to electoral success. Our results show that the largest advantage in electoral competition is provided by a candidate's previous experience as an incumbent MP. Furthermore, previous participation in local elections also helped candidates in attracting more votes.

While political experience is important, this does not mean that the organizing of the election campaign does not matter. On the contrary, we found that expenditure on political advertising plays a major role in affecting a candidate's vote. Certainly, this was the case for newspaper advertising; however, television and radio advertising were not found to have any significant effect on the vote. This latter point is rather surprising, given that advertising in these media constitutes a large and growing share of candidates' campaign expenditure. Liberalized regulations for election advertising on the electronic media do not seem to have led to any increase in the importance of this kind of mediated campaign communication for the outcome of elections in Finland.

The high probability of success for incumbents and the important role of (newspaper) media advertising highlight the increasing significance of media coverage in election campaigns. While outgoing MPs may receive 'free' media publicity in the newspapers, newer candidates can use local politics or buy advertising space to attract their own share of media visibility. This trend is consistent with the debates surrounding image politics and the media-ization of politics. Success in elections requires ever more publicity and the taking of positions in the public arena. The role of active and sustained activity in less visible arenas, such as in party organizations, is clearly less important. On the one hand, such a development is positive, because 'media representatives' do not 'live on' politics in the same way as the traditional professional politicians; they can be more independent of the political parties, and thus more independent representatives in the constituency. On the other hand, this development might lead to short-term policy making and to a weakened ability to take responsibility, because the politician must constantly pay attention to variations in popular opinion, as measured by opinion polls, in order to harmonize statements in line with trends in popular opinion.

It is not enough for a candidate to simply buy visibility through newspaper advertisements. Our results show that – in addition to large advertising budgets and political experience – the way the election campaign is organized matters. If a candidate uses a wide variety of different forms of campaigning his/her likelihood of success is (all other things being equal) better than that of a candidate who tries to succeed using only one or two campaigning methods. In practice, this means that a successful election campaign is still at least partly based on more traditional campaigning forms, such as election rallies, visits to workplaces and so on.

On the whole, the results of our regression analysis endorse – albeit not exclusively – the political experience and resources models. In particular, the role of the candidates' advertising resources has grown over recent decades, indicating how campaigns have become more and more candidate-centred. This reflects a new kind of elitism in Finnish politics. The traditional 'party elitism' is increasingly being replaced by candidates who either have partially free access to publicity on the grounds of non-political merit (such as sports stars and other celebrities) or can raise private campaign funding. In the long run this kind of development suggests that the traditional political class of party professionals – who tended to train for several years in the party organizations – may lose out to political amateurs. Indeed, just such a development has already started, not only in the Finnish national parliament but also among Finnish MEPs (Ruostetsaari 2001).

Notes

1 Party support (per cent) in Pirkanmaa was as follows (SVT 1991; comparisons with national trends in 1999 are shown in brackets). Social Democrats 23.8 (+0.9); Centre Party 14.7 (−7.7); National Coalition Party (the Conservatives) 24.1 (+3.1); Left Alliance 16.0 (+5.1); Green League 7.0 (−0.3); Swedish People's Party in Finland 0 (5.1); Christian League of Finland 4.6 (+0.4); Progressive Finnish Party 1.4 (+0.4); True Finns 0.6 (−0.4); Reform Group 0.9 (−0.2); Communist Party of Finland 1.3 (+0.5); Ecological Party 3.4 (+3.0); Alliance for Free Finland 0.4 (−); Pensioners for the People 0.3 (+0.1); Liberal Party 0.8 (+0.6); Finland's Pensioners' Party 0.4 (+0.2); Natural Law Party 0.1 (−); For Peace and Socialism – Communist Worker's Party 0 (−0.1); other 0.2 (−0.6).

2 In order to save expenses, candidates occasionally publish a common advertisement even if they are competitors. The usual presumption here is that they are not seeking the support of the same groups of voters.

3 The survey data and information on press advertising were collected by a seminar group of twelve students of political science at the Department of Political Science and International Relations, University of Tampere.

4 Examples of forms of campaign tactics asked about in the questionnaire included: 'advertising in the press', 'advertising on television', 'participation in election rallies', distribution of material on the streets', 'information on the internet', 'visits to workplaces', 'visits to hospitals or schools'.

5 When examining the figures one should bear in mind that as many as 30 per cent of all candidates did not spend any money at all on electioneering. These candidates are included in the calculations, meaning that the figures are somewhat 'biased' downwards, i.e. if a candidate decided to use money on advertising, the average amount spent is bigger than the figures in Table 6.4 indicate.

6 It is important to note that there were no legal regulations or limits on advertising in 1999. Only in May 2000 was legislation introduced requiring candidates to inform public authorities of their total expenses and the financing of their election campaigns. The share of support received from private individuals, firms, party organizations and other sources must be specified. For instance, in the case of private donations, the amount of money and the name of the donor are supposed to be provided in cases where the size of the donation exceeds €3,364 (FIM 20,000) in presidential and European Parliament elections and €1,682 (FIM 10,000) in parliamentary and local elections. However, if the information is not provided or is incorrect, there are no legal sanctions.

7 We repeated the same analysis in linear form with the raw number of votes as the dependent variable, but the logarithmic transformation performed better. The coefficients in our log-lin model specification have the following interpretation: if the coefficient of the independent variable is b, one unit increase in this variable means that the value of the dependent variable grows e^b units. For instance, if the coefficient on a dummy variable has a value 0.1 this means that the dependent variable is 11 per cent ($e^{0.1} = 1.11$) higher when the dummy variable is coded 1 than when it is coded 0.

8 This is a dummy variable that is coded 1 if the candidate has participated in national parliament, European Parliament or presidential (as a candidate for the electoral college) elections, and otherwise zero.

7   Post-Fordism in the constituencies?

The continuing development of constituency campaigning in Britain

David Denver and Gordon Hands

As Chapter 1 in this volume suggests, there have been important recent changes in the style of election campaigning – amounting broadly to a process of 'modernization' – and authors have used various conceptual frameworks to describe and explain this process. This chapter focuses on constituency-level campaigning in British general elections. We describe how this too has changed, in line with the developments summarized in Table 1.1, and also consider conceptual frameworks used to understand these changes. In addition, we present some evidence about the effectiveness of new campaigning techniques in improving electoral performance.

Pippa Norris distinguishes three phases in the development of campaigning in Britain – pre-modern, modern and post-modern. Pre-modern or traditional campaigning was low budget, *ad hoc*, local and decentralized and was characterized by 'direct communications between citizens and their representatives' (Norris 1997a: 76), but this declined after 1945 to be replaced by modern campaigning. The latter involved a longer time scale, was dominated by television, opinion polls and daily press conferences and was nationally co-ordinated by specialists and professionals from central party headquarters. In the 1990s, however, campaigning in Britain began to move into a 'post-modern' phase, coming to be characterized by 'specialized narrowcasting leading to a greater fragmentation of media outlets, messages and audiences' (ibid.: 87). We now have the permanent campaign, nationally co-ordinated but with decentralized operations, extensive media management, greater use of focus groups and selective mail shots and advertisements.

Norris's focus is almost entirely upon campaigning at national level and the kinds of changes that she identifies have been well documented (see Kavanagh 1995; Scammell 1995; Rosenbaum 1997). In the major parties national campaigning has become highly professionalized and is now a sophisticated exercise in political marketing. The parties employ professional experts to develop a 'media strategy', to give advice on how to improve the image of party leaders (including how they should dress, speak and have their hair cut), to design posters and logos, to devise slogans, to suggest who should (and should not) appear on television and which policies should be stressed. Party election broadcasts are made by professional film directors. Daily press conferences are carefully managed and other campaign events planned to ensure the best possible media coverage. Certainly as compared with the 1960s it would be fair to say that national-level campaigning has been revolutionized.

Our concern here, however, is with campaigning at constituency level. During British general elections, in every constituency many volunteers trudge the streets delivering leaflets, knock on voters' doors, staff street stalls and participate in get-out-the-vote efforts on polling day, while candidates go on walkabouts, visit local institutions and so on.[1] But despite being a traditional, familiar and essential aspect of British elections constituency campaigning has a much lower profile in the mass media and, until recently, has been all but ignored by academics. Indeed, the development of election campaigning over most of the twentieth century has involved, broadly speaking, a switch in focus by the political parties themselves from constituency campaigns to the national campaign.

With respect to constituency campaigning we might elaborate, and perhaps clarify, Norris's insight by using the related terminology of Fordism and post-Fordism. Sociologists and economists have used these concepts to distinguish different phases in the development of the capitalist production process (Amin 1994). Fordism refers essentially to mass production – production designed to achieve economies of scale by manufacturing a relatively undifferentiated product in very large numbers for an undifferentiated mass market, using dedicated machinery operated by relatively unskilled labour. This can be distinguished from an earlier period of craft production, in which individually differentiated products were produced, 'hand made', by skilled craftsmen using general tools; and a later period of post-Fordism, characterized by the use of hi-tech multi-purpose machines, batch production of diverse specialized products and a versatile work force with some control over its work patterns. Post-Fordism involves flexible specialization and niche marketing – identifying particular consumer demands and adjusting the productive process to meet them.

The Fordist/post-Fordist distinction provides a suggestive framework within which to examine the development of election campaigning in the second half of the twentieth century. In particular, the standard constituency campaign that had developed by the late 1950s and 1960s shared features of the mass-production Fordist model, and it is tempting to think of changes since then as marking a move into a post-Fordist period.

Norris's categorization suggests a qualitative change – the post-modern campaign is not just 'the same only more so', but qualitatively different from the modern campaign. We want to ask whether there is evidence of such a qualitative change in campaigning at constituency level. In the two elections of the 1990s there was undoubtedly something of a resurgence of local campaigning. Significantly greater resources were poured into the constituencies by all the major parties and this renewed effort has been matched by a renewed interest in this aspect of electoral politics on the part of academics (see, for example, Whiteley and Seyd 1992; Pattie *et al.* 1995; Denver and Hands 1997). Like national campaigning but somewhat belatedly, constituency campaigning was revamped and modernized. But has there been anything amounting to a qualitative change? Later in this chapter we explore these developments in constituency campaigning before going on to examine the impact of the new campaigning style on party performance. First, however, it is useful to provide a brief account of local campaigning as it was in the Fordist phase.

Constituency campaigning in the Fordist phase

There were many features of the standard local campaign between the 1950s and 1980s which could be seen in terms of a mass-production Fordist model. Elsewhere we have distinguished between four aspects of campaigning – informing, persuading, mobilizing and reinforcing (Denver and Hands 1997). By the 1960s, with the emergence of television as the dominant means of political communication, it was clear that informing, persuading and reinforcing activities were best carried on at the national level – a huge mass audience could be addressed economically and effectively. Increasingly, therefore, local campaigning focused on the one activity that could best be done locally – mobilizing voters to go to the polls. It is, after all, in local constituencies that voting takes place and it is constituency results that determine the outcome of elections. The 'Fordist' local campaign was, therefore, concerned with identifying supporters and making sure that they turned out on polling day.

The classic mobilizing campaign focused on known supporters and concentrated on building an effective organization to ensure that as many as possible of them voted (see Holt and Turner 1968). In all parties the central mobilizing technique was canvassing, carried out by teams of volunteers calling on voters in their homes and attempting to ascertain their intentions in the forthcoming election. Usually there was no attempt to solicit support or persuade opponents – 'arguing on the doorstep' was explicitly discouraged in party handbooks of the time. Rather the purpose was simply to compile a list of potential supporters which was as full and accurate as possible. The relevant names, with electoral registration numbers, were then transferred to specially prepared sheets. On polling day 'number takers' recorded the registration numbers of electors as they went in to vote and these numbers were relayed to a central location where those who had voted were crossed off the prepared lists. Teams of volunteers would then 'knock up' or 'fetch out' those who hadn't voted, often offering a lift to the polling station. In a well run campaign, this continued until well into the evening to ensure that as many as possible of those on the list had been prevailed upon to vote.

The role played by national party headquarters in these campaigns was modest. Party professionals provided routine services, such as training for campaign workers, leaflets and posters but constituency campaigns remained just that – campaigns organized and run by constituency parties or associations with some help and guidance from the centre. The organizational effort was planned and headed by a local campaign organizer, known as the election agent, with the help of a few key local party officers.

Although the 'canvass and knock-up' campaign required a lot of volunteer workers and a fairly complex organization, it was a relatively straightforward operation in principle. As a technique for ensuring that as many supporters as possible went to the polls it is difficult to see how it could be improved upon, and in many ways it can be seen as the application of Fordist methods to the task of constituency campaigning. The central aim is stripped down to its essentials – getting supporters to the polls on polling day – and the work necessary to achieve this is split into a number of simple repetitive tasks to be carried out by (relatively) unskilled workers – canvassing, making lists of supporters, taking polling numbers and knocking up on polling day. It is perhaps not entirely accidental that the organization created to do this was known as the party's election machine.

Recent developments

We now turn to look at developments in constituency campaigning over the general elections of the 1990s. There have been two major sets of changes: some concerning the relationship between party headquarters and local campaigns and others relating to the development of new campaign techniques.

The role of the centre

The Fordist model would lead one to expect that constituency campaigns would be fairly tightly co-ordinated from the centre – in the economic sphere mass production would be controlled by specialized central management. In practice, even in the 1960s and 1970s the role of the centre in constituency campaigning was largely restricted to giving advice and providing services. On the whole, local campaigns were locally organized and locally run. Officials at party headquarters were, of course, well aware that elections were decided in a relatively few marginal seats and attempted to improve the local campaign in these seats – making extra resources available, for example. For a variety of reasons, however, attempts by the parties to target their efforts on key constituencies were not always successful. As Butler and Kavanagh pointed out in their report of the 1983 election, 'Parties have always had target seats, but this often meant little in practical terms' (Butler and Kavanagh 1984: 212–13). Even relatively modest measures, such as urging volunteer workers from safe or hopeless seats to go to neighbouring marginal constituencies, sometimes met with resistance from local party activists.

During the 1990s, however, there was renewed emphasis on targeting, but it was now much more rigorous and far-reaching (see Denver and Hands 1998b). In the 1992 election the parties' national campaign teams gave much greater attention to constituency campaigns in marginal seats (see Denver and Hands 1997: 159–61). The aim was to ensure that the best possible campaigns were mounted in these seats, and in practice that meant well organized and well resourced campaigns, using the most up-to-date campaigning techniques. Additional resources and effort were clearly brought to bear by Labour and the Liberal Democrats in their targeted seats: campaigns were much stronger and more intense in marginal seats than in those which were safe or hopeless prospects. Despite the efforts of central party officials, however, the Conservatives were less able to focus resources and effort into the seats that mattered – partly because local Conservative associations have traditionally been more autonomous than the constituency organizations of the other parties, but also because associations in safe seats in 1992 were so well endowed with resources that it was easy for them to mount strong campaigns.

In 1997 targeting reached new peaks of sophistication – with both Labour and the Conservatives targeting individual voters as well as constituencies – and this has transformed the relationship between local and national levels in running constituency campaigns. This process has gone furthest in the Labour Party and a brief account of Labour's campaign strategy in 1997 illustrates this new approach in its most developed form so far.

The basis of Labour's strategy – code-named Operation Victory – was the ruthless targeting of national and local resources on about ninety key seats. National headquarters sought to ensure that candidates were selected early in these seats, that a campaign organization was in place with either a trained agent or alternatively a special organizer 'parachuted' in from national party headquarters.[2] Canvassing was now renamed 'voter identification', and the central element in the strategy was a mass telephone voter identification campaign in the key seats during the eighteen months before the election. Telephone banks were established across the country and volunteers (using a centrally written script) contacted key seat voters. On the basis of the telephone interview, voters were divided into one of a number of categories, depending on whether they were reliable Labour supporters, had a weak Labour preference, were potential switchers, and so on. Reliable Labour supporters received little more attention and firm opponents were subsequently ignored, while potential switchers, first-time voters and weak Labour supporters were then the subjects of a direct mail campaign and further telephone calls. During the 'short' campaign before the election, candidates and party workers were directed to individual voters whom they should contact personally. Finally there was a massive get-out-the-vote operation on polling day, based on the detailed canvass returns. This whole operation was tightly managed from the centre by a 'Key Seats Unit' at national headquarters. To a large extent in the target seats, then, the initiative in local campaigning had ceased to lie with the local candidate and agent. Equally, by categorizing other seats as non-targets and prescribing the nature of the campaigns that should be run in them – high-profile but low-cost and low-energy – the influence of the centre was felt in these as well.

The change in the extent of centre involvement in Conservative and Labour campaign planning is illustrated by the fact that, whereas in 1992 in marginal seats 22 per cent of Conservative ($n = 54$) and 16 per cent of Labour agents ($n = 69$) reported that they were contacted weekly by party headquarters in the six months before the election, the 1997 figures for target seats were 61 per cent ($n = 61$) and 58 per cent ($n = 64$) respectively.[3]

The effects of the parties' efforts at targeting in 1997 are shown in Table 7.1. Constituency spending was highest in the parties' target seats and much lower in non-targets which they did not hold, most of which would be hopeless seats for the party concerned.[4] Conservative and Liberal Democrat spending in non-target seats that they held, however, was close to the levels of target seats.[5]

In terms of directing volunteer workers to key areas, all parties had some success but Labour was clearly best at getting workers out of safe and hopeless seats and into the targets. Whiteley and Seyd (1998) have suggested, on the basis of a survey of Labour Party members, that Labour's strategy was not particularly effective in this respect since 'only' 3 per cent of Labour members

Table 7.1 Campaigns in target and non-target seats, 1997

	Con.	*Lab.*	*LibDem.*
Mean % of permitted expenditure (all seats)			
Target seats	91.1	93.0	95.0
Non-targets won in 1992	88.6	76.1	90.6
Non-targets not won in 1992	54.0	62.9	30.4
Index of worker transfers			
Target seats	+54	+92	+35
Non targets won in 1992	−48	−76	a
Non-targets not won in 1992	−23	−57	−67
Mean index of overall campaign strength			
Target seats	0.758	1.218	1.288
Non-targets won in 1992	0.773	0.351	a
Non-targets not won in 1992	−0.368	0.146	−0.763

Notes
'Index of worker transfers' is the percentage of campaigns which received volunteers minus the percentage which sent volunteers elsewhere. Overall campaign strength is measured by a standardized index (see note 6).
a Too few cases for analysis. For the survey-based data the *N*s for the three categories used are: Conservative 64, 166, 204, Labour 65, 168, 222 and Liberal Democrats 29, 1, 380.

reported campaigning in another constituency most or all of the time. However, given that the party's average membership in non-target seats was about 600 at the time of the election and that there were six non-target seats for every target, each target constituency could have received about 108 campaign workers. By any standard that is a very significant addition to a campaign work force!

The final comparison shown in Table 7.1 is in terms of an overall index of campaign intensity[6] and the data show that, as in 1992, the Conservatives still had difficulty targeting resources. Their campaigns were strongest in seats that they held but did not target, although non-target seats not won in 1992 had relatively weak campaigns. The strongest Liberal Democrat campaigns were in their targets while campaigns where their prospects were poor were very weak. Labour's targeting was highly effective, campaigns in their target seats easily outstripping those in other seats.

New campaigning techniques

The nature of local campaigning has changed a good deal since the 1950s. One early casualty of the advent of television was public election meetings (especially in urban areas) which were once a standard feature of all campaigns. In his account of the 1950 election, Nicholas (1951: 235) suggested that candidates addressed an average of about twenty public meetings in urban areas and over eighty in rural areas. By 1992 candidates of the three main parties averaged only 2.5 meetings and this fell further to 1.2 in 1997. This form of face-to-face communication with electors is largely now confined to some rural areas. On the other hand, the continuing modernization of local campaigns has involved the use of personal computers, direct mail and telephone canvassing, which we will consider in turn.

Use of personal computers

Personal computers can take the drudgery out of many routine aspects of the traditional canvass and knocking-up campaign. Computerized electoral registers can be used to prepare the necessary lists of voters, to maintain records of individuals canvassed and responses received, and to prepare knocking-up lists for use on polling day. In addition, computers can be used to print address labels for the delivery of campaign material to voters, for correspondence and to produce leaflets at local level. Distributing leaflets has always been an important part of the conventional constituency campaign but in the past they were usually produced by professional printing firms and were relatively expensive. As a consequence, local parties frequently bought standard leaflets printed in large numbers for their regional or national headquarters. Now, highly professional leaflets can be produced by the local parties themselves relatively quickly and cheaply, and so they can deal with locally relevant issues.

Table 7.2 Use of computers in constituency campaigns

	Con.		Lab.		LibDem.	
	1992	*1997*	*1992*	*1997*	*1992*	*1997*
% used PCs	79	88	77	90	68	77
% (of all) used party software	45	56	48	69	15	42
Mean number of PCs (of users)	1.6	1.8	2.9	3.7	2.4	3.6
% (of all) used for:						
Canvass records	60	75	45	67	29	50
Knocking-up lists	46	48	47	44	30	22
Correspondence	61	78	54	73	48	61
Address labels	67	69	45	58	35	47
Targeted leaflets	46	a	47	a	30	a
Targeted direct mail	a	56	a	50	a	31
Desk-top publishing	a	59	a	66	a	68

Notes
a Was not specifically asked about in relevant survey. Number of PC users are: Conservative 376, Labour 393, Liberal Democrat 294. Otherwise *N*s for this and subsequent tables involving all respondents are as given in note 3.

Table 7.2 gives details of the use of PCs by the local constituency organizations of the major parties in 1992 and 1997. Computer use was already widespread by 1992, but it increased further in 1997 – well over three-quarters of all campaigns used PCs, and the figure was virtually 100 per cent for all three parties in marginal seats. The figures in the second row of the table, showing sharp increases in the proportions of constituency campaigns using their party's specially designed software, reflect the efforts made by party headquarters to assist and encourage their constituency organizations. Where computers were used, there was also an increase in the number of machines available. The Conservatives lagged somewhat, but by 1997 Labour and the Liberal Democrats, on average, used over three PCs per constituency (and over four in their marginal seats).

The uses to which computers were put is in line with the discussion above and in almost all cases there was a clear increase between the two elections. The relatively low figures for producing knocking-up lists may reflect a lack of confidence in computers on the part of campaign organizers. This is understandable, given that knocking up is the climax of a constituency campaign and it is vital that nothing goes wrong at this stage, otherwise a vast amount of effort will have been wasted.

Direct mail

A major innovation in British campaigning during the 1990s has been the use of direct mail techniques. This too is a consequence of the development of computers and appropriate software packages. Given an adequate database, customized letters containing appropriate information and appeals can be sent to specific groups or individuals. Direct mail of this kind is such a recent innovation at constituency level that we did not ask about it in our 1992 study. In 1997, however, we directly asked election agents whether they targeted 'special communications (direct mail) to individual voters previously identified as supporters or potential supporters'. Twenty-eight per cent of Conservative respondents indicated that they did 'a substantial amount' of this, as did 29 per cent of Labour respondents and 10 per cent of Liberal Democrats. As we have seen (Table 7.2), even larger proportions reported that they used computers to undertake some direct mail activity (56 per cent of Conservative, 50 per cent of Labour and 31 per cent of Liberal Democrat campaigns).

There is no doubt, however, that the main direct mail effort was made by the parties centrally, as can be illustrated by consideration of the Conservatives' efforts in this direction in 1997. Beginning just after the 1992 election, Conservative Central Office embarked on a strategy called Battleground Voters. This involved building up a database of 2 million target voters – 20,000 from each target constituency. This was developed partly on the basis of door-to-door inquiries, supplemented by increased use of telephone canvassing – Central Office helped financially with the installation of telephone lines and provided training in telephone canvassing techniques. In addition, however, a major effort was put into a series of mail surveys. Lists of potential supporters were initially compiled from computerized electoral registers using geo-demographic data based on postcodes and 'lifestyle' data supplied by commercial firms. Over a period of two and a half years these voters were sent mail surveys designed to identify previous Conservative voters and possible future supporters, and also to get information about voters' concerns on key political issues. Particular efforts were made to identify 'soft' Conservative supporters – those who had voted for the party in the past but were now worried about some aspects of the government's performance. This combination of canvassing, survey and other techniques allowed the database to be refined into what was potentially a very powerful electoral weapon and it was used in the pre-election period to send direct mail from the centre to target groups. Thus, in September and November 1996 and in January 1997, Central Office sent out 2 million personalized letters to their target voters. In addition, however, candidates and party workers were expected to use the information available from the database and make special efforts to personally visit 'swing' voters and to respond to their particular concerns.

As with Labour's Operation Victory, the Conservatives' strategy in 1997 demonstrates the tendency for control and direction of constituency campaigning to move from the localities to the centre. In addition, it illustrates the move to more or less continuous campaigning which is thought to be typical of 'post-modern' campaigning.

Telephone canvassing

Like direct mail, telephone canvassing is a campaign technique imported from the United States. It has a number of advantages over traditional 'doorstep' canvassing. It can be undertaken in bad weather and by people who would be unable or unwilling to meet voters face-to-face, and it enables the parties to contact voters who live in remote areas or are otherwise difficult to reach in person. Perhaps most important, telephone canvassing can be done from anywhere in the country. Parties can set up central or regional telephone 'banks' from which teams of volunteers can ring voters. What has made this method of canvassing feasible is the explosive growth in ownership of telephones in Britain, which stood at only 42 per cent of households in 1972, but had reached 91 per cent by 1994 (OPCS 1978: table 4.28, 1994: table 6.8).

The first use of telephone canvassing on a significant scale was in the 1992 election but it became much more extensive in 1997, as shown in Table 7.3. About a quarter of Labour and Conservative campaigns did a substantial amount of telephone canvassing during the campaign itself – a sharp increase from 1992 – but this is clearly an activity which the Liberal Democrats eschew (probably for financial reasons). There were also very large increases in the proportions of campaigns using telephones to call out supporters on polling day – now a very well established practice in the Conservative Party.

In our 1997 survey we asked more detailed questions about telephone canvassing. Table 7.4 shows the responses for all campaigns and also for target constituencies. As we have seen, the national strategies of both the Conservatives and Labour involved a good deal of telephone canvassing well in advance of the election. This is reflected in the first row of the table, which shows the proportions of constituency campaigns which did a substantial amount of telephone canvassing in the year before the campaign began.

Table 7.3 Telephone canvassing, 1992–97 (%)

	Con.		Lab.		LibDem.	
	1992	*1997*	*1992*	*1997*	*1992*	*1997*
Did 'a substantial amount'	15	25	8	26	1	1
Did telephone 'knocking up'	37	66	7	32	6	15

The huge concentration in target seats is evident, especially in the case of Labour. However, the arduous and time-consuming nature of even telephone canvassing is illustrated by the relatively small proportions of the electorate reached in this way. Even in their targets Labour only managed to canvass 38 per cent of the electorate by telephone. The third row shows mean scores on a scale of 1 (very little) to 5 (very substantial) when agents were asked to rate the effort that was put into telephone canvassing in their constituency campaign. When all campaigns are considered the scores are towards the 'weak' end of the scale, but in their targets the Conservatives and Labour clearly made greater efforts. Labour had by far the greatest number of telephone canvassers at work during the campaign – reaching almost forty in their target seats. Fewer Labour people were at the end of a telephone line on polling day – as noted above, this appears to be a technique especially favoured by the Conservatives. The last row of the table shows the proportions of agents who were aware of telephone canvassing of the electorate in their constituency having been organized at regional or national level in 1997. The striking figure is for Labour's target seats (88 per cent). This is probably a reflection of the fact that (in contrast to previous elections) the list of targets and the campaign strategy were effectively communicated to the grass roots and campaign organizers were, therefore, aware of activities affecting their constituency going on at other levels.

The development of telephone canvassing has encouraged other important changes in campaigning. First, parties no longer wait until an election is in the offing before they start to gather information about voters' preferences. Rather, the operation begins months or years before an election is due.

Table 7.4 Telephone canvassing, 1997

	Con.		Lab.		LibDem.	
	All	Targs	All	Targs	All	Targs
% 'a substantial amount' pre-campaign	24	48	24	84	1	10
% elect canvassed by telephone	15	19	19	38	6	6
Mean effort telephone canvassing (1–5)	2.4	3.1	2.2	4.0	1.2	1.9
Number of telephone canvassers (in campaign)	12	17	19	39	6	10
Number of telephone canvassers (on polling day)	13	15	8	8	5	7
% telephone canvassing from outside constituency	8	31	16	88	9	14

Note
Numbers for target seats are as in Table 7.1.

Secondly, more detailed information is now sought from voters. In addition to their current voting intention, those staffing the telephones typically now also collect demographic details, such as age, sex and occupation, and ask voters about their past voting record, opinions on issues, current concerns and evaluations of the party leaders. Subsequently, as explained above, voters can be sent targeted direct mail specifically tuned to their situation and, if necessary, arrangements can be made for party workers in the locality to pay a visit. We described the classic 'Fordist' constituency campaign above as essentially involving mobilization. These developments clearly reintroduce elements of persuasive communication into canvassing, and also involve feedback from voters to parties.

An index of post-Fordism

In order to obtain an overall impression of the extent of recent changes we computed a simple index of the use of recent developments in campaigning, which we tentatively label an index of 'post-Fordism', based on our 1997 survey. We used fourteen variables relating to work done well in advance of the election (to capture the idea of continuous campaigning) and to the use of telephone canvassing, direct mail and computers.[7] This is, of course, a far from ideal measure but it is a useful rough-and-ready summary. Table 7.5 shows the distribution of constituency campaigns on the index and the data suggest that we should not overestimate the extent to which constituency campaigning has entered a new phase, since the distance that constituencies have travelled down the post-Fordist road varies a good deal. More than half of the campaigns of each party (and 85 per cent of Liberal Democrat campaigns) scored less than seven out of fourteen while only 14 per cent of Conservative, 17 per cent of Labour and 2 per cent of Liberal Democrat campaigns are at the top end of the scale.

To compare the extent to which campaigns in different types of seat were post-Fordist, the scores were converted to percentages and means computed. Details are shown in Table 7.6. Clearly much greater efforts have been made by all parties to update campaigning in target seats. In contrast, in

Table 7.5 Scores on index of post-Fordism (%)

Score (out of 14)	Con.	Lab.	LibDem.
0–2	18	23	43
3–6	33	36	42
7–10	36	24	13
11–14	14	17	2
N	434	455	411

Table 7.6 Mean scores on index of post-Fordism in different types of seat

Type of seat	Con.		Lab.		LibDem.	
All	45.9	(434)	45.5	(455)	24.7	(411)
Target seats	67.1	(64)	84.3	(65)	56.2	(29)
Non-target seats	42.2	(370)	35.5	(390)	22.3	(382)
Very safe	50.5	(119)	26.0	(82)	28.6	(1)
Comfortable	56.7	(47)	44.7	(47)	50.0	(5)
Marginal	62.3	(121)	71.2	(94)	52.0	(14)
Possible	36.3	(46)	66.9	(35)	50.6	(24)
Hopeless	19.9	(101)	30.8	(197)	21.6	(367)

Note
The numbers on which the calculations are based are shown in brackets.

weaker Conservative seats, and very safe and hopeless Labour and Liberal Democrat seats, the scores suggest that little has changed.

The electoral impact of constituency campaigning

For most of the post-war period, the dominant view among academics was that constituency campaigns were old-fashioned rituals that parties indulge in out of habit. As early as the 1951 election David Butler suggested that 'the quality of the candidate and his organization matter remarkably little' (Butler 1952: 4), and during the 1992 campaign Ivor Crewe asserted that 'constituency organization counts for next to nothing' (*The Times*, 24 March 1992). The orthodoxy was that modern election campaigns were so dominated by the national mass media and the national party leaders that what happened on the ground in the constituencies was of little or no consequence.

During the 1990s, however, revisionist researchers began to devise measures of the intensity and organizational effectiveness of local campaigns that could be applied across a large number of constituencies and could be used to investigate the effects of campaigning in ways that had been impossible before. Johnston and Pattie (1995) argued that campaign spending was a useful surrogate indicator of the strength of a campaign and, on this basis, provided evidence that campaigning had a significant effect on election results, especially improving the performance of non-incumbent candidates. Whiteley and Seyd (1992); Whiteley *et al.* (1994) used nation-wide surveys of Labour and Conservative party members to derive an indirect measure of the intensity of campaign activity and found that this too suggested that local campaigning affected constituency results. Finally, we ourselves constructed a direct measure of the strength and intensity of local campaigning on the basis of surveys of local campaign organizers at the 1992 and 1997 general elections. We found clear evidence that in 1992 Labour and Liberal Democrat campaigning improved their performance and, despite Labour's landslide victory, there was evidence that all three parties' local campaigns were effective in 1997 (Denver and Hands 1997, 1998a, b).

We do not repeat these analyses here but present a brief analysis of the impact of the new developments that we have discussed. Did constituency campaigns making use of the most up-to-date (post-Fordist) campaigning techniques achieve better results than those which did not? We compare the impact of the most recent changes (using the simple index of post-Fordism described above) with the effects of more traditional methods of mobilization, using a modified version of the more elaborate index of campaign intensity developed in previous work and explained above.[8] The modification makes the latter now more clearly an index of the intensity of Fordist mobilization techniques.

In Table 7.7 we present a series of simple multiple regression models with change in each party's share of the vote between 1992 and 1997 as the dependent variable. In each case the first model (a) has the index of modernization as an independent variable together with two other variables that might be assumed also to have affected changes in vote share – region and whether the candidate was an incumbent MP. In addition, we include each party's share of the vote in 1992 as controls. Previous party strength could itself be associated with change in the 1997 election but it also correlates strongly with a large number of socio-economic variables such as class structure, housing patterns, proportion of ethnic minority voters, indicators of poverty and affluence and the rural–urban dimension. Thus including previous vote shares is an economical way of controlling for a large number of socio-economic variables.

The figures for the Conservatives' campaigns show, first, that they did relatively worse where they were previously strong and also where Labour was previously strong. They also had poorer results in London than in the Midlands (the comparator region) but stemmed the tide somewhat when their candidate was an incumbent MP. Once these variables are taken into account more modern campaigning made no significant difference to their performance at constituency level. When the Fordist mobilization index is incorporated into the model (equation b) this did have a positive significant effect on Conservative performance – the greater the mobilizing effort the better the result – but post-Fordist campaigning now has a significant negative impact. In the case of Labour campaigning, the post-Fordism index has a significant positive effect on performance in both equations. In other words, after taking other factors into account, variations in the strength of traditional campaigning help to explain variations in performance but, in addition, the more that post-Fordist techniques were used the better the result for Labour. In equation (a) for the Liberal Democrats, the most important predictor is the post-Fordism index. We have already seen, however, that relatively few Liberal Democrat campaigns scored high on this index (Table 7.5) and its effect is swamped when the measure of traditional

Table 7.7 Multiple regression analyses of changes in vote share, 1992–97

	Con.		Lab.		LibDem.	
	(a)	(b)	(a)	(b)	(a)	(b)
Post-Fordism	−0.06	−0.12**	0.28**	0.15**	0.40**	0.13
Fordism (mobilization)	–	0.18**	–	0.20**	–	0.60**
Incumbent MP	0.21**	0.21**	0.00	0.00	0.32**	0.31**
% Con. 1992	−0.96**	−1.05**	0.10	0.08	0.23	0.20
% Lab. 1992	−0.33*	−0.33*	−0.14	−0.19	0.09	0.13
% LibDem. 1992	0.10	−0.01	−0.30**	−0.29**	−0.29*	−0.53**
North	−0.37	−0.05	0.05	0.06	0.11	0.03
South	0.00	−0.02	0.12	0.10	−0.10	−0.09
Greater London	−0.22**	−0.23**	0.19**	0.19**	−0.04	−0.02
Scotland	−0.05	−0.07	−0.12	−0.13	0.12	0.07
Wales	−0.05	−0.05	−0.19**	−0.20**	0.11	0.11
Constant	1.35	2.69	10.05	11.1	−5.01	−0.12
Adjusted R^2	0.49	0.50	0.29	0.31	0.17	0.26
N		429		439		404

Notes
The coefficients shown are standardized ('betas'). ** Significant, $p < 0.01$; * significant, $p < 0.05$.

campaigning is introduced (equation b) which now becomes the most significant predictor.

The strength of local campaigning, then, affected the performance of all three parties in 1997. In the case of the Conservatives and the Liberal Democrats, however, the extent to which techniques that might be described as post-Fordist were used did not make a significant difference. The change in Labour's share of the vote, on the other hand, was positively influenced not just by the intensity with which traditional mobilizing techniques were employed but also by the use of post-Fordist campaigning.

Table 7.7 is concerned with the effects of each party's constituency campaigning separately. It is likely, however, that a party's performance will also be affected by the campaigns of the other competing parties, and in order to take account of this we need to incorporate scores on the strength of campaigning indices for all three major parties into the analysis. This is done in Table 7.8 which relates only to constituencies for which we had survey responses from all three parties and which, for clarity of presentation, shows only the equation in which both campaigning indices are involved.

Focusing on the first six rows, which contain the coefficients relating to campaigning, it can be seen that Conservative campaigning had mixed effects. Post-Fordist Conservative campaigning had no effect on their own performance, was associated with better Liberal Democrat results but affected the Labour vote in the expected way. As in Table 7.7, traditional

Table 7.8 Multiple regression analyses of changes in vote share, 1992–97 (campaigns of all three parties)

	Con.	Lab.	LibDem.
Post-Fordism – Con.	−0.08	−0.19*	0.17*
Post-Fordism – Lab.	0.05	0.22**	−0.19*
Post-Fordism – LibDem.	0.01	0.14	0.27**
Fordism (mobilization) – Con.	0.22**	−0.10	0.08
Fordism (mobilization) – Lab.	−0.12	0.25**	−0.17*
Fordism (mobilization) – LibDem.	−0.11	−0.46**	0.58**
Con. incumbent MP	0.02	0.07	−0.04
Lab. incumbent MP	−0.23**	0.06	0.11
LibDem. incumbent MP	−0.24**	−0.08	0.34**
% Con. 1992	−0.89**	0.59**	0.14
% Lab. 1992	0.02	0.05	0.09
% LibDem. 1992	0.28	0.40*	−0.77**
North	−0.05	0.07	0.03
South	−0.02	0.11	−0.13
Greater London	−0.28**	0.22**	−0.07
Scotland	−0.02	0.22	−0.06
Wales	−0.04	0.06	−0.05
Constant	−2.69	−6.33	2.49
Adjusted R^2	0.47	0.41	0.34
N	198	198	198

Notes
The coefficients shown are standardized ('betas'). ** Significant, $p < 0.01$; * significant, $p < 0.05$.

campaigning by the Conservatives improved their performance but it had no impact on that of the other parties. Labour campaigning of both the traditional and post-Fordist kind affected their own vote and that of the Liberal Democrats in the expected ways but had no effect on the performance of the Conservatives when the other variables are taken into account. Similarly, Liberal Democrat campaigning did not affect the change in the share of vote obtained by the Conservatives but improved their own performance and (at least in terms of traditional mobilization) weakened Labour's. For all parties the coefficients relating to traditional mobilization in campaigns are signed as expected and in most cases they indicate a more powerful effect than those related to post-Fordist campaigning.

We have provided persuasive evidence, then, that local constituency campaigning affected electoral outcomes in 1997. The evidence relating specifically to what we have called post-Fordist campaign techniques is more mixed. In part this is because the two are related – campaigns scoring well on the use of post-Fordist techniques also tend to score well on the use of classical mobilizing techniques. When the Fordism index is entered into regression equations predicting change in share of vote, it tends to make the coefficient for the post-Fordism index non-significant. On the other hand, post-Fordist campaigning by Labour does seem to have some independent effect, and Labour was the party which had the most sophisticated and powerful local campaigns in the 1997 election.

Conclusion

Having considered recent changes in constituency campaigning in some detail we need now to return to our original question. Do the changes in local campaigning that have taken place over the 1990s amount to a qualitative change into a new post-Fordist phase? It would, of course, be foolish to press analogies of this kind too far or to expect anything like a perfect fit between the implicit models and how campaigning has developed in practice. None the less, it seems clear that the terminology does capture an aspect of what has been going on, since some of the changes we have described appear to fit well with the post-Fordist model. This applies, in particular, to the use of computers, telephone canvassing and the use of direct mail. In some ways the use of computers and telephone canvassing simply allows the classic modern campaign to be conducted more effectively but they also bring in new and distinctively post-Fordist features. The Fordist constituency campaign focused on identifying supporters, who were then all treated alike – this is reminiscent of the application of the Fordist mass-production system to achieve economies of scale. The combination of computers and telephone canvassing has allowed well organized campaigns not only to identify potential supporters but to differentiate them and then treat them differently. So, as we have seen, Labour in 1997 identified various categories of supporters by telephone canvassing and these were then handled in different ways during the campaign proper. Moreover, the maintenance of computerized records allows the generation of direct mail customized for different groups, for example on the basis of demographic characteristics or known support for different causes. So there is some evidence here of post-Fordist development.

On the other hand, what is arguably the most important single development in constituency campaigning in the 1990s – greatly increased central control, seen particularly in Labour campaigns but also to some extent in those of the Conservatives – does not fit so well with the post-Fordist model.[9] The latter would, if anything, lead us to expect some relaxation of central control and an extension of local autonomy. Constituency parties and local campaign organizers would be given some freedom to adjust their methods, using new techniques, to the particular circumstances facing them. As Table 1.1 puts it, we might expect 'decentralization of operation with central scrutiny'. Certainly in the case of Labour what we have seen is a move to greater central direction and control. This perhaps represents the belated perfection of the Fordist campaign, rather than any move in a post-

Fordist direction. Local campaigns in key seats are now seen as too important to be left to volunteers in the constituencies.

There have undoubtedly been significant changes in constituency campaigning in Britain over the last decade. Whether these amount to a revolution or a qualitative change is less certain. Furthermore, the impact of the changes that have taken place should not be overplayed. In seats where parties see themselves as having little chance of winning, campaigns remain fairly perfunctory and, at best, consist largely of going through the motions of 'modern' campaigning. The same may be said of safe Labour seats. It is generally less true of safe Conservative seats and is certainly not the case in seats held by the Liberal Democrats. None the less, post-Fordism in terms of techniques, if not management, has clearly emerged in key seats and it seems likely that the relevant techniques will slowly spread to the others.

Notes

The research on which this chapter is based was supported by the ESRC (grant reference number R000222027).

1 We estimate that in 1992 about 280,000 people across Britain helped one or other of the three major parties on polling day; in 1997 the figure fell to about 205,000 (see Denver and Hands 1998a: 79).
2 Interestingly, in a very significant new development, Conservative Central Office ensured that trained agents were in place in key seats by appointing and paying half or more of an agent's salary where the local association could not afford it.
3 All data presented in this chapter are derived from postal surveys of party agents conducted shortly after the appropriate election. From 634 constituencies the 1992 survey produced responses from 266 Conservative, 356 Labour and 386 Liberal Democrat agents. In 1997 there were 434 Conservative, 450 Labour and 410 Liberal Democrat responses from 639 constituencies.
4 There were significant changes to the boundaries of parliamentary constituencies between 1992 and 1997. All references to 1992 results are, therefore, based on estimates of what the 1992 result would have been in the new constituencies (Rallings and Thrasher 1995).
5 The spending data are not survey-based but derive from official returns. The numbers for target seats, non-targets won in 1992 and non-targets not won in 1992 are 85, 257 and 297 for the Conservatives; 91, 262 and 286 for Labour; 54, 2 and 583 for the Liberal Democrats.
6 The index of campaign intensity summarises seven dimensions of campaigning, as follows.
   1 *Preparation* – when serious campaign planning started; how far advanced various aspects of pre-campaign preparation were when the election was called.
   2 *Organization* – when the organizer was in place; whether there were other campaign officers; the proportion of the constituency covered by active campaign organization.
   3 *Election workers* – the number of volunteer workers on a typical campaign day and on polling day.
   4 *Canvassing* – the proportion of the constituency electorate canvassed face-to-face.

5   *Literature* – the number of leaflets distributed in the constituency, as a proportion of the electorate.
6   *Use of computers* – whether a computerized electoral register was used; whether computers were used for various campaign tasks; whether there was a specialized computer officer.
7   *Polling day operation* – whether last-minute leaflets were distributed; whether there was knocking-up from canvass records; proportion of the electorate covered by polling station number takers; whether the number of polling day workers was relatively large or small.

A factor analysis of these data generated factor scores for each case which are taken as campaign intensity scores. For further details see Denver and Hands (1997: chapter 8).

7 Details of the variables used are as follows. In each case the responses in brackets scored 1 and other answers 0.
   1   *Work in advance of the election*
       Identifying supporters through canvassing. (Scored 4 or 5 out of 5.)
       Contact from national headquarters in the six months before. (Once a week or more.)
   2   *Telephone canvassing, etc.*
       How much in the year before? (Substantial amount.)
       How much during the campaign? (Substantial amount.)
       Whether organized nationally/regionally. (Yes.)
       Whether telephoned promises on election day. (Yes.)
       Effort on telephone canvassing. (Scored 4 or 5 out of 5.)
   3   *Direct mail*
       How much during campaign? (Substantial amount.)
       Used computer for direct mail? (Yes.)
   4   *Computers*
       Used computer? (Yes.)
       Had computer officer? (Yes.)
       Used for canvass returns? (Yes.)
       Used for knocking-up lists? (Yes.)
       Had computerized electoral register? (Yes.)

All these variables are positively intercorrelated and on a principal component analysis all score positively on the first factor extracted. The index is the sum of the scores.

8 For the purpose of this analysis the index described in note 6 was modified by excluding the computing components.
9 The 'post-Fordism' index includes a measure of contact with party headquarters in the period before the election but we interpret this as an indicator of continuous campaigning rather than central control.

8 Do campaign communications matter for civic engagement?

American elections from Eisenhower to George W. Bush

Pippa Norris

Who killed civic engagement? During the 1990s multiple voices on both sides of the Atlantic have blamed campaign communications for fuelling public cynicism. In particular, *political actor* accounts claim that links between politicians and voters have been weakened by the adoption of professional marketing techniques, including the mélange of spin, packaging and pollsters. In contrast, *media actor* accounts hold journalistic practices in campaign coverage liable for growing public disengagement from civic affairs, and this thesis has developed into something of an unquestioned orthodoxy in the popular literature. The arguments are hardly new, but are these claims correct? Previous work by the author has argued that the process of campaign communications by politicians and journalists has not contributed to civic disengagement (Norris 2000). This chapter, based on analysis of long-term trends in political communications in US election campaigns from the Eisenhower era in 1952 until the Bush–Gore contest in 2000, confirms that the indictment remains unproven. The chapter draws upon fifty years of National Election Surveys. Many popular commentators suggest that the US public was exceptionally disenchanted by the 2000 presidential election but, in contrast, this chapter demonstrates that (1) contrary to popular opinion, the electorate did not display exceptional levels of disaffection in the 2000 campaign, in fact according to the standard indicators, American faith and confidence in government have been progressively restored in successive elections from 1994 to 2000; (2) overall levels of political activism, interest in elections and public affairs, and attention to the news media display trendless fluctuations in successive US campaigns during the last twenty years, not a steady secular decline; and lastly that (3) at individual level, channels of campaign communications directly initiated by politicians and indirectly mediated by journalists are positively associated with levels of civic engagement.

To develop this argument, the next section briefly summarizes the theoretical framework, including conceptual models of how the process of political communications in election campaigns has been transformed over the years and theories about how these developments may have fuelled public cynicism. The subsequent section examines whether there has been a long-term decline in civic engagement in the United States, as many claim, monitoring trends in party canvassing, campaign activism, political interest, trust in government, and attention to the news media, drawing from the series of surveys in the US National Election Studies. The third section examines the impact of attention to the campaign on public engagement, with models conducted at individual level. The conclusion outlines the theory of a 'virtuous circle' to explain the pattern we find. Rather than mistakenly criticizing the process of campaign communications, the chapter concludes, we need to understand and confront more deep-rooted flaws in American democracy.

The theoretical framework

At the most general level, and as outlined in the first chapter, campaigns can best be understood as *organized efforts to inform, persuade and mobilize*. Using a simple model, campaigns include four distinct elements: the messages that the campaign organization is seeking to communicate, the channels of communication employed by these organizations, the impact of these messages on their targeted audience and the feedback loop from the audience back to the organization. Some messages are conveyed *directly* from politicians to voters, such as through door-to-door canvassing, advertising and internet websites, but most are communicated *indirectly* via the prism of the news media. This process occurs within a broader social and political environment. Effective campaigns also include a dynamic feedback loop as campaign organizations learn about their targeted audience and adapt their goals and strategies accordingly. Indeed, the most dramatic effect of campaigns may be evident at elite rather than mass levels, for example if electoral defeat leads to parties adopting new policies and leaders. Understood in this way, campaigns essentially involve the interaction of political *organizations*, the *news media* as prime intermediary and the *electorate*. Studying these phenomena systematically is difficult because effective research designs require analysis of dynamic linkages among all three levels and often data are available only at one, namely post-election cross-sectional surveys of the electorate.

Although we commonly think of elections as the prime arena for political campaigns in fact, and as pointed out in Chapter 1, these come in a variety of shapes and forms, such as AIDS prevention and anti-smoking campaigns by public health authorities, environmental recycling campaigns by environmentalists and attempts to win hearts and minds in the debate between transnational advocacy groups and anti-globalization movements and government and business proponents of free trade in the 'battle for Seattle' or Quebec. Campaigns can be regarded as 'political' when the primary objective of the organization is to influence the process of governance, whether those in authority or public opinion and behaviour. As other chapters in this volume discuss, the primary impact of this process may be *informational*, if campaigns raise public awareness and knowledge about an issue like the dangers of smoking, or problems of the ozone layer. Or the effect of a campaign may be *persuasion* in terms of reinforcing or changing public attitudes and values, such as levels of support for the major parties or the popularity of leaders. Or campaigns may have an effect upon *mobilization* – the focus of this chapter – typified by behaviour such as voting turnout and party volunteer work. Many accounts emphasize how the process of campaign communications has been transformed during the twentieth century, but nevertheless the impact of these changes upon the *contents* of the messages has not been well established, still less the *impact* of the process upon mobilizing or demobilizing the general public.

Many fear that common developments in election campaigns have undermined their role as mobilizing processes. The last decade has seen growing concern in the United States about civic disengagement fuelling a half-empty ballot box. The common view is that, faced with the spectacle of US elections, the public turns off, knows little, cares less and stays home (Nye *et al.* 1997; Ladd and Bowman 1998; Putnam 2000). Similar fears are widespread in many other democracies (Pharr and Putnam 2000). The growth of critical citizens is open to many explanations that have been explored elsewhere (Norris 1999), linking public confidence with levels of government performance and value change in the political culture. One of the most popular accounts blames the process of political communications for public disengagement, especially the changing role of politicians and journalists within election campaigns. The idea that typical practices in campaign communications have fostered and generated civic malaise originated in the political science literature in the 1960s, developed in a series of scholarly articles in the post-Watergate 1970s, and rippled out to become the conventional wisdom today. The chorus of critics is loudest in the United States but similar echoes are common in Western Europe. There is nothing particularly novel about these arguments but their widespread popular acceptance means that the evidence for these claims deserves careful examination. Two main schools of thought can be identified in the literature. Political actor accounts emphasize the decline of traditional face-to-face campaigns, eroding direct voter–politician linkages, and the rise of 'spin' and strategic news management by politicians, reducing public trust in parties and confidence in governments. Journalist actor accounts stress the shift within the news media towards covering political scandal rather than serious debate, policy strategy rather than substance and conflict rather than consensus. These developments can be regarded as complementary, with the shift towards strategic news management by government prompting a journalistic reaction, or as two autonomous changes.

Campaign demobilization?

In theorizing about these developments, campaigns can be understood to have evolved through three primary stages. *Pre-modern* campaigns are understood to display three characteristics: the campaign organization is based upon direct and active forms of interpersonal communications between candidates and citizens at local level, with short-term, *ad hoc* planning by the party leadership. In the news media the partisan press acts as core intermediary between parties and the public. And the electorate is anchored by strong party loyalties. During this era, which predominated in Western democracies with mass branch party organizations at least until the rise of television in the 1950s, local parties selected the candidates, rang the doorbells, posted the pamphlets, targeted the wards, planned the resources, and generally provided all the machinery linking voters and candidates. For citizens the experience is essentially *locally active*, meaning that most campaigning is concentrated within communities, conducted through more demanding activities like rallies, doorstep canvassing and party meetings.

Modern campaigns are defined as those with a party organization coordinated more closely at central level by political leaders, advised by external professional consultants like opinion pollsters. In the news media, national television becomes the principal forum of campaign events, a more distant experience for most voters, supplementing other media. And the electorate becomes increasingly decoupled from party and group loyalties. Politicians and professional advisers conduct polls, design advertisements, schedule the *thème du jour*, leadership tours, news conferences and photo opportunities, handle the press and battle to dominate the nightly television news. For citizens, the typical experience of the election becomes more *centrally passive*, in the sense that the main focus of the campaign is located within national television studios, not local meetings, so that the experience becomes more distant.

Lastly *post-modern campaigns* are understood as those where the coterie of professional consultants on advertising, public opinion, marketing and strategic news management become more co-equal actors with politicians, assuming an increasingly influential role within government in a 'permanent' campaign, as well as co-ordinating local activity more tightly at the grass roots. The news media fragment into a more complex and incoherent environment of multiple channels, outlets and levels. And the electorate become more dealigned in their party choices. The election may represent a return to some of the forms of engagement found in the pre-modern stage, as the new channels of communication allow greater interactivity between voters and politicians. Post-modern types of communication can be conceptualized to fall somewhere between the locally active dimension of traditional campaigns and the centrally passive experience characteristic of television-dominated elections. Case studies suggest that political campaigns in many nations have been transformed by the widespread adoption of political marketing techniques, although countries have not simply imported US practices wholesale. According to the 'shopping' model, politicians adopt whatever techniques seem well suited to their particular environment, supplementing but not discarding older forms of electioneering (Plasser *et al.* 1999).

The extent and pace of these developments can be expected to vary from one context to another. Rather than claiming that all campaigns are inevitably moving into the post-modern category, contests can continue to be arrayed from the pre-modern to the post-modern, due to the influence of a range of intermediary conditions such as the electoral system, campaign regulations, and organizational resources. Even within the United States, where these developments have perhaps gone furthest, all forms of campaigning remain evident, from the face-to-face, yard-sign, retail politics of primaries in New Hampshire to the capital-intensive, poll and ad-driven campaign in California. A series of case studies have documented the deployment of new campaign techniques in many established and new democracies around the world (Bowler and Farrell 1992a; Butler and Ranney 1992; Swanson and Mancini 1996; Gunther and Mughan 2000). The move towards strategic communications represents part of the 'professionalization' of campaigning, giving a greater role to technical experts in public relations, news management, advertising, speech writing and market research.

The rise of modern and post-modern campaigns has been widely blamed for encouraging cynicism. The most common concern is that the techniques of 'spin', selling and persuasion may have undermined the credibility of parties and political leaders (Jones 1995; Rosenbaum 1997). If everything in politics is designed for popular appeal then it may become harder to trust the messages or messenger (Franklin 1994; Pfetsch 1996; Siune 1998). Many believe that this process has reduced the importance of traditional activities such as local party meetings, door-to-door canvassing and direct voter–politician contact. The use of 'negative' or attack advertising by parties and candidates has also raised anxieties that this practice may demobilize the electorate (Ansolabehere and Iyengar 1995).

News demobilization?

Another related perspective commonly blames journalists rather than politicians. Kurt and Gladys Lang (1966) were the first to connect the rise of network news with broader feelings of disenchantment with US politics in the 1960s. The Langs proved an isolated voice at the time, in large part because the consensus in political communications stressed the minimal effects of the mass media on public opinion. The idea gained currency in the mid-1970s since it seemed to provide a plausible reason for growing public alienation in the post-Vietnam and post-Watergate era. Michael Robinson (1976) first popularized the term 'video-malaise' to describe the link between reliance upon US television journalism and feelings of political cynicism, social mistrust, and lack of political efficacy. Greater exposure to television news, he argued, with its high 'negativism', conflictual frames and anti-institutional themes, generated political disaffection, frustration, cynicism, self-doubt and malaise. During the 1990s the trickle of complaints about the news media became a popular deluge. For Thomas Patterson (1993) the press, in its role as election gatekeeper, has become a 'miscast' institution, out of order in the political system. Cappella and Jamieson (1996) found that strategic news frames of politics activate cynicism about public policy. Dautrich and Hartley (1998) conclude that the news media 'fail American voters'. James Fallows (1996) argues that down-market trends have produced the relentless pursuit of the sensational, superficial and populist, at the expense of serious coverage of public affairs.

Eleswhere similar voices can be heard. Blumler and Gurevitch (1995) believe that a 'crisis of civic communication' has afflicted Western Europe. Achille and Bueno (1994) fear that growing competition from commercial channels has undermined the quality and diversity of public service television. Dahlgren (1995) argues that the displacement of public service television by commercial channels has impoverished the public sphere. Schulz (1997) warns that the decline of public service broadcasting and the rise of commercial channels in Germany, the latter emphasizing the more sensational and negative aspects of political news, may have increased public cynicism. Kaase (2000) fears that these developments may produce audiences segmented according to the amount of political information to which they are exposed, possibly reinforcing a 'knowledge gap'. There is widespread concern that increased competition for readers has increased the pressure on traditional standards of news in the print sector, leading to 'tabloidization' or 'infotainment'. While hardly a new practice, many believe that today routine and daily front-page news about government scandals appears greater than in previous decades (whether sleaze in Britain, Tangentopoli in Italy or *l'affaire* Lewinsky in America) (Lull and Hinerman 1997). This coverage is believed to corrode the forms of trust underpinning social relations and political authority. Many hope that the internet can escape these problems, but others fear that new media may simply reinforce political cynicism (Murdock and Golding 1989; Hill and Hughes 1998; Owen and Davis 1998: 185).

Of course there are counter-claims in the literature and the number of sceptics questioning the evidence media malaise has been growing in recent years. The most recent examination of the US evidence, by Bennett *et al.* (1999), found that trust in politics and trust in the news media went hand in hand, with no evidence that use of the news media was related to political cynicism. Kenneth Newton (1997, 1999) showed that reading a broadsheet newspaper in Britain, and watching a lot of television news, was positively associated with political knowledge, interest and understanding of politics. Christina Holtz-Bacha (1990) demonstrated similar patterns in Germany, while Curtice *et al.* (1998) reported similarly positive findings in a five-nation study from elections in the early 1990s. Until recently, however, counter-claims have usually been published in scattered scholarly journals and thereby drowned out by the Greek chorus of popular lament for the state of modern campaign communications. In work elsewhere (Norris 2000) I have argued that the media malaise thesis remains flawed on multiple grounds.

Since the argument is based on historical shifts in the nature of campaign communications, then at diffuse level there should be evidence from longitudinal indicators of public opinion. If modern campaigns have weakened direct voter–party linkages, then there should be evidence of lower levels of *electoral canvassing*. And there should be a steady erosion of conventional *political participation*, measured by traditional activities such as involvement in political discussion, attending party meetings, working for a party, contacting elected representatives and donating money to a candidate during the election. If negative and strategic news has turned people off, then the public should be *less attentive to the news media*. There should be a long-term decline in *public interest* in government, civic affairs and political campaigns. And standard measures of *political trust* should show a steady and significant fall. On the other hand, if indicators of American civic engagement display a pattern of stability or trendless fluctuations over time, rather than a steady fall, then this throws doubt on the core thesis.

Trends in civic engagement

Party canvassing

First, to consider the evidence for these claims, this study can examine long-term trends in reported party–voter contact and levels of participation in US campaigns, drawing upon National Election Studies since 1952. If US parties have progressively abandoned traditional campaign techniques, exemplified by grass-roots meetings and local get-out-the-vote drives, then we might expect to see lower levels of canvassing over the years. Figure 8.1 shows the proportion of Americans who said that someone from the political parties had called them by phone or someone had come round to talk to them about the campaign during successive elections. The results according to the NES figures show that party-initiated contact activity surged from 1956 to 1972, despite coinciding with the era when television took off rapidly in US households as a popular medium, and therefore when political ads gradually reached a wide audience. It is true that trends suggest a subsequent decline in contact activity from 1972 to 1990, but this was followed by a major recovery in successive elections. The level of contact activity generated in the 2000 campaign was the highest ever recorded in the series, with almost one-third of all Americans talking about the election with parties. The major parties have been broadly balanced in their contact activities over the years, with the Democrats marginally more energetic in many

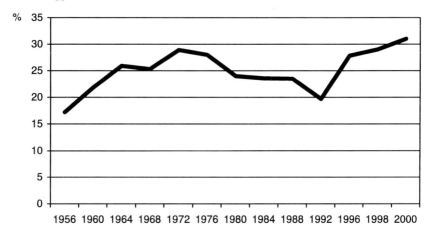

Figure 8.1 Percentage canvassed by the major parties, United States, 1956–2000.

Source: American National Election Studies, 1956–2000.

Note
Question: 'As you know, the political parties try to talk to as many people as they can to get them to vote for their candidate. Did anyone from one of the political parties call you up or come around and talk to you about the campaign this year?'

years although the GOP has outpaced them occasionally in the early 1960s and again in the mid-1990s. Moreover this underestimates the total amount of contact activity since about one in ten Americans regularly reports being called to talk about the election by someone not from the major parties, and this proportion has also increased in recent years. The form of contacting may now be conducted more by telephone than by the traditional face-to-face meeting, but what this trend suggests is that in recent decades US parties and candidates have been investing greater energies in the attempt to mobilize individual voters through calling them directly, not less.

Campaign activism

Figure 8.2 presents the trends in campaign activism in US presidential elections. The pattern shows trendless fluctuations from 1952 to 2000 in many of the items, rather than a clear secular decline. The sharpest fall is in the proportion of Americans wearing a button or displaying a bumper sticker, both minor activities that have become unfashionable. Since the 1960s there has also been a modest long-term decline in activism within parties, although the proportion of party workers today is similar to the situation in the 1950s. The proportion of Americans engaged in other types of campaigning remains fairly stable, such as those contributing money or going to a political meeting. Today the internet provides new channels of communication, such as the use of candidate websites for fund raising and e-mail for networking,

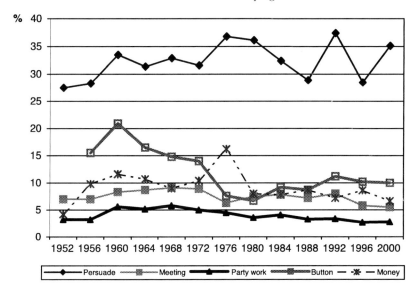

Figure 8.2 Trends in campaign activism, United States, 1952–2000.

Source: American National Election Studies, 1952–2000.

Notes

NES 2000 version of questions Persuade: 'We would like to find out about some of the things people do to help a party or a candidate win an election. During the campaign, did you talk to any people and try to show them why they should vote for or against one of the parties or candidates?' Meeting: 'Did you go to any political meetings, rallies, speeches, dinners, or things like that, in support of a particular candidate?' Party work: 'Did you do any (other) work for one of the parties or candidates?' Money: 'During an election year people are often asked to make a contribution to support campaigns. Did you give money to an individual candidate running for public office?' 'Did you give money to a political party during this election year?' Button: 'Did you wear a campaign button, put a campaign sticker on your car, or place a sign in your window or in front of your house?'

discussion groups for chat and electronic payments for donations (Norris 2001a), but the figures suggest that older forms of campaigning continue, with new technologies supplementing rather than replacing older channels.

Attention to campaign news

As discussed earlier, many believe that the public has been turned off from the campaign by strategic and negative coverage in the news media. These fears have been fuelled by broader trends as many Americans leave network television evening news for cable channels like MSNBC and CNN, as well as alternative news sources available via the internet. The secular erosion in overall network news viewership recorded by Nielsen figures persists in non-election as well as election years, as Americans find access to cable news more convenient for their working schedules (Norris 2001b). Newspaper circulation figures, which have long been weak in comparison with similar

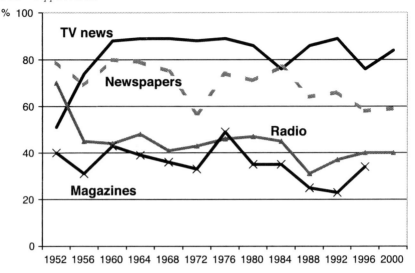

Figure 8.3 Attention to the news media, United States, 1952–2000.

Source: American National Election Studies, 1952–2000.

Notes
Television news: 'Did you watch any programs about the campaign on television?' Radio: 'How about radio – did you listen to any speeches or discussions about the campaign on the radio?' Magazines: 'Did you read about the campaign in any magazines?' Newspapers: 'Did you read about the campaign in any newspaper?'

post-industrial societies, have also been steadily falling in the United States. Yet when asked how much attention they pay to news about the campaign for President, the trends in Figure 8.3, from 1960 to 2000, show a picture of trendless fluctuations. The main change occurred earlier, in the 1950s, as television came into the living room, displacing the role of radio news that had been popular in the inter-war years. Once widely available, television news shows a fairly stable plateau over successive elections, with two temporary dips in 1984 and again in 1996. Use of newspapers shows a slightly more pronounced decline since the early 1980s but it also remains unclear whether this has now stabilized or whether it will fall further.

Political interest

If traditional forms of campaign activism have not fallen, what about general interest in election campaigns, as well as in government and public affairs? If election coverage became more negative in the 1960s and early 1970s, then plausibly people could switch off from politics. Figure 8.4 shows long-term trends in these indicators, in presidential and mid-term elections. The results show that interest in the campaign was slightly stronger in successive

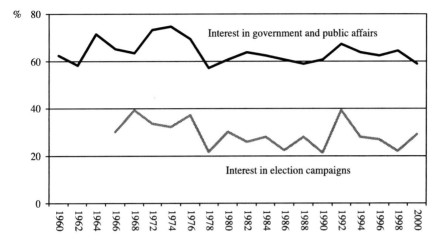

Figure 8.4 Interest in campaigns and in government, United States, 1952–2000.

Source: American National Election Studies, 1952–2000.

Notes
Interest in government and public affairs: 'Some people seem to follow what's going on in government and public affairs most of the time, whether there's an election going on or not. Others aren't that interested. Would you say you follow what's going on in government and public affairs most of the time, some of the time, only now and then, or hardly at all?' (percentage 'Most/some' of the time). Interest in campaigns: 'Some people don't pay much attention to political campaigns. How about you? Would you say that you have been very much interested, somewhat interested, or not much interested in following the political campaigns so far this year?' (percentage 'Very' interested).

elections from 1952 to 1976, and then fell to a lower level from 1978 to 2000 (with the exception of the 1992 election, where attention rose again). The pattern is far from uniform, for example interest in the 1956 campaign proved similar to that in 1996. Variations over time could plausibly be produced by many factors, including the closeness of the race, whether an incumbent President was standing for re-election, competition from third party candidates, the salience of the political issues, and so on (Rosenstone and Hansen 1993). The decline of political interest indicates a period-specific shift, but this change seems to have occurred between 1976 and 1978. In addition, the decline in political interest could be attributed to many things beyond changes in campaigning, for example the heightened generational and racial tensions in US politics could have increased political interest during the 1960s, producing a fall thereafter.

Trends in attention to government and public affairs, rather than campaigns, present a similar picture. The proportion of Americans who follow government and public affairs either 'most' or 'some' of the time in the 1990s is similar to the situation in the early 1960s. The main exceptions to the overall trend concern heightened attention in the 1964, 1972, 1974, and

1976 elections. As many have observed, the events of these years stimulated political awareness – from conflict over civil rights and urban riots to anti-Vietnam demonstrations, political assassinations, the rise of second-wave feminism, generational culture wars and the aftermath of Watergate. From 1976 to 2000 attention returned to the 'normal' level evident in the early 1960s. There is no linear decline in interest in US politics. The 1992 Bush versus Clinton versus Perot election, for example, registered the fifth highest level of interest in the entire series. The common assumption that Americans have become increasingly bored with government and turned-off from public affairs in recent years, and that this can be attributed to increasingly negative, trivial or strategic coverage in the news media, or to changes in party campaigning, receives no support from this evidence.

Political trust

Yet the effects of a more cynical culture in journalism should be evident more directly in indicators of political trust in US government and politicians. After all, much of the concern about growing alienation has been generated by the long-term slide in the standard NES indicators of civic malaise. The key question here is whether the timing of the decline in political trust mirrors the events that are believed to have transformed the news culture.

Figure 8.5 maps trends in the standard NES indicators of trust in government, from 1958 until 2000. The pattern confirms relatively high levels of trust from 1958 to 1964, the sharp plunge from 1964 to 1974, the modest slide until 1980, then the revival under Reagan's first term in the early 1980s, the slide again from 1984 to 1994, then a distinct revival during Clinton's second term. While earlier observers saw only a linear decline, the most recent figures suggest a far clearer pattern of fluctuations. The key question for this study is how far these patterns can be related to the timing of any assumed changes in political campaigning. The pattern in the 1980s and 1990s, with the rise and fall and rise again in US political trust, strongly suggests that rather than a secular phenomenon, driven by cultural or structural trends, this represents a more events-driven or performance-driven political explanation. If 'negative' campaign coverage increased in the early 1980s, as Patterson (1993) suggests, or if news of political scandals commonly became front-page headlines in the 1990s, this may be associated with the popularity of presidential candidates, but it is unrelated to broader trends in political trust, which became more positive during these eras. Of course we cannot assume that there is any simple and direct link between attitudes towards the political system and the broader pattern of campaign coverage, since multiple factors can influence political trust. But at the same time if the timing of trends in these indicators of civic engagement fails to match the timing of any hypothetical change in the campaign communications, even with lags, then we have failed to establish convincing evidence for these hypothetical effects at diffuse level.

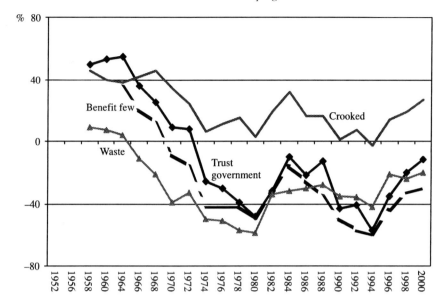

Figure 8.5 Trends in trust in government, United States, 1958–2000.

Source: American National Election Studies, 1952–2000.

Notes
Crooked: 'Do you think that quite a few of the people running the government are [1958–72: a little] crooked, not very many are, or do you think hardly any of them are crooked [1958–72: at all]?' Benefit few: 'Would you say the government is pretty much run by a few big interests looking out for themselves or that it is run for the benefit of all the people?' Waste: 'Do you think that people in the government waste a lot of the money we pay in taxes, waste some of it, or don't waste very much of it?' Trust government: 'How much of the time do you think you can trust the government in Washington to do what is right — just about always, most of the time, or only some of the time?'

The impact of exposure to campaign communications

So far we have examined diffuse patterns at aggregate level, but what is the evidence of the effects of exposure to campaign communications on civic engagement at individual level? Table 8.1 displays the results of a regression model analysing the effects of attention to the campaign news media and party canvassing on campaign activism. The model controls for the standard factors commonly found to be associated with political participation, including demographic background (age, gender, income, education and race) and political attitudes (including political interest and strength of partisanship), as well as the year of the survey in the merged NES 1948–98 data set. The results in Table 8.1 confirm that attention to campaign communications in newspapers, radio news and magazine news, as well as being canvassed by parties, are all significantly associated with greater campaign activism, even after controlling for social background and political attitudes. Attention

140   *Pippa Norris*

to television news about the campaign is also positive but proves a statistically insignificant predictor of activism. Other variables point in the expected direction, with greater levels of political participation among men, older citizens, the well educated and the more affluent, as well as among stronger partisans and those who are politically interested. The year of the election proves insignificant, confirming the earlier observation that there has not been a secular slide in overall levels of campaign engagement. Moreover the indicator of party canvassing proved more strongly related to participation than any of the demographic variables.

Similar models are run using a single media attention scale with measures of campaign activism, external efficacy, trust in government and govern-

Table 8.1 Regression model predicting campaign activism, United States, 1948–98

	B	(SE)	Beta	Sig.	Coding
Year	0.00	(0.00)	0.003	0.802	Year of the election
Demographic controls					
Gender	0.03	(0.01)	0.02	0.018	Male (1)
Race	−0.02	(0.03)	−0.01	0.485	White (1)
Age	−0.03	(0.01)	−0.06	0.000	Years
Education	0.05	(0.01)	0.06	0.000	Four categories
Household income	0.02	(0.01)	0.03	0.022	Five categories
Attitudinal controls					
Political interest	0.12	(0.01)	0.26	0.000	Seven-point scale
Strength of partisanship	0.01	(0.00)	0.03	0.002	Seven-point scale
Attention to campaign news					
Television news	0.04	(0.02)	0.02	0.108	See Fig. 8.3 caption
Newspapers	0.04	(0.02)	0.03	0.024	See Fig. 8.3 caption
Radio news	0.08	(0.01)	0.05	0.000	See Fig. 8.3 caption
Magazine news	0.12	(0.02)	0.08	0.000	See Fig. 8.3 caption
Party contact	0.22	(0.02)	0.14	0.000	Contacted (1)
Constant	0.20				
Adjusted R^2	0.184				
N	42,908				

Source: American National Election Studies, 1948–98, merged dataset.

Notes
The model predicts campaign activism based on ordinary least-squared regression models with columns reporting the unstandardized (B) coefficients (with the standard errors in parenthesis), the standardized beta coefficients, and significance. The model was tested for collinearity. Campaign activism: a four-point scale measuring attending a political meeting, working for a candidate or party, displaying a campaign button, and talking to others about parties or candidates. This scale is available for all elections except 1954, 1958, and 1966. For details see Figure 8.2. It should be noted that similar results were replicated using the longer six-point scale of campaign activism. Party contact: see Figure 8.1.

ment responsiveness as alternative indicators of civic engagement, with the summary results presented in Table 8.2. The models confirm that Americans who are most exposed to direct and indirect channels of campaign communications, because they pay attention to campaign news and they are canvassed by parties, prove consistently more *active, efficacious* and *more positive about government responsiveness*. This relationship remains significant even after introducing a battery of controls in the multivariate regression models. There is a modest negative effect between exposure to the news and trust in government but this proves statistically insignificant despite the large sample size.

Moreover, far from a case of 'American exceptionalism', this pattern is found in the United States *and* in Western Europe (for full details see Norris 2000). The evidence strongly suggests that the public are not simply passively responding to political communications being presented to them, in a naive 'stimulus–response' model; instead they are critically and actively sifting, discarding and interpreting the available information. A more educated and literate public is capable of using the more complex range of news sources and party messages to find the information they need to make practical political choices. The survey evidence suggests that news exposure was not associated with civic disengagement in America.

Conclusion: a virtuous circle?

Why should we find a positive link between civic engagement and attention to campaign comunications? There are three possible answers, which cannot be resolved with the available evidence here.

One interpretation is *selection effects*. In this explanation, those who are most predisposed to participate politically (for whatever reason) could well be more interested in keeping up with current affairs, so the direction of causation could be one-way, from *prior attitudes to attention to campaign communications*. This view is consistent with the 'uses and gratification' literature, which suggests that media habits reflect prior predispositions in the audience: people who love football turn to the sports results, people who invest on Wall Street check the business pages and people interested in politics read about government and public policy (Blumler and Katz 1974). But if we assume a purely one-way selection effect, this implies that despite repeatedly turning to campaign messages, the public learns nothing whatever from the process, a proposition that seems inherently implausible.

Another answer could be *campaign effects*. In this explanation, the process of attending to campaign messages (for whatever reason) can be expected to increase our interest in, and knowledge about, government and elections, thereby facilitating political participation. The more we watch or read, in this interpretation, the more we learn. News habits can be caused by many factors such as leisure patterns and broadcasting schedules: people may catch the news because it comes on after a popular sit-com, or because radio

Table 8.2 The relationship between media attention, party contact and civic engagement, with controls, United States, 1952–98

	Campaign media attention				Party contact				
	B	(SE)	Beta	Sig.	B	(SE)	Beta	Sig.	R^2
Campaign activism	0.07	(0.01)	0.11	0.000	0.22	(0.02)	0.14	0.000	0.183
External efficacy	1.21	(0.46)	0.03	0.008	2.81	(0.98)	0.03	0.004	0.149
Trust in government	−0.46	(0.27)	−0.02	0.095	0.18	(0.59)	0.00	0.763	0.090
Government responsiveness	1.50	(0.32)	0.06	0.000	1.29	(0.32)	0.06	0.000	0.064

Source: American National Election Studies, 1948–98, merged dataset.

Notes

$N = 42.908$. For the design of the full model see Table 8.1. The results presented here show the effects of media exposure and party contact on selected indicators of civic engagement in multivariate ordinary least-squares regression models which control for the year of the survey, the standard socio-demographic characteristics (gender, race, age, income and education) and political attitudes commonly associated with civic engagement (the political interest scale and the strength of partisanship). The columns present the unstandardized regression (B) coefficients, the standard error (SE) in parenthesis, the standardized beta coefficients, the significance of the association, and the adjusted R^2 for the whole model. All models were tested for collinearity. Campaign media attention: this scale is based on attention to the campaign in television news, newspaper, radio news, and magazines. See Figure 8.3 caption. Party contact: see Figure 8.1 caption. Campaign activism scale: see Figure 8.2 caption. External efficacy: 100-point scale 'Public officials don't care much what people like me think' and 'People like me don't have any say about what the government does.' Trust in government: see Figure 8.5 caption. Government responsiveness: 100-point scale 'Over the years, how much attention do you feel the government pays to what the people think when it decides what to do – a good deal, some, or not much?' and 'How much do you feel that having elections makes the government pay attention to what the people think – a good deal, some or not much?'

stations air headline news between music clips or because the household subscribes to home delivery of a newspaper. In this view, the direction of causality would again be one-way, but in this case running *from prior exposure habits to our subsequent political attitudes.*

Both these views could logically make sense of the associations we establish. One or the other could be true. It is not possible for us, any more than for others, to resolve the direction of causality from cross-sectional polls of public opinion taken at one point in time. But it seems more plausible and convincing to assume a two-way interactive process or a *virtuous circle.* In the long term, through repeated exposure, like the socialization process in the family or workplace, there may well be a 'virtuous circle' where the news media and party campaigns serve to activate the active. Those most interested and knowledgeable pay most attention to campaign communications. Learning more about the election (the policy stances of the candidates and parties, the record of the government, the severity of social and economic problems facing the nation) reduces the barriers to further electoral turnout and civic engagement. In this interpretation, the ratchet of reinforcement thereby moves in a direction that is healthy for public participation.

In contrast, the news media have far less power to reinforce the disengagement of the disengaged, because, given the easy availability of the multiple alternatives now available, and minimal political interest, when presented with campaign messages this group is habitually more likely to turn over, turn off or surf to another web page. If the disengaged do catch the news, they are likely to pay little attention. And if they do pay attention, they are more likely to mistrust campaign information. Repeatedly churning out political messages inoculates against their potential impact. This theory cannot be proved conclusively from the available cross-sectional survey evidence, any more than can alternative theories of blaming campaign communications for the ills of the body politic, but it does provide a plausible and coherent interpretation of the associations confirmed in this chapter.

Claims of campaign-induced malaise are methodologically flawed, so that they are at best unproven, to use the Scottish verdict, or at worse false. As a result too often we are 'blaming the messenger' for more deep-rooted ills of the body politic. This matters, not just because we need to understand the real causes of civic disengagement to advance our knowledge, but also because the correct diagnosis has serious implications for public policy choices. 'Blaming the messenger' can prove a deeply conservative strategy, blocking effective reforms, especially given a First Amendment tradition that idealizes the protection of media mega-corporations from public regulation.

This study does not seek to claim in la-de-da fashion that all is for the best in the best of all possible political worlds. If not 'broken', there are many deep-rooted flaws embedded in the core institutions of representative democracy; we are not seeking to present a Panglossian view. The important point for this argument is that many failings have deep-seated structural causes, whether the flood of dollars drowning US campaigns, the bungling and incompetence evident in the Florida recount, or the lack of viable third parties competing in US elections (for details see Norris 2001c). If we stopped blaming the news media's coverage of campaigns, and directed attention to the structural problems in ensuring free, fair and competitive democratic elections, perhaps effective remedies would be more forthcoming.

9   Referendums and elections

How do campaigns differ?

Lawrence LeDuc

A referendum presents a different set of choices than does an election. No political parties or candidate names appear on the ballot, and voters must choose among alternatives that are sometimes unfamiliar and perhaps lacking in partisan cues. One might therefore expect a greater degree of volatility and uncertainty in referendum voting than is typically found in elections. Particularly in those instances where the issue(s) of the referendum are new to the voter, the campaign dynamic which ensues becomes critical to the determination of the outcome. Only through the various information sources available to them over the course of a campaign will voters be able to form opinions on new and unfamiliar (or only partly familiar) ballot questions. As Bützer and Marquis show in Chapter 10, this process of opinion formation is of primary importance for the wide variety of issues which Swiss voters are routinely asked to consider. Applying Zaller's (1992) model of communication flows, they show that information communicated by elites during the course of a referendum campaign is often crucial to the outcome of a vote on an issue about which voters may have little prior information. This view is also supported by evidence from US studies (Lupia 1994; Bowler and Donovan 1998; Lupia and McCubbins 1998). Voters draw upon a variety of sources in forming opinions about the sometimes complex and confusing initiatives which routinely appear on many US state ballots.[1] Among the most frequently mentioned sources of such information are campaign pamphlets, newspaper and television editorials, and direct mailings from campaign organizations. Voters take their cues from these and other campaign sources, as well as from individuals, groups and organizations with which they identify.

In other situations, however, voters may be able to make up their minds much more quickly on the basis of partisan or ideological perceptions, or familiarity with one or more positions in a long-standing political debate. Strong supporters of the Parti québécois, for example, would hardly have needed a campaign in order to make up their minds how to vote in the 1995 Quebec sovereignty referendum, given that the 'sovereignty' issue has been debated for more than twenty years and itself forms the basis on which the party system in Quebec is aligned. Referendums such as the 1980 vote on nuclear power in Sweden, the several votes on EU issues in Denmark (1986, 1992, 1993, 1998, 2000) or the two Irish referendums on abortion (1983, 1992), may also serve as examples of instances in which a significant part of the electorate could be expected to have strong existing views. As Zaller (1992) notes, the process of opinion formation proceeds from an inter-action of *information* and *predisposition*. When strongly held predispositions are merely reinforced by the campaign, referendums begin to take on some of the characteristics of elections. But when parties are internally divided, ideological alignments are unclear or an issue is new and unfamiliar, voters may be expected to draw more of their information from the campaign dis-course, and the outcome of the contest becomes highly unpredictable. Although models of electoral behaviour that are familiar to election scholars work reasonably well in explaining referendum voting in some instances, the relative weight of campaign effects can vary substantially as the context in which a referendum takes place changes. Because referendums are rela-tively rare events in most countries, this contextual variation is most easily operationalized in a broadly comparative study. In this chapter, I examine the effects of the campaign in twenty-three national or sub-national referen-dums held in fourteen different countries or provinces.[2] This set of cases pro-vides sufficient diversity to permit an analysis of the dynamics of referendum campaigns within a broadly comparative context.

The theoretical issues

At least some of the factors which political scientists are accustomed to considering in studies of elections also arise in referendums. However, these might be expected to vary considerably from one referendum case to another, because the political context in which one referendum takes place can be very different from another. The context of the referendum, therefore, itself becomes a variable, which in turn will affect the weight which even familiar elements of electoral models such as partisanship or ideology might carry in explaining behaviour and outcomes.

Referendum campaigns can easily become entangled with a range of other political factors, above and beyond the issue presented on the referendum ballot. In this respect, they may be somewhat like 'second order' elections (Reif and Schmitt 1980; van der Eijk *et al.* 1995). Examining the 1992 Danish and French referendums on Maastricht, Franklin *et al.* (1995) con-cluded that shifting attitudes toward domestic political actors, or the relative popularity or unpopularity of the government of the day, can sometimes provide a more plausible explanation of changes in voter sentiment than feelings about the referendum issue itself. Heath and Taylor (1999) advance a similar view in their analysis of the 1997 referendums in Scotland and Wales, noting that the popularity of the newly elected Blair government was a positive element for the 'yes' side in both of these campaigns. However, the relative weight of such factors in a referendum campaign can vary

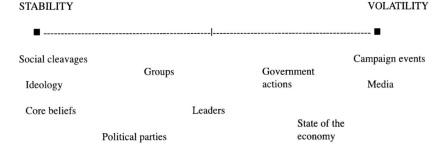

STABILITY   VOLATILITY

Social cleavages   Campaign events
                    Groups   Government
Ideology   actions   Media

Core beliefs   Leaders
                                                        State of the
            Political parties   economy

Figure 9.1 Elements leading towards stability or volatility in referendum voting.

considerably from one context to another. Feelings about certain types of issues may change less readily than attitudes toward individual politicians or even political parties. For some voters, opinions on Quebec sovereignty or European integration might reflect fundamental beliefs about the nation or a sense of political community. For others, such attitudes are less the product of deeply held beliefs than a shorter-term electoral decision based on the persuasive arguments of an advertising campaign, apprehensions about the state of the economy, or judgements about the relative credibility of those delivering the message.

As Tonsgaard (1992) has argued, the extent to which basic values and beliefs are linked with the referendum issue in the public debate, and the relative strength and stability of those beliefs, is a key starting point for any theoretical understanding of referendum voting. Factors such as party identification, linkage of the referendum issue with particular groups, or its identification with established political actors, might also provide examples of Zaller's 'predispositions'. Figure 9.1 outlines a conceptual map, on which a number of the variables which are familiar from the study of election campaigns are rearranged to fit the more widely varying context of referendum voting. I will argue here that the closer a particular referendum comes to involving elements at the left-hand side of the diagram, the more foreseeable its outcome should be and the more limited (or reinforcing) the effects of the campaign. As one moves towards the right hand side of the diagram, the greater the potential for volatility and the more inherently unpredictable the outcome. Thus a referendum which involves a cleavage or ideological issue, and/or in which political parties take well known and predictably opposite positions, ought to see the least volatility. One which involves a new or previously undiscussed issue, or in which parties line up in a non-traditional manner, is more likely to promote some of the short-term variables towards the right side of the diagram. Of course this schematic, when applied to real cases, may somewhat understate and minimize the potential for campaign effects, even in instances where the initial configuration of forces would seem to fall more towards the 'stability' end of the continuum. For, as we shall see subsequently, an important part of the dynamic of a referendum campaign involves changing and redefining the subject matter of the referendum through the campaign discourse. Hence the 1986 Irish divorce referendum might have seen *less* movement over the course of the campaign had it been fought solely along religious or partisan lines. But the rather dramatic shift which took place in voter sentiment during that campaign was attributable in part to the success of certain campaign actors in redefining the issue for the voters, i.e. in persuading them to view the matter as something *other* than a traditional cleavage issue (Darcy and Laver 1990). To frame this question properly, we must consider how an issue comes to be on the ballot in the first place.

Why governments call referendums

The origin of a referendum is nearly always found in a conscious political decision taken by a party, organization or group. Even in the case of 'citizen initiated' referendums, the undertaking generally requires the political and financial resources of a well organized group in order to collect the thousands of signatures needed to get a proposed measure on to the ballot. The question therefore is often clearly identified at an early stage with the group or organization that initiated it. In virtually all of the cases to be considered here, however, the decision to hold a referendum was taken by a governing political party (or parties). Sometimes this occurred because the governing party concluded that a particular political agenda required demonstrated public support in order to carry it through. No British government today, for example, would risk joining European monetary union without obtaining public approval in a referendum, even though such a course is not legally required. Similarly, none of the governments of the Nordic countries in 1994 was willing to undertake the historic decision to join the European Union without the concurrence of its citizens. A referendum may also involve other strategic considerations. The 1992 Irish abortion referendum took place because of the government's desire to separate the contentious abortion issue from the debate on the Maastricht treaty, for which the government wanted a smooth ratification process. In each of these instances, and in dozens of others that might be used as examples, the political chain of events that led up to the decision to hold a referendum can be easily reconstructed.

The reasons why a governing party or coalition might opt for a referendum strategy are many and varied. Morel (1993) notes that divisions *within* a party on a sensitive issue are one of the most common reasons. By tossing the 'hot potato' to the electorate, party leaders may hope to be better able to manage dissent within the party on a divisive issue. The Swedish and Austrian referendums on the divisive issue of nuclear power provide one such illustration of circumstances in which a popular vote was used to prevent a difficult issue from tearing a party apart. A referendum may also be part of some larger political objective. The 1997 Scottish and Welsh devolution referendums, together with the 1998 referendum on local government in London, were clearly part of the Blair government's wider constitutional agenda, which also included Northern Ireland, restructuring of the House of Lords and electoral reform.

When a governing party chooses a referendum strategy, it generally does so in the expectation that it will win. Even in those instances where a party is internally divided, it is generally possible to discern the preferred outcome of those who planned and organized the referendum. Harold Wilson saw the referendum as a means of sustaining British membership of the European Community in 1975, even though many prominent members of his party continued to oppose it. Similarly, Felipe Gonzalez used the 1986 Spanish referendum on NATO as a means of quelling opposition to NATO membership within his own governing party. But such strategies can easily fail. François Mitterrand may not have fully anticipated the high degree of political risk involved in putting the Maastricht treaty to a referendum in 1992, believing as he did that the treaty would be readily endorsed by French voters. Neither did Canadian political leaders, having committed themselves to a referendum following the 1992 constitutional agreement, anticipate that the electorate would ultimately reject their carefully balanced package of reforms. While the strategy behind calling a referendum may be clear, the outcome of the venture, once undertaken, is much more uncertain. The volatility of a campaign can place at risk even the most carefully thought out referendum strategy.

The campaign and the vote decision

One indicator that is suggestive of the role played by the campaign is the amount of time that voters require in order to reach a decision about how to vote in a referendum. As noted earlier, we would expect that in those instances where the issues of the referendum are entirely new to the voter, the learning process of the campaign will be more critical for deciding how to vote and therefore also more important in determining the outcome. In those cases where voters clearly need the campaign in order to form an opinion on the issue(s) of the referendum, we might expect more actual voting decisions to be made late in the campaign, after a sufficient amount of information about the issue has become available. When voters are able to make up their minds on the basis of clear partisan or ideological cues, or where there is a high degree of prior familiarity with the referendum issue(s), we might expect voting decisions to be made earlier. The timing of the vote decision therefore may be a useful indicator of the role of the campaign in affecting the outcome of a given referendum.

Survey data on reported time of vote decision are available for ten of the referendums considered here (Table 9.1). The cases presented cover a range of different contexts in terms of the amount of prior knowledge that a voter might be expected to have regarding the issue being voted upon in the referendum. The 1992 Canadian constitutional referendum provides a fairly

Table 9.1 Reported time of vote decision in ten referendums (%)

Where	Year	Long before	At call	During campaign	Final week
Quebec[a]	1995	70	5	14	11
Finland[b]	1994	62		16	22
France[c]	1992	60		20	20
Norway[b]	1994	59		24	17
Sweden[b]	1994	58		17	25
Quebec[d]	1980	49	19	27	5
Australia[e]	1999	42	19	20	19
Scotland[f]	1997	40	21	16	24
Wales[f]	1997	32	20	16	33
Canada[g]	1992	–	38	33	29

Sources: a 1995 Carleton ISSP Study. b Comparative Nordic Referendums Study (Pesonen 1998). c SOFRES/*Le Figaro* (Franklin *et al.* 1995). d 1980 Canadian National Election Study. Quebec referendum wave. e 1999 Australian Constitutional Referendum Study. f 1997 CREST surveys. g 1992 Carleton Referendum Study.

extreme example, because that referendum could not have been anticipated in advance and voters could not have been expected to have a high degree of prior knowledge of the content of a complex constitutional agreement which had been negotiated in closed sessions. Not surprisingly, therefore, nearly two-thirds of those voting in that referendum made their decisions over the course of the campaign, a substantial number of these as late as the final week. By contrast, voters in the second (1995) Quebec sovereignty referendum were able to come to a decision much more quickly on the issue, in part because the subject matter of the referendum was well known, but also because the campaign provided strongly reinforcing partisan cues for many voters. While the campaign was still important to the outcome, in part because of the closeness of the result, fewer voters needed the additional information provided by the campaign in order to reach a decision. Three-quarters of the Quebec electorate had already made up their minds how to vote at the time that the referendum was called.[3]

The 1994 EU membership referendums in the Nordic countries provide examples which fall clearly between these two extremes. While a majority of the voters surveyed in all three countries reported having made their decision how to vote 'long before' the campaign had begun, substantial numbers also decided how they would vote at some point during the course of the campaign. In Sweden, 25 per cent reported that they made their decision in the final week. The fact that parties that are normally opponents in election campaigns were campaigning together in support of EU membership in these referendums may have served to present voters with new information, in which it could be expected that more time might be required for this to be factored into their decisions. In Sweden, divisions among the governing

Social Democrats spilled over into the campaign, with the government actively supporting the 'yes' side but others campaigning against it under the umbrella group 'Social Democrats against the EU'. Listhaug *et al.* (1998) found that partisanship played an important role in voting in the 1994 EU referendums in all of the three Nordic countries, but also discovered that the strength of this relationship varied substantially both between the countries and between parties. In Sweden, the correlation between feelings toward the Social Democratic Party and feelings about the European Union was in fact moderately negative, in spite of the party's official endorsement of EU membership.[4] Listhaug *et al.* show that the party was able to win back some of its supporters to the 'yes' side over the course of the campaign, perhaps making the difference between victory and defeat for the proposal.[5] But the circumstances of the 1994 EU referendums in the three Nordic countries present a quite different picture from the Quebec case, in which parties with well known and strongly held positions on the sovereignty issue were putting forward highly familiar arguments right from the beginning.

Campaign effects

The measurement of campaign effects is not an easy task, either in the study of elections or in the case of referendums. Sometimes, studies which have employed rolling cross-section survey designs over the length of a campaign have been successful in isolating the effects of particular campaign events. But such studies are even rarer in referendum campaigns than in election research.[6] Public opinion polls, however, can sometimes provide circumstantial evidence of similar shifts over the course of a campaign.

Polls on the issue of the referendum taken either at the beginning of, or in advance of, a campaign provide a benchmark against which outcomes can be compared in attempting to estimate campaign effects. Of course, such a comparison measures only *unidirectional* shifts in public sentiment. Movement of voters in equal and opposite directions over the course of a campaign would not be captured by such an indicator. Nevertheless, such a measure is appealing, in spite of its limitations, because it is readily available for many of the cases considered here and because it can be applied in a broadly comparative manner. Computed as an absolute value, the net shift from the poll percentage to the final result is conceptually similar to a Pedersen index, which is commonly computed to measure electoral change.[7] It is thus an approximation of the net level of volatility generated by the campaign.

Table 9.2 compares the estimate of vote share based on a poll taken early in the campaign, or in advance thereof, on the issue of the referendum for a number of the cases examined here. Comparing this indicator with the actual outcome of the referendum provides a useful surrogate for campaign effects. To permit a statistically legitimate comparison with the referendum outcome, the poll figure displayed in the table excludes undecided respondents. These, however, are shown in a separate column, labelled 'DK'. The

Table 9.2 Net change from pre-campaign/early-campaign poll to referendum outcome

Country	Issue	R%	P%	+/-	DK%	Ref. date	Poll date	Organization	Source
Australia	1988 rights and freedoms	31	71	−40	a	1988 09 03	1989 08	Morgan Gallup	Hughes (1994: 163)
	1999 republic	45	63	−18	14	1999 11 06	1999 08	A.C. Nielsen	Sydney Morning Herald
Austria	1994 European Union	67	61	+6	25	1994 06 12	1994 03	Fessel	Gallagher and Uleri (1996: 27)
Canada	1992 constitutional agreement	45	67	−22	24	1992 10 26	1992 09	Environics	Johnston et al. (1996: 148)
Denmark	1992 Maastricht treaty	49	60	−11	32	1992 06 02	1992 04	Eurobarometer 37	Franklin et al. (1994b: 113)
	1993 Edinburgh agreement	57	67	−10	22	1993 05 18	1993 02	Gallup	Siune et al. (1994: 74)
Finland	1994 European Union	57	52	+5	23	1994 10 16	1994 08	Taloustukimus Oy	Jenssen et al. (1998: 19)
France	1992 Maastricht treaty	51	78	−27	39	1992 09 20	1992 04	Eurobarometer 37	Franklin et al. (1994a: 113)
Ireland	1986 divorce amendment	37	61	−24	7	1986 06 26	1986 04	MRBI	Darcy and Laver (1990: 3)
	1992 Maastricht treaty	69	91	−22	32	1992 06 18	1992 04	Eurobarometer 37	Franklin et al. (1994a: 113)
	1992 abortion (restrict)	35	67	−32	a	1992 11 25	1992 11	MRBI	Gallagher and Uleri (1996: 97)
	1995 divorce amendment	50	69	−19	a	1995 11 24	1995 05	MRBI	Gallagher and Uleri (1996: 93)

		R%	P%	+/−						
New Zealand	1992 electoral system (change)	85	69	+16	15	1992 09 19	1992 07	Heylen	–	
	1993 electoral system change	54	63	−9	18	1993 11 06	1993 09	Heylen	–	
Norway	1994 European Union	48	41	+7	22	1994 11 28	1994 10	MMI	Jenssen et al. (1998: 19)	
Quebec	1980 sovereignty-association	40	62	−22	18	1980 05 20	1979 09	CROP	Cloutier et al. (1992: 53)	
	1995 sovereignty	49	46	+3	16	1995 10 30	1995 06	Léger and Léger	Clarke and Kornberg (1996: 678)	
Scotland	1997 Scottish parliament	74	78	−4	4	1997 09 11	1996 11	System 3	Mitchell et al. (1998: 173)	
Sweden	1980 nuclear power (line 3)	39	40	−1	5	1980 03 23	1980 03	Central Statistical Bureau	Granberg and Holmberg (1988: 383)	
	1994 European Union	52	51	+1	22	1994 11 13	1994 09	SIPO	Jenssen et al. (1998: 19)	
Uruguay	1994 electoral reform	31	80	−49	65	1994 08 28	1994 08	NA	Qvortrup (1997: 551)	
	1996 electoral reform	50	64	−14	44	1996 12 08	1996 10	Cifra	Qvortrup (1997: 552)	
Wales	1997 devolution	50	65	−15	26	1997 09 18	1997 08	Western Mail	Broughton (1998: 205)	
Mean absolute change				17						

Notes

R% denotes percentage voting *for* the option specified in the referendum. P% denotes the percentage found supporting the same position in the poll cited. +/− records the difference between the two figures. Respondents classified in the poll as 'undecided', 'no opinion', or 'don't know' are shown in the column labelled 'DK' but are not included in the computation of percentages in P%. a Polls where such a figure was not available.

percentage of such 'undecided' respondents is often quite high, a pattern not unexpected in a poll taken in the early stages of a campaign.

The average absolute shift of seventeen percentage points found for these twenty-three cases taken together is impressively high, but by itself may actually understate the degree of movement occurring in some of the referendum campaigns. In the 1988 Australian campaign, for example, all four constitutional proposals enjoyed the support of a majority of the electorate according to polls taken about a month in advance of the referendum (Hughes 1994). The campaign waged by the opposition Liberals in that referendum was very effective in raising doubts among voters about the measures, in the end bringing about the defeat of all four proposals by wide margins.[8] Similarly large shifts are found in other cases such as the 1992 Canadian constitutional referendum, the 1992 French referendum on the Maastricht treaty, or the 1994 Uruguayan referendum on electoral reform. In all of these cases, the effectiveness of campaign actors in raising doubts about what was actually being proposed may have accounted for a substantial share of the decline in support (Appleton 1992; Johnston *et al.* 1996; Qvortrup 1997). This pattern is similar to that found by Darcy and Laver (1990) in their study of the 1986 Irish divorce referendum campaign. In that case, the ability of fringe groups who became involved in the campaign to effectively 'change the subject' of the debate in the minds of voters introduced a new campaign dynamic. As voters began to have doubts about what was actually being proposed, support for a proposal which once seemed solid quickly evaporated.

Another important element of the dynamic in these cases is the perception developed over the course of the campaign that the referendum is really a battle of 'the people' against 'the establishment', a perception encouraged by the entry of groups that do not normally play an active role in election campaigns. In the case of the 1992 Canadian constitutional referendum, the constitutional proposal was supported by all three major national parties and by all ten provincial premiers. Yet this seemingly broad phalanx of cross-party support was unable to save the agreement, and may in fact have actually contributed to its defeat (LeDuc and Pammett 1995). A similar pattern emerged in the case of the French Maastricht referendum, in which the treaty enjoyed the support not only of President Mitterrand, but also of his predecessor (Giscard), of Mitterrand's 1988 presidential opponent (Chirac), the leaders of all of the mainstream political parties, most of the business establishment, many trade unions and a wide variety of prominent figures in French society. The 'no' side, consisting mainly of the political fringes (Communists, National Front) and a handful of party dissidents, had little in common politically except for their opposition to Maastricht. But the opponents' ability to portray themselves as political 'outsiders' captured the mood of disenchantment with the political class which was widespread in France at the time. Mitterrand's own unpopularity and the perceived deficiencies of his government were also weaknesses that could be readily exploited by the treaty's opponents (Franklin *et al.* 1995). An intense campaign waged in the final week by the 'yes' side, including an unprecedented nation-wide television appearance by German Chancellor Helmut Kohl, barely saved the treaty from defeat, as the polls shifted from forecasting a narrow 'no' victory to a narrow 'yes' in the last few days.[9]

Of course, while the average degree of movement in referendum campaigns as documented in Table 9.2 is substantial, not all of the cases considered here conform to identical patterns. Particularly in the case of the 1994 EU membership referendums (Austria, Finland, Norway, Sweden), the amount of movement in the campaign appears to have been much smaller, and was found to be in a positive rather than a negative direction. Here, the issue of EU membership was well known, and had been actively debated in the political arena for some time. Norway had voted narrowly against membership in a previous (1972) referendum. These were not cases where 'changing the subject' or 'raising doubts' about what was actually being proposed was as likely to prove an effective campaign tactic. In all four cases, also, the governments involved had initiated the referendums, and were actively campaigning for a 'yes' vote. In the cases of Norway and Sweden in particular, the Euro-scepticism of their electorates was well known, and it had been important to lay the political groundwork for proposing EU membership carefully. But while the vote was particularly close in both Norway and Sweden, the evidence does not suggest that the campaign itself accounts for the outcome in either case. The vote in Norway was in fact considerably closer than was predicted by most of the pre-referendum polls, but this may have been due as much to the 'domino effect' of the Swedish vote two weeks earlier as to the overall effectiveness of the government's campaign in support of the 'yes' (Jahn and Storsved 1995).[10] The two effects are virtually inseparable here, since the likelihood of a Swedish 'yes' vote was in fact an important part of the Norwegian government's own campaign strategy.

The two Quebec sovereignty referendums provide a particularly good test of the potential of campaigns to sway public opinion on different types of referendum issues. As is seen in Table 9.2, the two Quebec referendums display a very different dynamic, even though the issue was essentially the same in both instances. This is because the context in which they occurred was quite different, given the fifteen years of debate over Quebec sovereignty which had taken place in the interim between the two votes. In the first (1980) referendum, the sovereignty issue in Quebec was still a new political phenomenon, and the campaign represented an important part of the learning process for many voters. The product of extensive public opinion polling, the question put to the electorate in the 1980 referendum was widely thought at the time to be a 'winning' question.[11] It provided the reassurance of a continued economic association with Canada and a common currency and asked only for a 'mandate to negotiate' an agreement with the rest of Canada and not for sovereignty itself. Further, it specified that any agreement that might be achieved through such negotiations would have to be approved in another referendum. Polls commissioned by the Quebec government suggested that this strategy was capable of attracting the support of well over 50 per cent of the electorate. Yet the proposal ultimately went down to a rather decisive defeat. In part, this was because the federalist side was able to effectively shift the terms of the debate over the course of the campaign, arguing instead for 'renewed federalism' as an alternative to the Quebec government's sovereignty-association proposal. The message of 'renewed federalism' was delivered to a receptive electorate by a respected and credible federal Prime Minister, Pierre Trudeau – still at that time popular in Quebec. While 'renewed federalism' as such was not on the ballot, the 'no' campaign ultimately persuaded voters to view the choice in these terms rather than as the *status quo* versus sovereignty-association.

Opinion shifted steadily away from the 'yes' side over the course of the 1980 Quebec referendum campaign, reflecting in part the struggle between the two sides to redefine the issue in their own competing terms. The relative newness of these issues at the time, the complexity of the ballot question (see note 11), and the nature of the discourse itself meant that the decision was not a clear-cut or easy one for many Quebec voters. The context in which the second Quebec sovereignty vote took place in 1995 was very different. Partisan positions on the sovereignty issue by that time were well known and well entrenched. The federal Prime Minister, Jean Chrétien, was highly unpopular among Quebec francophones and widely mistrusted. An electorate frustrated with the record of failed constitutional initiatives of the previous fifteen years was much more prepared to listen to the arguments put forward by more popular Quebec leaders over the course of the campaign. But, as Table 9.2 shows, the total amount of movement during the 1995 campaign was much less than had been the case in 1980, and it was in a different direction. It was important to the outcome nevertheless because of the closeness of the vote. But there were simply fewer voters in 1995 who had not already made up their minds on an issue that had by that time become *the* defining cleavage of Quebec politics.

Because these contextual factors vary more widely in referendum campaigns than in elections, the potential for volatility is greater in many referendums. Table 9.3 compares the average absolute amount of change over the course of some of the referendum campaigns discussed here with a Pedersen volatility index, which measures the absolute change in party shares of the vote for pairs of elections. The election pairs have here been chosen to represent time periods reasonably close to those of the referendums. By this measure, the amount of volatility found in referendum campaigns is, on average, about 50 per cent higher than that calculated for the election pairs. It also varies considerably between countries and cases. In Australia, Canada and Ireland, for example, the amount of volatility found in referendum campaigns appears to be substantially greater than that typically occurring in elections, while in Norway and Sweden it is less. In Denmark,

Table 9.3 Comparison of net change in campaign with Pedersen index

Country	Issue	R%	P%	+/−	PED	Elections
Australia	1988 rights and freedoms	31	71	−40	10	1987–90
	1999 republic	45	63	−18	10	1996–98
Austria	1994 European Union	67	61	+6	8	1995–99
Canada	1992 Charlottetown agreement	45	67	−22	8	1993–97
Denmark	1992 Maastricht treaty	49	60	−11	9	1990–94
	1993 Edinburgh agreement	57	67	−10	12	1994–98
Finland	1994 European Union	57	52	+5	7	1995–99
France	1992 Maastricht treaty	51	78	−27	14	1993–97
Ireland	1986 divorce amendment	37	61	−24		
	1992 Maastricht treaty	69	91	−22	15	1989–92
	1992 abortion (restrict)	35	67	−32		
	1995 divorce amendment	50	69	−19	9	1992–97
New Zealand	1992 electoral system (change)	85	69	+16	15	1993–96
	1993 electoral system change	54	63	−9	16	1996–99
Norway	1994 European Union	48	41	+7	17	1993–97
Quebec	1980 sovereignty-association	40	62	−22	14	1981–85
	1995 sovereignty	49	46	+3	6	1989–94
Scotland	1997 Scottish parliament	74	78	−4	8	1992–97
Sweden	1980 nuclear power (line 3)	39	40	−1	9	1982–85
	1994 European Union	52	51	+1	15	1994–98
Uruguay	1994 electoral reform	31	80	−49	13	1989–94
	1996 electoral reform	50	64	−14	10	1994–99
Wales	1997 devolution	50	65	−15	9	1992–97
Mean absolute change				17	11	

Note
See note on Table 9.2. PED is Pedersen index for election pairs shown.

Finland and Austria, on the other hand, the statistics for referendums and elections are roughly comparable.

Using these measures of overall campaign volatility, the referendum cases considered here might be arranged along a continuum in a manner suggested in Figure 9.2. Referendums with relatively little movement in public opinion over the duration of the campaign are grouped towards the left side of the continuum; those with greater volatility towards the right.[12] Some patterns quickly suggest themselves. Referendums involving well known issues, on

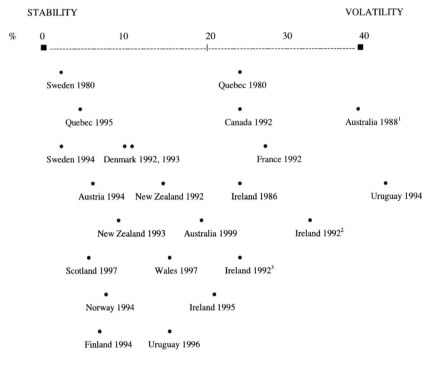

Figure 9.2 Categorizing selected referendum campaigns by degree of volatility.

Notes
1 Constitutional referendum, 1988, 'rights and freedoms' item. 2 Abortion referendum, 1992, substantive item (no. 1). 3 Referendum on the Maastricht treaty, 1992.

which voters might be expected to have already formed opinions, tend to be found on the lower end of the distribution. Those involving new issues, or areas of political debate in which the mass public is not highly engaged, tend to display more volatility. Principal among these are constitutional referendums in which elite-driven projects were suddenly thrust upon the public for ratification. In many of these instances, initial public support deteriorated rapidly once the campaign began. When an issue has been widely debated in other political arenas, or where links with partisanship or ideology are stronger, the potential for movement resulting from the campaign is much less.

Conclusion: three types of referendum campaign

As we begin to pull together the theoretical threads of this analysis, we can see that the types of referendum campaign that are *least* like those of elections are the ones in which there is little partisan, issue or ideological basis on which voters might tend to form an opinion. Lacking such information, they take more time to come to a decision, and that decision becomes highly unpredictable. Where an issue is a familiar one, or where parties take clear competing positions, the voting decision is easier and tends to be made earlier in the campaign. We might here distinguish between three distinctly different types of referendum campaign, all of which are amply represented among the cases examined. In the first of these, termed *opinion formation*, voters cannot be expected to have fully formed opinions on a issue that has not previously been a subject of political debate in arenas such as those of elections. As the campaign progresses, opinions gradually begin to form. Many of these cases also involve elites taking strong positions at the beginning of the campaign, to which voters gradually begin to react. As noted earlier, the Australian, Canadian and Uruguayan constitutional referendums seem to conform to this pattern, in which elite-driven projects were decisively rejected once voters had learned enough about them.

A second type of dynamic occurs when a referendum on a reasonably well known issue suddenly takes on a new direction over the course of a campaign. Often this occurs when opposition groups are successful in 'changing the subject' of the referendum, or in raising doubts about the issue that is *really* being discussed. Darcy and Laver (1990) documented this type of campaign in their study of the 1986 Irish divorce referendum, coining the term *opinion reversal* to describe that dynamic. Prior to that campaign, public opinion polls had shown substantial support for a change in the laws governing divorce, and there was initially little organized opposition to the referendum. But the campaign took on an unexpected direction when non-party groups became involved and began to refocus the debate in terms of the rights of women and the integrity of family life. Support for the proposed change in the divorce law declined rapidly. Within a few months after the referendum, public opinion polls in Ireland had returned to a 'normal' reading on the issue of divorce. But the rapid shift in the discourse over a short campaign had been enough to defeat the proposal. Raising doubts about the motives of those proposing the referendum, or changing the subject of the debate in mid-course, can often be a highly effective campaign tactic. In the 1999 Australian republic referendum, polls indicated that a majority of Australians favoured ending the monarchy, both before *and* after the referendum. But opponents of the change were successful during that campaign in shifting the debate on to the terrain of an elected versus appointed President, thereby dividing potential 'yes' voters. Persuaded that the 'politicians' republic' deserved to be defeated, many republicans who would otherwise have supported the 'yes' voted 'no'.[13]

Finally, we come to a third type of referendum campaign which might seem more familiar to students of elections. Here, opinion is much firmer and less subject to rapid change or sudden reversal. Voters will often have strong cues based on partisanship or ideology, and be receptive to arguments presented by familiar and trusted political leaders. In such a campaign, much of the attention is directed towards wavering or 'undecided' voters, in the knowledge that a swing of only a few percentage points might make the crucial difference in the outcome. The government of Felipe Gonzalez was successful in mobilizing partisan voters to support his NATO position in the 1986 Spanish referendum, and the Swedish government successfully overcame opposition to EU entry in its 1994 referendum. In both of these cases the votes were extremely close, and might conceivably have gone either way. The 1995 Quebec sovereignty referendum also stands as a good example of a campaign in which the separatist provincial government knew that it could count on the support of the partisan voters who had brought it to power, but also needed the votes of 'soft nationalists' in order to secure a majority for its sovereignty proposal. The fact that it was nearly successful in that effort was due more to effective campaign leadership than to the underlying fundamentals of opinion on the issue (Pammett and LeDuc 1998). I term this type of campaign dynamic the *uphill struggle*. The party initiating the referendum knows that it can count on the votes of its core supporters. It knows also where the additional votes may lie that it needs in order to security a majority, and that it can win these only through a hard-fought campaign. But, as the Norwegian and Quebec cases demonstrate, such a strategy is not always successful even when it is well conceived and well executed.

Figure 9.3 presents a graphic illustration of these three types of referendum campaign, and of the dynamic of opinion formation or change that might be expected to occur in each of them. To a large extent, these are representations of pure type, that may portray only an abstraction of the reality of many actual referendum campaigns. In fact, some campaigns may readily combine elements of more than one type. Yet the typology shown in Figure 9.3 seems to capture the essential characteristics of many of the specific campaigns discussed in this chapter. Research on elections teaches us that 'campaigns matter', but the extent to which this is true in any given setting is likely to depend on the overall volatility present in the party

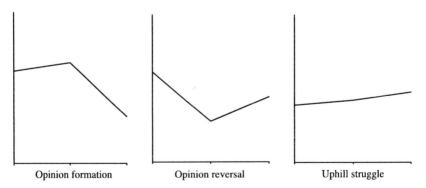

Opinion formation   Opinion reversal   Uphill struggle

Figure 9.3 Three types of referendum campaign dynamics.

system to begin with. Levels of volatility in elections vary considerably from one system to another, and even within a particular system over time. Referendums display the same sort of variation, but across a much wider range. The 'opinion formation' model resembles that of the most highly dealigned polities, in which short-term variables become the dominant element in understanding and explaining electoral outcomes. Theories of direct democracy presume that referendum voters are 'issue' voters. But the evidence examined here suggests that attitudes towards issues are only one of the variables affecting voting choice, and not always the most important one in determining the outcome of a referendum.

Notes

The support of the Social Sciences and Humanities Research Council of Canada (grant #410-98-4161) for this research is gratefully acknowledged. I also wish to thank Michael Harvey, Josh Koziebrocki and Helder Marcos for their work on this project.

1 In the November 2000 US presidential election, there were over 200 citizen initiatives or legislative propositions on the ballot in forty-one states. There were twenty-six such proposals on the Oregon ballot alone, dealing with issues such as gun control, utility rates, tobacco settlements, campaign finance, education and taxation. Initiative and Referendum Institute (http://www.iandrinstitute.org).

2 This material was compiled as part of the Comparative Referendums Project at the University of Toronto. The referendums considered here were chosen to represent a wide diversity of countries and issues, but the inclusion of particular cases also reflects the availability of sufficient data.

3 The categories found in the surveys do not always coincide perfectly with the labels employed in Table 9.1. In the CREST surveys in Scotland and Wales, for example, the categories were: *before the general election* (i.e. 1 May 1997); *between the general election and the referendum*; *in the month before*; *in the week before*. The category *when the referendum was called* was not used in the SOFRES or the Nordic countries surveys, but the other categories utilized in those instances were similar to those shown in the table.

4 A special party congress held in June 1994 voted to support EU membership by a margin of 232 to 103 (Jahn *et al.* 1998).

5 The vote in Sweden on EU membership in the 1994 referendum was 52.3 per cent 'yes', 46.8 per cent 'no'. The remaining 0.9 per cent of the ballots were recorded as blank.

6 But see the study by Johnston *et al.* (1996) of the 1992 Canadian constitutional referendum campaign. In this study, a rolling cross-section sample of 2,530 respondents was interviewed over a thirty-two-day period, at the rate of approximately eighty interviews per day.

7 The Pedersen index computes the difference in the share of votes received by political parties across any pair of elections as a summed absolute value. It thus has a 'base 100' comparability to the measure employed here. See Pedersen (1983).

8 The percentage of 'yes' votes cast for the four proposals in the 1988 referendum was: 'Fair elections' (37.6 per cent), 'Local government' (33.6 per cent), 'Parliamentary terms' (33.0 per cent) and 'Rights and freedoms' (30.8 per cent). None of the four proposals carried a majority of the votes in any state (Galligan 1990; Hughes 1994).

9 The treaty was approved in the referendum by a vote of 51.0 per cent to 49.0 per cent.
10 The vote in Norway was 52.3 per cent 'no' to 47.7 per cent 'yes'.
11 The text of the 1980 Quebec referendum question was as follows: 'The Government of Quebec has made public its proposal to negotiate a new agreement with the rest of Canada, based on the equality of nations; This agreement would enable Quebec to acquire the exclusive power to make its laws, levy its taxes, and establish relations abroad – in other words, sovereignty – and at the same time, to maintain with Canada an economic association including a common currency; No change in political status resulting from these negotiations will be effected without approval by the people through another referendum. On these terms, do you agree to give the Government of Quebec the mandate to negotiate the proposed agreement between Quebec and Canada?'
12 The difference between the percentage vote in the referendum and a pre-campaign poll is used as the metric here. See Tables 9.2 and 9.3.
13 The proposal put to Australian voters in the 1999 referendum was: 'To alter the constitution to establish the Commonwealth of Australia as a republic, with the Queen and Governor General being replaced by a President appointed by a two-thirds majority of the members of the Commonwealth Parliament.' The overall national vote was 54.9 per cent 'no' to 45.1 per cent 'yes'.

10 Public opinion formation in Swiss federal referendums

Michael Bützer and Lionel Marquis

Direct democracy is central to Swiss politics (Trechsel and Kriesi 1996). Three to four times a year, citizens are asked to express their opinions in popular votes on ballot proposals. It is this important stage of the political decision-making process, the stage when voters and public authorities are confronted with referendum campaigns, that is the focus of attention here.[1] In Chapter 1 of this volume it was noted that the general view on whether campaigns actually matter could best be described as 'undecided'. This is particularly so for referendum campaigns (as also shown by Chapter 9). Whereas some authors underline the voters' limited cognitive capacity and the decisive impact of the ballot propaganda (Converse 1964; Hertig 1982; Cronin 1989; Saris 1997), others, while acknowledging the important role of campaigning, point out that voters are not quite so ignorant as is often believed (Kriesi 1994; Dubois and Feeney 1998; Klöti and Linder 1998; Norris *et al.* 1999).

Referendum campaigns provide a good illustration of the complexity of the public opinion formation process, showing how the relevant characteristics can change from one issue to the next. This chapter aims at analysing this fundamental link between discourse at the macro-level of political elites and cognitive mechanisms at the micro-level of individual electors. How do voters form their opinion on ballot issues? What factors determine the people's reaction to communications of the political elite? And to what extent do campaigns influence the ballot outcomes? In the next section, we present our theoretical model, based upon John Zaller's research (1992), which we believe elucidates well the mechanisms at work in referendum campaigns. Indeed, during these campaigns, advocates and opponents of the ballot measures are foremost in using propaganda techniques to try to influence the voters' decision. A top-down approach is therefore appropriate. Moreover, Zaller's 'RAS model' (receive–accept–sample) – combining, as it does, the communications of the political elite with just two individual characteristics, political awareness and personal predispositions – is both parsimonious and sophisticated enough to account for the voter behaviour in *any* ballot measure, independently of the issue at stake.

Having set out the theoretical framework, we then proceed with a description of the data used and the operationalization of the main variables, where necessary adapting Zaller's model to the Swiss context. (This is consistent with Zaller's claim of the general applicability of his model, see Zaller 1992: 301–8.) At the macro-level, we analyse the level and nature of conflict between the political elite – taking into account campaign intensity – with political conflict measured by two indicators: vote cues of the political parties and the balance of press advertisements. At the micro-level, we develop the concepts of political awareness and individual predispositions. The chapter concludes with an empirical test of Zaller's opinion formation model, making use of individual-level data gathered by VOX surveys of voter opinion conducted after each federal referendum vote.[2] We test voter behaviour in consensual and conflicting vote situations in relation to both political awareness and personal predispositions. This analysis thus allows us to link campaign effects at the macro-level to voter behaviour at the micro-level.

Theoretical framework

Building on the early scholarly work of Converse and McGuire, John Zaller (1992) developed a theoretical model for the study of mass communications. At the core of his model are four ideas. First, citizens vary considerably in their habitual attention and exposure to political information in the media. Second, people are only able to react critically to the arguments they encounter to the extent that they are knowledgeable about political affairs. Third, citizens do not typically carry around in their heads fixed attitudes but construct opinion statements on the fly as they confront each issue. And fourth, people make greatest use of ideas that are most immediately salient to them when constructing their political opinion statements, which is typically the case in survey responses. For the models' key axioms – reception and acceptance of political communications – two auxiliary assumptions are developed (Zaller 1993). According to the reception axiom, the greater a person's level of general political awareness or attentiveness, the greater the likelihood of *reception* of mass communication. Reception depends thus on the individual level of political awareness and involves both exposure to and comprehension of a given communication. Regarding the acceptance axiom, the greater a person's political awareness, the less likely he or she is to uncritically accept the contents of mass communications. Thus *acceptance or resistance* brings one's values in line with the contents of the communications.

If the individual level of political knowledge determines the reception of information in Zaller's theory, it is political predispositions that become crucial for the degree of acceptance of a received message. Political predispositions are conceptualized as stable, individual-level values or ideological orientations. In interaction with political awareness, predispositions constitute the critical intervening variable between the communications people encounter in the mass media and their political values (Zaller 1992: 23).

More precisely, people tend to resist arguments that are inconsistent with their predispositions to the extent that they possess the contextual knowledge to assess the arguments in the light of their predispositions. In other words, the most aware citizens receive most campaign messages, but they are also the most critical and selective citizens as they scrutinize the message's conformity to their own ideological backgrounds (Marquis and Sciarini 1999). The least aware pay little attention to politics and receive only a few messages. Furthermore, they change their opinions on the spot when confronted with new messages as they lack the contextual information for analysing them in the light of their beliefs. This does not imply that referendum campaigns do not matter to them. On the contrary, non-aware citizens are easily influenced and most affected by the mass media in general, as they accept most messages uncritically. Yet often this influence is hard to measure, since conflicting messages may neutralize each other and *net* media effects may appear considerably smaller than the *total* media impact (Zaller 1996: 37).

In addition to the two micro-level variables, Zaller's model (1992: 97) also refers to elite discourse. The political elite can either be unanimous or divided about a certain issue, with consequences for how the RAS model operates at the voter level (see also Chapter 9 of this volume). In the case of consensus, a *mainstream effect* is likely to occur, whereby public support of the elite tends to increase with the degree of political awareness, independently of the ideological predispositions. In conflictual cases, however, voters are exposed to competing elite arguments and rival flows of communications. In such situations, a *polarization effect* is likely to occur, whereby support for a given position tends to increase or decrease with a higher level of awareness, depending on political predispositions.

Operationalization

The focus of our empirical study is on Swiss federal referendums between 1981 and 1996. Of the 118 federal referendums during this period, we have selected thirty-two for our analysis.[3] Half of the ballot measures which we selected were on foreign policy issues, half concerned domestic policies. Where these tended to differ was with respect to the general *conditions* under which the public opinion formation takes place; in general, the opinion formation *processes* were the same across both types (Marquis and Sciarini 1999: 23).[4] With regard to the sixteen domestic votes, we deliberately selected cases in which party cues and vote results differed substantially. The underlying idea was that advertising campaigns could have influenced voter behaviour between the announcement of party recommendations and the voting day. This particular mode of selection does not interfere with our analyses, however, since we are assembling all ballots in broader vote categories and testing the general opinion formation process, independently of the context of the issues at stake.[5]

As far as opinion *formation* is concerned, the distinctive parsimony of Zaller's model makes the operationalization of the two key independent variables – political awareness and ideological predispositions – quite straightforward. However, with respect to the level and nature of conflict among the political elite, we will need to explain the details of variable construction at greater length. The vote decision, our dependent variable, will be presented last.

Political awareness. The keystone in Zaller's model is the concept of political awareness. However, his operationalization of awareness is not optimal for our purposes, as it provides 'a measure of general, chronic awareness' (1992: 43). Instead, with the help of three 'factual' questions, we will first determine the voters' knowledge of each ballot proposals, or their *issue-specific* knowledge. The three questions are: (1) recall of the ballot title, (2) recall of its basic content and (3) recall of the vote recommendation issued by the Federal Council. The resulting 'cognitive' scale ranges from 0 to 3. In addition, in so far as awareness can be defined as 'intellectual engagement with politics' (Zaller 1992: 21), we also wanted our indicator of awareness to convey a sense of 'practical competence' (Bütschi 1993). By this concept we mean the capacity of motivating a vote decision correctly. More concretely, VOX respondents were asked to give two *justifications* for their vote decisions. The scores on this 'motivational' scale range from 0 (no justification, or no valid justification)[6] to 2. Figure 10.1 summarizes how the cognitive and motivational components of awareness have been combined to produce our composite index of political awareness.[7]

Political predispositions. In line with Zaller's definition of political predispositions (1992: 228), we first considered using voters' self-positioning on the left–right scale as a possible indicator, but this variable was missing for a good many votes in the VOX surveys. We therefore used the *party identification* question instead. Admittedly, this variable is not ideal either, because 50 per cent of the respondents did not express any partisan preference whatsoever;[8] however, we will systematically compare the voting behaviour of 'apartisans' and 'party identifiers'. We next assigned the different parties to broader political categories. The left–right cleavage is widely regarded as the most salient dividing line in Swiss politics (Linder 1998). However, for some issues, a clash emerges inside the right camp, setting moderate parties

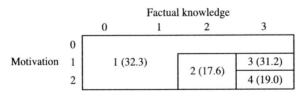

Figure 10.1 Composite index of political awareness ($N = 30,000$): percentage of voters per category.

against extreme parties (Sciarini and Marquis 2000). In such cases, the former take a common stance with the left parties, while the latter are prone to advance drastic solutions in opposition to the other parties. Consequently, if Zaller is correct in asserting that citizens follow 'their' political elite, then a threefold classification of predispositions (left, centre right, far right)[9] incorporates all major cleavage configurations in Switzerland. The share of each political category in our sample is, therefore, as follows: left 20.7 per cent, centre right 22.2 per cent, far right 9.6 per cent, apartisan 47.5 per cent.

Level and nature of conflict among the elite. In his fullest description of the RAS model, Zaller (1992) does not provide any consistent method of how the *level of conflict* among the political elite should be measured. On occasion he draws a distinction between mainstream and conflicting politics by simply looking at the degree of 'congressional criticism' against an administration's policies (1992: 103). Alternatively, he accounts for elite consensus and division by counting magazine cover stories that either promote or condemn the government's actions (1992: 102). Given the large number and diversity of policies dealt with in this chapter, we cannot rely on *ad hoc* estimates of elite divisions. Instead, we shall employ a *three-stage filter* to distinguish between 'consensual' and 'conflicting' ballot proposals, which will then allow us to categorize our thirty-two ballots into 'mainstream' and 'polarization' groups. This fairly demanding method implies the prior collection of specific data about each proposal, as follows:

1   We consider the *vote recommendations* of the main political parties, issued on every ballot proposal. The twelve main parties are included, accounting for more than 95 per cent of the votes at national elections: their voting cues (weighted by their electoral result) are compiled into an indicator of *support for the government's position* on the ballot proposal. This procedure amounts to calculating the share of 'yes' cues in the case of referendums, and the share of 'no' cues in the case of popular initiatives.[10] The resulting measure provides a rough estimation of the support authorities enjoy in the 'parliamentary arena'.

2   We measure the *intensity of the advertising campaign* in the month prior to the poll. The purpose of analysing the advertising campaign is to take into consideration the general referendum campaign and the role of actors other than political parties. Our attention is focused on just one means of campaigning, namely *political ads* placed in six major Swiss newspapers.[11] Although advertisements are also used by political parties, it has been shown elsewhere (Sciarini and Marquis 2000) that their messages can be overwhelmed by the advertising messages of other actors.

3   We consider the *directional thrust of the advertising campaign*. Here our aim is to assess the margin by which the 'yes' or the 'no' side prevails in the advertising campaign. This requires adding the *size* of all advertisements endorsing both positions, and then converting the figures so as to produce an indicator of governmental support, as we do for party cues. The

resulting measure provides a rough estimation of the support authorities enjoy in the 'referendum arena'.

Taking into account the intensity of advertising campaigns (Table 10.1) shows an increased erosion of support for the government when campaigns exceed a certain threshold.[12] In such cases, on average, no more than 58.6 per cent of newspaper advertising space endorses its position, as do 52.3 per cent of the people at the polls. These figures illustrate that a wide consensus in the partisan arena does not preclude a strong opposition in the referendum campaigns, in particular in high-intensity situations.

According to our theoretical model, campaign intensity has an influence on the reception of messages by the voters (Zaller 1992: 154). We assume therefore that the impact of referendum campaigns on voters is more important when campaigns are intensive. In other words, we believe that the elite conflict is more accurately represented when taking into account the referendum campaign in high-intensity situations. Conversely, we believe that partisan cues become more important to the electorate when the advertising campaign is weak, as then the parties are often the only active actors. The direct measure of the vote recommendations of all parties is, then, a more precise indicator of the actual elite conflict. In short, with respect to the *level of conflict* among the political elite, we draw a distinction between 'high-intensity' and 'low-intensity' campaigns, and we measure the degree of elite division among those elites who are most likely to take the crucial part in the process of opinion formation, i.e. *parliamentary elite* or *advertising elite*. More formally, we classify the thirty-two votes under study into 'consensual' and 'conflictual' categories by applying two sorting rules:

1   When the parliamentary elite command control over the campaign – i.e. when referendum campaigns remain below the mean intensity in our database (16,390 cm^2; see note 10) – we use the *party cues* as an indicator of elite support for government's policies.
2   When referendum campaigns reach a high intensity (over 16,390 cm^2), we use the percentage of advertising space endorsing the government's position as an indicator of elite support.

Table 10.1 Support for government and campaign intensity (%)

Support for government measured as	Average	Low-intensity campaigns (0–16,390 cm^2)	High-intensity campaigns (16,390 cm^2+)
Party cues	77.38	76.55	78.2
Ads' surface	63.1	67.6	58.6
Popular vote	53.98	55.65	52.3
N	32	20	12

Regardless of the method of elite support, we calculate an index of *tightness of majority view*, which estimates the closeness of the actual majority to a situation where both camps would be exactly matched (i.e. where 50:50 would be a situation of maximal conflict): therefore, tightness = majority − 50. Next, we consider as 'conflicting' all ballot proposals in which the majority has a smaller lead than the average. All other objects are classified as 'consensual'. This sorting procedure leaves us with twelve consensual and twenty conflictual cases in our sample of Swiss federal referendums.

With one exception, all consensual cases display a majority in favour of the government's position both in the parliamentary and in the referendum arena. However, in the case of the vote on Swiss accession to the United Nations, a solid partisan majority (79 per cent) approving the policy could not prevent an unprecedented reversal of opinion in the referendum campaign, with only 23 per cent of advertising space advocating a 'yes'! This fact alone reveals a major conflict between the party establishment and other actors from civil society, leading us to classify the UN vote as highly conflictual.[13] As for the other conflictual objects, they all display *party* majorities supporting the government's position, while *advertising* majorities are almost balanced between support and refusal. In the light of all this, we ultimately define *eleven policies as consensual and twenty-one as conflicting*.

We now turn to the *nature of the conflict*. This concept seeks to determine who is responsible for the conflict at stake and, in turn, which voters might be most sensitive to their claims. Consider the example of a conflict situation produced by a left-wing referendum. Clearly, it does not take on the same meaning for voters of different ideological groupings. We expect the supporters of left parties to *decrease* their governmental support as a function of their level of awareness, because higher knowledge and attentiveness to the issues correlate with a better reception of cueing messages. By contrast, the supporters of right parties should offer a reverse image to left-wing citizens, *increasing* their governmental support as competence rises.

Our concern with the nature (or localization) of conflict is to anticipate the directional effect of the *resistance mechanism* among different ideological groups (Zaller 1992: 448). We want to avoid aggregating different types of ballot proposals for which the cueing messages pushed the *same* ideological groupings of citizens in *opposite* directions. The consequence of assembling such votes is that the particular effects of political awareness in each situation would cancel one another across the whole range of votes.

We can operationalize the *nature of the conflict* by looking at the configuration of voting cues in the partisan arena. We focus here on party recommendations because the evidence is readily available and the identification of the dissenters is an easy task. Also, it is hardly conceivable that opponents to the governmental policies should change their basic political orientation as we move from the parliamentary to the referendum arena. Thus we classify the opponents of government again into three categories: left, centre right,

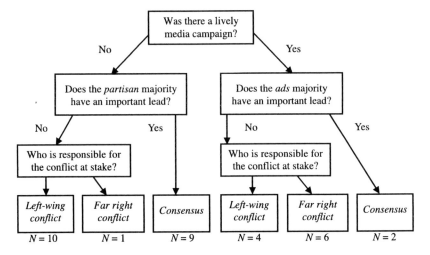

Figure 10.2 Procedure for determining the level and nature of conflict among the political elite.

far right. All possible combinations of either two or three categories were also considered,[14] but in fact only two simple configurations emerged:[15] left-wing opposition to government (fourteen cases) and far right opposition (seven cases).

Adding these cases to the eleven consensual policies outlined above, Figure 10.2 defines three basic configurations of conflict at the elite level. We should underline that our classification procedure is essentially a heuristic device providing an automatic way of discriminating ideal types of elite division within a large pool of objects.

Vote decision. Finally, the dependent variable in our analysis is the vote decision made by the citizens at the polls.[16] This is converted into an indicator of voting *support for the government's position*, so as to match the construction of the variables at the elite level. It should be noted that it also includes the decision of people who actually abstained, but who indicated their 'virtual' choice. Although the participants and non-voters do not reach completely similar decisions,[17] the main reasons for keeping the latter in our analysis are to avoid our sample shrinking by nearly a third, and to increase the degree of variance in the level of awareness.[18]

Mainstream and polarization effects

According to the categories established above and as summarized in Figure 10.2, we can test voting behaviour in one consensual and two conflicting situations, in the latter distinguishing between cases where left-wing parties opposed the government position and cases where the far right parties

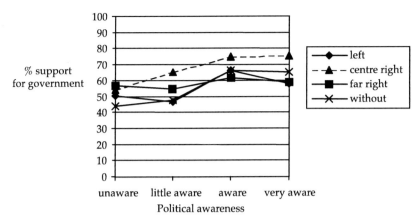

Figure 10.3 Consensus: influence of political awareness and predisposition on support for government.

Note
Gammas: left 0.142** ($N = 1{,}464$), centre right 0.257** ($N = 1{,}653$), far right 0.048 ($N = 730$), apartisan 0.285** ($N = 3{,}172$).

were in opposition. We start with consensual ballot measures, for which our model predicts a mainstream effect.

Figure 10.3 reveals overall voter support for the government position, which tends to increase with the level of political awareness. Political predispositions do not matter for voter behaviour, except for centre right voters, who are most in support of the government position. But, given that all voter groups support the government position in an increasing trend, this reflects a 'mainstream' effect. However, general support for the mainstream measures is pretty low – around 60 per cent – and fluctuates within the voter categories. These effects might be due to our rather permissive definition of elite consensus. Some of the nine cases in our mainstream situation are, indeed, characterized by a modest conflict among the elite, either from the left or from the far right, and therefore voter behaviour is somewhat more volatile and general support a bit lower than predicted. But none the less, we can affirm that political awareness is the single most significant predictor of individual voter behaviour and that the elite's discourse seems to be of prime importance for the opinion formation process.

Turning, next, to ballots with a conflictual elite discourse, we start with those cases of challenge by left-wing groups. Figure 10.4 reveals a very explicit polarization between the voters of different political orientations. On the one hand, the gap between groups tends to increase with the level of political awareness. For leftist voters, the more aware one is, the less one supports these measures; inversely, for rightist voters, the more aware one is, the more one supports them. On the other hand, even the least aware citizens were able to scrutinize the messages of their respective elite. In other words,

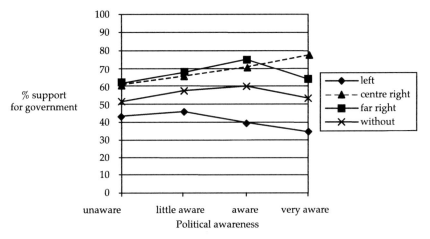

Figure 10.4 Left-wing conflict: influence of political awareness and predisposition on support for government.

Note
Gammas: left 0.113** ($N = 2{,}382$), centre right 0.208** ($N = 2{,}545$), far right 0.053 ($N = 1{,}020$), apartisan 0.037 ($N = 4{,}450$).

they did not uncritically accept all the messages they received. Thus, whatever their level of awareness, a majority of left-wing voters disavowed the government, whereas a majority of both right and far right voters supported the authorities' position. Clearly, the dissident campaigns of left-wing groups seem to have been received and accepted by their voter bases and rejected by the other voters. As expected, citizens without an ideological preference took a middle stance between the two camps. Moreover, there is a sharp decline in governmental support among very aware far right voters. The nature of these ballots and our classification criteria could explain this behaviour. Together with leftist organizations, the far right elite on occasions take stances on environmental and social matters against the government.[19] This atypical elite position is very poorly received by its voter base and is accepted only by the most aware voters.

To sum up, ballots facing opposition from the left produce a polarization effect at the voter level. The level of political awareness and ideological predispositions jointly determine individual voter behaviour, according to our theoretical model – although, undeniably campaigns do not have the same impact on all voters, and even the least aware citizens seem to be capable of scrutinizing elite communications. For this ballot category, however, we find support for the assumption that elite discourse is a determinant of individual opinion formation.

The third category is ballots facing opposition from far right groups. We expect far right voters to decline in their government support as a function of their level of political awareness. In Figure 10.5 the gap between ideological groups tends to increase with a higher level of political awareness.

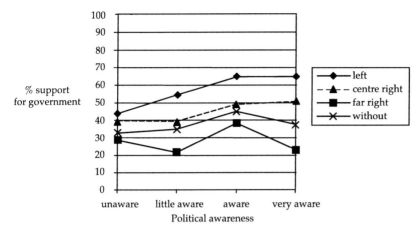

% support
for government

Figure 10.5 Far right conflict: influence of political awareness and predisposition on support for government.

Note
Gammas: left 0.162** ($N = 1,184$), centre right 0.128** ($N = 1,653$), far right 0.066 ($N = 599$), apartisan 0.034 ($N = 2,546$).

For far right voters, the more aware one is the more one rejects the government's position. But given the very low level of far right support – around 30 per cent – the decline in support is only slight. For left and centre right voters, the support tends to increase with the level of awareness. Strikingly, only leftist voters with a certain competence are in majority support of the proposed measures. Moreover, we notice again that even citizens with little awareness are able to scrutinize campaign communications. Voters must therefore be considered as competent enough to receive and evaluate elite messages according to their ideological beliefs. This evidence corroborates the decisive effect of elite discourse on voter behaviour for those ballots opposed by far right groups. Again voter support depends unmistakably on the interaction of individual competence and political predisposition.

Taken together, we have observed the same underlying mechanism regarding the public opinion formation process in all of our three ballot categories. However, when comparing the two conflictual categories, we see a noticeable difference with respect to the *level of governmental support*. Ballots opposed by far right groups are generally poorly supported, not only by their voters but also by all other voters. By contrast, leftist groups have less success in influencing the other voters to such a low level of support. In other words, leftist chances of successfully opposing a ballot measure at the polls seem to be lower than those of far right groups. The *resources available to groups and the nature of the opposition* in the campaign could explain this phenomenon. Whereas leftist groups primarily try to *promote* ecological or social measures, resourceful far right groups are more likely to want to *preserve* the *status quo* with opposition campaigns. Thus 'negative' spending seems to attract voters more easily than 'positive' campaigning. This assumption is supported by empirical evidence from several US campaigns, where large amounts of money can increase the likelihood of a negative outcome at the polls (Dubois and Feeney 1998: 185; Gerber 1999: 137).

Clearly, the RAS model has proved to be a robust predictor of voting behaviour at the aggregate level. In particular, the expected interaction between political awareness and partisanship – regardless of how one may question the measuring of these two variables – was clearly displayed in Figures 10.3–5). But the model needs a more straightforward test at the individual level, employing logistic regression to account for individual differences in voting. The dependent variable is a dummy indicating whether a person voted according to the government's recommendation (1) or not (0). The model consists of three independent variables: political awareness, partisanship and an interaction term (awareness × partisanship). However, because our measure of partisanship does not qualify as a continuous variable, we construct three dummy variables for left, centre right and far right partisanship, with the apartisans defined as the reference category. Accordingly, the interaction between awareness and partisanship produces three variables (one for each partisanship category). In any event, awareness *per se* is also included at this first step, since the RAS model predicts a direct effect of awareness in mainstream situations.

In a second step, we control for other effects than those of awareness and partisanship. The model, therefore, includes the following: (1) the global intensity of the advertising campaigns (measured in square metres of newspaper space); (2) the familiarity of ballot proposals (measured by the mean level of awareness of voters in our surveys); and two individual-level variables that traditionally exert a strong influence on voting behaviour: (3) education levels and (4) linguistic region.[20] If the RAS model really applies to the Swiss case, the introduction of these control variables should not remove the effects of its basic components.

As before, the model was tested separately for the three types of situations (mainstream, left-wing and far right conflicts). All variables in the three models were standardized,[21] so that the impact of the independent variables can be roughly compared within and across models. Table 10.2 displays the results of the two-step logistic regression analysis for each category. With respect to the coding of the dependent variable, positive coefficients indicate the factors increasing the government's chances of success at the polls.

A final commentary is in order before presenting our results. Throughout this analysis, we have been concerned about the risk that our results could be plagued by multicollinearity problems, particularly because some basic elements of the model are partial combinations of others. In fact, whereas this risk was found to be negligible for our first two models (mainstream and left-wing conflict situations), the threat is more serious with respect to far right conflict situations. On occasions, more specifically among partisanship variables and interaction terms, the proportion of an independent variable's variance not accounted for by the other independent variables in the model sinks to nearly 10 per cent, which indicates sizeable risks of multicollinearity (see Gujarati 1995: 338–9).[22] At the same time, the most frequent and conspicuous signs of excessive collinearity – unreasonably large regression coefficients, large standard errors (see Menard 1995: 65–6) – were not found in our results.[23] It seems, therefore, that high collinearity did not entail major computational problems or fully unreliable estimates. With these considerations in mind, we can proceed to an interpretation of our regression coefficients.

To begin with, the results for *mainstream situations* correspond rather closely to our observations at the aggregate level (Figure 10.3). First, at step 1, awareness exerts a highly significant effect on the vote: the more people are aware of issues, the more they follow the government position. Furthermore, regardless of awareness, partisans of each camp are more prone than apartisans to support the government. Next, with respect to the interaction terms, we can see that awareness plays a lesser role in boosting the support of left and far right citizens than it does for people without partisan affiliation. This pattern probably reflects the fact that several objects, although defined here as consensual, gave rise to some moderate opposition from either groups (see above). Hence, overlapping a general mainstream baseline, there is a tendency for left and far right partisans to be less driven by awareness toward approval of government than are more neutral apartisans.

At step 2, the main effect of awareness remains highly significant, a result which conforms with the predictions of the RAS model. Likewise, partisanship remains a significant factor of the vote decision, centre right and far right citizens being more favourable to the government than apartisans. As for the interaction between awareness and partisanship, it also retains significance in the face of the control variables.

The impact of awareness is all the more remarkable given that the variables added to the model are quite strong explanatory factors of the vote. In particular, education plays an important role in increasing government support. Since education and awareness measure partly the same dimension, we are not surprised to find parallel effects. However, even though education might capture some of the explanatory power of awareness, the latter remains relevant for predicting votes in mainstream situations. Likewise, the government clearly gets more support when objects are more familiar to the public. Yet, strong as it is, this effect does not take away the impact of awareness.

In contrast to education and familiarity, increasing the space of the advertising campaign seriously *depresses* the share of votes in support of the government. This effect of advertisements seems to be intrinsic to mainstream situations. The explanation lies perhaps in the fact that parties and resourceful 'organized interests' (such as business organizations, labour unions, etc.) engage less in referendum campaigns when the outcome seems predetermined by the absence of sizeable opposition, at least in the parliamentary

Table 10.2 Multivariate model of vote in support of government

	Consensus (N = 6,816)		Left-wing conflict (N = 9,910)		Far right-wing conflict (N = 5,619)	
Step 1						
Constant	0.33*** (0.03)	0.36*** (0.03)	0.29*** (0.02)	0.29*** (0.02)	−0.27*** (0.03)	−0.26*** (0.03)
Awareness	0.41*** (0.04)	0.23*** (0.04)	0.07* (0.03)	0.09** (0.03)	−0.05 (0.05)	0.06 (0.05)
Left partisanship[a]	0.16* (0.07)	0.10 (0.07)	−0.07 (0.06)	−0.07 (0.06)	0.09 (0.10)	0.11 (0.09)
Centre right partisanship[a]	0.20** (0.07)	0.14* (0.07)	0.00 (0.06)	0.00 (0.06)	−0.01 (0.10)	−0.03 (0.10)
Far right partisanship[a]	0.22*** (0.06)	0.18** (0.06)	0.13* (0.06)	0.12* (0.06)	−0.08 (0.10)	−0.05 (0.10)
Left × awareness	−0.19*** (0.07)	−0.15* (0.07)	−0.22*** (0.06)	−0.22*** (0.06)	0.24** (0.10)	0.24** (0.09)
Centre right × awareness	−0.03 (0.07)	0.06 (0.08)	0.24*** (0.06)	0.24*** (0.06)	0.15 (0.10)	0.16† (0.09)
Far right × awareness	−0.24*** (0.06)	−0.21*** (0.06)	0.01 (0.05)	0.01 (0.05)	−0.05 (0.10)	−0.08 (0.09)

Step 2

Surface of advertising campaign		−0.32*** (0.02)		0.11*** (0.03)		0.12*** (0.04)
Familiarity (mean awareness)		0.41*** (0.03)		−0.11*** (0.03)		0.10** (0.04)
Educational level[b]		0.20*** (0.03)		−0.07** (0.02)		0.43*** (0.03)
Linguistic region (French)		−0.12*** (0.03)		−0.06** (0.02)		0.11*** (0.03)
Chi-square (df)	245.7*** (7)	417.6*** (11)	569.4*** (7)	599.7*** (11)	250.8*** (7)	526.8*** (11)
-2LL	9,509.4	9,091.8	14,175.7	14,145.3	7,834.6	7,558.6
Nagelkerke R²	0.05	0.12	0.07	0.07	0.06	0.12

Notes

*** $p < 0.001$; ** $p < 0.01$; * $p < 0.05$; † $p < 0.10$. Entries are B coefficients from logistic regression; standard errors are in parentheses. a Apartisans as reference category. b Coded as a five-category variable (1, lowest educational level, to 5, highest educational level).

arena. In turn, challengers (such as minor parties, ecological organizations or xenophobic groups) can seize this opportunity to make their voices heard more easily, especially through alternative channels like newspaper advertisements. In passing, we should also note a small effect of the linguistic cleavage, as French-speaking people are less prone to follow the government than their German-speaking and Italian-speaking counterparts.

The results for *left-wing conflict situations* show that the interaction posited by the RAS model outperforms the direct effects of awareness and predispositions in explaining vote behaviour, although it does not supersede them completely. In line with Zaller's assumptions, awareness contributes to decreasing the agreement with the government among left citizens (assuming that it has no effect on apartisans),[24] while it contributes to increasing the support among centre right citizens. The interaction term indicates no effect on far right partisans; for them, a significant main effect of partisanship simply reveals that their support is higher than the support of apartisans, regardless of awareness. Globally, then, a clear polarization effect arises between the voting behaviour of left and centre right partisans. Finally, we should note that awareness *per se* contributes little to predicting the vote decision.

Adding the control variables at step 2 does not change the impact of awareness and predispositions. Moreover, it does very little to improve the fit of the model, and there remains a large amount of variance in vote decision to be explained. Contrary to mainstream situations, it appears that an intensification of advertising campaigns tends slightly to profit the government. Conversely, education and the familiarity of ballot proposals tend to be detrimental to the authorities, and thus to favour left-wing disagreement. Compared with mainstream situations, though, their impact on the vote decision is quite negligible. This suggests that, when the political debates take the form of a classical left–right conflict, neither awareness nor education produces a sizeable *net* impact on the vote. Rather, specific political skills (i.e. awareness) or general cognitive capabilities (i.e. education) are assumed to help people assess the consistency with their values of messages they receive, and so to foster an indirect, *interactive* effect.

Finally, the model for *far right conflict situations* yields some mixed results. On the one hand, it bears some resemblance to left-wing conflict situations in that awareness plays a role mainly through its interaction with partisanship. Indeed, awareness contributes to increasing the agreement with the government among left citizens (assuming again that it has no effect on apartisans). On the other hand, contrary to the predictions, there is no polarization effect *stricto sensu*, since awareness exerts no specific effect on centre right and far right partisans, as compared with apartisans.

Moreover, the introduction of the control variables yields a pattern of results that is fairly reminiscent of mainstream situations. As a matter of fact, education again proves to be a strong and direct predictor of voting: people with higher educational levels, whatever their ideological orientation, are more likely to reject far right stances and to adopt the more moderate position of government. Likewise, when far right parties are the only challengers of national policy making, increasing the global intensity of the advertising campaigns (along with the familiarity of issues) is a means of preventing the public from accepting the minority view. Globally, then, information mediated through education or referendum campaigns seems to be rather 'enlightening' – in Gamson and Modigliani's (1966) sense of discrediting 'belligerent' or radical policies. There is also evidence of a moderate effect by the linguistic cleavage: French-speaking citizens are more likely to side with the government on such matters.

Conclusion

The purpose of this chapter was to use survey data to test a theoretical model of public opinion formation. Our empirical evidence supports the case that elite discourse in Swiss referendum campaigns can influence individual vote decisions. More precisely, the balance of communication flows of the elite determines the citizens' vote behaviour in a way which is regulated by the interaction of individual awareness and political predispositions. This interaction reflects a two-stage process at the voter level, involving reception and acceptance of persuasive messages (Zaller 1993: 381).

As has already been shown by Kriesi (1994: 255), newspaper advertisements have a direct influence on the individual vote decision in Switzerland, although not a large one. Indeed, advertising campaigns more distinctly reflect the *overall division of the political elite*, an aspect of the general referendum campaign that is of prime importance for the public opinion formation *process*. With our measures of advertising, therefore, we have considered the *balance* of referendum campaigns as a part of the global decision-making context and not their overall influence on the citizens.

To be sure, the campaign messages are communicated to voters in multiple ways in a total media flow, and in this chapter we have been investigating just one element of this. But our focus on the balance of power in political advertisements shows that citizens clearly take the position of *'their' elite* into consideration. Accordingly, the voters cannot be considered as ignorant, but must be credited with the cognitive capacity to receive and evaluate campaign messages. Thus Zaller's model of opinion formation turns out to be highly relevant in the context of Swiss referendum campaigns – although, in consensus and far right conflictual situations, some macro-level variables may have a greater direct statistical impact on vote outcomes. The *potential campaign effects* on voters must indeed be differentiated among our vote categories. In other words, voters' resistance to changing their opinion towards, or away from, the dominant elite position varies across the three categories (Zaller 1992: 118).

The potential impact of campaigns in shaping negative vote outcomes for government is biggest in *consensus situations*, as voters are, then, least likely to resist countervailing messages from minority groups. Given that consensus ballots are often over non-salient issues, of which the general level of awareness in the electorate is pretty low, as soon as persuasive campaigns by opponents exceed a minimal attention threshold, there is no solid basis for the public to resist countervailing arguments. As has been shown, the relative importance of peripheral actors in the referendum campaigns can therefore be considerable.

Campaign effects appear indirectly in *left-wing conflictual* situations to the extent that they are mediated through political predispositions. Individuals refuse to internalize new dominant messages that they recognize as inconsistent with their predisposition (Zaller 1992: 121). Ballots with such partisan resistance are similar to the US party context in which the RAS model originates. Thus, in this instance, the inclusion of macro-level variables does not increase the general model fit.

The potential for campaign effects is limited in *far right conflict* situations. Here, ballot proposals often concern very salient issues, such as foreign policy. Thereby, individuals possess large stores of pre-existing views, producing inertial resistance to campaign messages (Zaller 1992: 121). The individual vote decisions are therefore largely predetermined, and government faces considerable difficulty in breaking this baseline resistance in some policy domains. In addition, government opponents often successfully resort to populist and emotional campaigns in order to increase their impact on vote outcomes. Qualitative dimensions of campaigns, however, are not taken into consideration in the RAS model. Among others, this aspect deserves more attention in coming analyses on referendum campaigns.

Notes

We are grateful to the editors for their comments on a draft of this chapter and for their help in editing it.

1 Throughout this chapter, the term 'referendum' refers to compulsory and optional referendums, as well as to popular initiatives.
2 The VOX surveys are regular post-election surveys accompanying each federal referendum in Switzerland since 1981, usually conducted during the week following the referendum.
3 In some cases, the VOX surveys we use did not distinguish between the proposals being voted on, and as a result the number of ballot measures in our individual analyses is reduced to thirty. This particularly affects our consensual category, reducing the number of ballots from eleven to nine.
4 The most significant ways in which the conditions can vary is over the role of non-partisan actors, the intensity of the campaigns and, in general, a higher elite conflict in foreign policy.
5 Finally, for all individual analyses, we have weighted the VOX surveys so that the number of respondents equals 1,000 in each ballot. The weighting was necessary as sample sizes vary considerably among our selected proposals (600–1,000 respondents).

6 Justifications are considered as 'non-valid' if they conspicuously miss the point of the question asked (e.g. reasons for a 'yes' to motivate a 'no'), or if they are unrelated to the characteristics of the ballot proposal (e.g. 'I voted like my husband/wife'). Note that validity is independent of whether people actually voted in the first place. As we take into account the 'virtual' decisions of non-voters (see below), similarly we retain their 'virtual' motivations ('Which are the main reasons why you would have accepted / refused the ballot proposal?').

7 Note that the mean level of awareness is slightly higher in our ballot sample ($\mu = 2.37$, thirty-two votes) than that for all ballots held between 1981 and 1996 ($\mu = 2.23$, 118 votes). This is due almost entirely to the inclusion of foreign policy ($\mu = 2.85$, four votes), immigration policy ($\mu = 2.45$, five votes) and defence policy ($\mu = 2.50$, seven votes) in our sample.

8 In fact, 45 per cent declared that they had no preference, while 5 per cent did not give any answer.

9 For more details see Marquis and Sciarini (1999).

10 With respect to compulsory or optional referendums, the Federal Council and the Federal Administration (in rarer instances, the parliament) initiate the legislative process and have control over the content and formulation of ballot proposals. As a result, supporting referendum proposals amounts to a backing of the authorities' policies. In addition, each citizen is entitled to launch a popular initiative and to put a proposal on the vote agenda, provided he or she meets the legal requirements. Popular initiatives are thus meant to challenge or oppose governmental action in some domain, and the Federal Council has almost always recommended their rejection at the polls.

11 *Neue Zürcher Zeitung, Tages-Anzeiger, Blick, Journal de Genève, Tribune de Genève, Le Matin*. Advertisements were selected because they can be seen as representative of the tenor of campaigns at a more general level, especially since broadcast political campaigning is prohibited by law. In contrast to television and radio programmes, newspaper editorials or the letters' page in the newspapers, political ads are very broad in scope (at least as concerns the social and political background of their users and the tone and content of the messages) and are used by almost all political actors.

12 This threshold is the mean intensity across all votes ($16,390 \text{ cm}^2$) excluding the campaign regarding participation in the European Economic Area. This case had to be set aside because on its own it nearly equalled the advertising space of all other campaigns.

13 The 'upheaval' of advertisers against UN membership was replicated later in the voting booth. However, so impressive was the tidal wave in the media that the outcome of the ballot – a clear rejection by 76 per cent of voters – was not surprising.

14 Our classification method is an automatic procedure taking into account the voting cues of the four main parties: Social Democratic Party (left); Christian Democratic Party *or* Radical Democratic Party (centre right); Swiss People's Party (far right). This method showed at once which ideological camps were at odds with the government's position. Only with respect to four votes did we have to take a closer look at the recommendations issued by smaller parties (i.e. when no main party took an anti-government stance) to get a picture of the dissenters.

15 The proposal to replace the old taxation system is an exception in this regard, as small parties on both the left and the right extremity of the political spectrum opposed the policy. However, since the share of the dissenting far right parties inside their own camp was noticeably greater than that of the dissenting left parties, and also for the sake of simplicity in the coming analysis, we decided to classify this case as one that elicited far right-wing opposition.

16 Of course, this is a *self-reported* decision, which might differ from the *actual* decision in some individual cases. We know from experience that the vote decision, as well as the reported participation in the ballot, is regularly biased in the VOX surveys; however, this should not alter our conclusions, since we are not primarily interested in the *absolute* level of support for the government.

17 Participants are somewhat more supportive of the government than the non-participants (respectively 55 per cent and 51 per cent in its favour; $\phi = 0.04$; $p < 0.001$), but in only two cases could the majority have changed sides if the non-voters had made their way to the voting booth.

18 Indeed, only 32 per cent of the participants (down to 27 per cent among the left-wing citizens) are classified within the two lower levels of awareness, which might prove problematic. In some conflict configurations (especially far right), this share is further reduced – with almost no one left in the lower categories – so that the uncovered relationships between awareness and voting would virtually bear on the differences between the two upper categories only. Taking the non-participants into consideration permits us to raise the proportion of least aware citizens from 32 per cent to 39 per cent.

19 In four out of fourteen votes, the Swiss Democrats (a xenophobic party) recommended rejection of the government position.

20 Unfortunately, other socio-demographic determinants of the vote decision (like age, or town versus countryside residence) were missing in the VOX surveys for several votes.

21 The SPSS z scores procedure was applied, which transforms any variable into a new variable with a mean of 0 and a standard deviation of 1. This standardization method was carried out *separately* for each sub-sample (mainstream, left-wing, far right conflicts), so that B coefficients can approximately be compared *across* models.

22 To evaluate multicollinearity, we entered all independent variables in a linear regression model and looked at the tolerance or VIF (variance inflation factor) statistics (see Menard 1995: 66). For the first two models, the VIF exceeds 7 only for two variables (left × awareness, centre right × awareness) and normally ranges between 1 and 6.5. For the third model, VIF values are generally higher, indicating risks of multicollinearity.

23 Neither was it the case when the unstandardized variables were entered in the models.

24 To be sure, this formulation is simplistic, since we do not know exactly the effect of awareness on apartisans. Thus a negative coefficient merely indicates that the effect of awareness is *less positive* on a given partisanship category than it is on apartisans. But because this kind of formulation is rather cumbersome, and provided that our preliminary analysis has found the relationship between awareness and voting to be virtually non-existent or non-monotonic, we will interpret the interaction effects without explicit reference to the category of apartisans.

11 Do political campaigns matter?

Yes, but it depends

Rüdiger Schmitt-Beck and David M. Farrell

The previous chapters have taken us on a Cook's Tour of different cases of campaign effects. The objective of this chapter is to draw the threads together, to show how collectively these chapters demonstrate some important steps forward in the comparative study of campaign effects, and to set out a stall for further possible research. Three major conclusions are drawn, namely: (1) campaigns do matter, but (2) how they matter can vary in a number of respects and (3) is contingent on circumstances.

Campaigns do matter

As John Zaller puts it in his path-breaking study on political influence, '[e]very opinion is a marriage of information and predisposition: information to form a mental picture of the given issue, and predisposition to motivate some conclusion about it' (1992: 6). Information is thus essential for any process of decision making. The information used by electors when deciding how to vote can come from many sources, and campaigns are only one of them. For instance, people may derive an impression of the political state of affairs from their experiences in everyday life. Are prices rising? Do I know many people who are unemployed? Have public services lately been improving or deteriorating? Such observations may help voters to draw conclusions about the performance of government (Popkin 1991). Voters also receive political cues from their social environment. They may see more and more people wearing lapel buttons, or cars displaying bumper stickers supporting a particular party or candidate. They may overhear political conversations in the tram on their way to work or afterwards at the pub. Or they may gather information by engaging in political discussions with their family, friends or co-workers. Last but not least, the mass media, especially television, must never be overlooked as a ubiquitous source of political information in modern democracies.

Hence voters constantly move in environments saturated with political information, even without the campaigns being waged by political actors. This means that, in their campaigns, the political actors have to compete with a range of other sources of potential influence over their target audiences. Campaign information is enmeshed in complex ways with information from other sources. In part, the campaigners' messages compete for (scarce and rather precious) voters' attention with other sources of information. In part, too, the information from other sources actually originates from, and is mediated by, campaigns, albeit modified through multi-step flows of communication, working through the mass media and stages of interpersonal communication. The point is nicely illustrated by Elisabeth Gidengil and her colleagues in Chapter 5, in their examination of how political discussions between voters can interfere with campaign information obtained from the mass media.

Studying the effects of campaigns requires us to disentangle this complex web of information flows, in order to isolate campaign information from all other kinds of information that fill both public and private spaces before the ballots are opened on election day. Only then is it possible to arrive at viable answers to the crucial question over whether political actors, by waging more or less sophisticated campaigns, can influence public opinion, increase their social support base and thus become, at least to some degree, masters of their own fate. Obviously, this is a challenging task, both theoretically and methodologically, and in part this difficulty explains why any answer to the question of whether campaigns matter must inevitably remain heavily qualified.

According to active participants in the political game – politicians, consultants, journalists – all in one way or another dealing each day of their professional life with strategic communications, campaigning is one of the biggest movers in the political process. In their view it plays a key role in determining voting behaviour and election outcomes. 'Election victories can be made,' as one German campaign consultant once self-confidently put it (Müller 1997). Sometimes even single campaign events, like a well designed television spot, are attributed the capacity to decide an election (Morris 1997). By contrast, there are those who believe that election results may be wholly explained by factors totally unrelated to the noisy rhetorical interludes preceding election day, such as the ups and downs of the economy, or the basic division of society in terms of political predispositions like social group identifications, ideology, basic value orientations or partisanship. According to this perspective, election outcomes are decided long before the election actually takes place, and remain unaffected by the communication strategies of political actors. As Newton (2000) argues, voters form their preferences on the basis of other information than that provided by campaigns, and against this information the biased messages thought up by marketing specialists cannot prevail. If this sceptical view entails any practical advice for politicians, it is to save their money for more worthwhile endeavours rather than habitually taking part in the frenzy of campaigning every four or five years.

As ever, there is a position in between these two extremes, in which it can be suggested that, while campaigns may not be of such predominant importance as is assumed by the political actors (whose outlook is glued to the superficial back-and-forth of day-to-day political debate), they do, none the less, count for something in the political process. They are one factor among many others that are important for how and what people decide. Parties trailing miles behind their competitors in terms of voters' support may not turn the tide simply by running a good campaign, but they may still have some effect on the vote. As Popescu and Tóka note in Chapter 4, the exclusive use of resources linked with their public office did not help the Hungarian government parties in 1994 and 1998 in their campaigns to gain re-election; however, at least it may have spared them even more painful defeats. Conversely, parties riding high on a tide of electors' esteem may well win even if they do not campaign at all. But certainly, in the case of close contests, campaigning may well be the pivotal force that in the end decides the contest.

In short, then, while it would be a clear exaggeration to state that campaigns are of *prime* importance in determining the election result, in the light of the research reviewed in this volume, it seems pretty incontrovertible that campaigns do, indeed, matter for the behaviour of citizens at elections and referendums. The rhetorical activities undertaken by political actors in order to improve their electoral prospects seem to matter to voters when they take their decisions. However, the extent of this influence varies between campaigns, as discussed below. In addition, and to return to a theme raised in Chapter 1, campaigns seem to have unintentional effects. They matter not only for citizens' votes but also for the wider polity, and thus are of consequence for politics in modern democracies more generally.

The potential for campaign influence is shown by Ian McAllister in Chapter 2 by the rising numbers of campaign late deciders in the United States, the United Kingdom and Australia, a proportion of whom – as 'calculating' voters – are open to campaign influence. In Chapter 3, Romain Lachat and Pascal Sciarini provide similar evidence from the 1999 Swiss general election showing how late-deciding voters are most responsive to campaign information. Other chapters in this volume present a range of different scenarios of campaign influence. For instance, Marina Popescu and Gábor Tóka, in Chapter 4, demonstrate that in Hungarian elections during the 1990s government parties, by instrumentalizing public television as channel of campaign communication, were able to influence those voters who were exposed to its programmes. In Chapter 5, Elisabeth Gidengil and her colleagues produce clear evidence of priming in recent Canadian elections, indicating how election campaigns can affect the bases on which people decide their vote. Findings from Finland, provided by Ilkka Ruostet-saari and Mikko Mattila in Chapter 6, suggest that both through advertising in newspapers and through applying a broad range of other direct campaign techniques, candidates can win votes in an environment of personalized campaigning. In Chapter 7, David Denver and Gordon Hands demonstrate how the local campaign efforts of political parties affected electoral outcomes in the constituencies during the British 1997 general election.

Turning to referendums and applying a wide-angle lens by looking at campaigns across a range of democracies, Lawrence LeDuc demonstrates how dramatic shifts in opinion on referendum issues can occur during campaigns, shifts which can be at least partially attributed to effects from the information infused through campaigns (Chapter 9). On the specific case of referendum campaigns in Switzerland, Michael Bützer and Lionel Marquis show in Chapter 10 how the degree of consensus or division between elites – in turn leading to very different campaigns – affects the way citizens make up their minds on the referendum proposals. Between them, and through a mix of micro-level and macro-level analysis, these chapters provide evidence supporting the notion that campaigns matter with regard to the aims for which they are fought, namely to obtain support for parties or candidates in elections or for issue proposals at referendums.

Chapter 8, by Pippa Norris, goes beyond this narrow instrumental focus. It addresses widespread worries, reviewed in Chapter 1, that campaigning, while perhaps being advantageous to some political actors, may also damage democratic political systems by contributing to growing civic disengagement and cynicism among the citizens. Yet, if anything, as Norris shows, the evidence points to a contrary conclusion, at least for the United States. The upshot of this is that, even if campaigns were irrelevant to electoral outcomes, they would still have relevance to democratic politics: rather than depressing citizens' political trust and involvement in the electoral process, they actually seem to enhance them. This is good news at least for one form of unintentional consequence of campaigns. However, this does not preclude the possibility that there are others, still in need of further study.

Variations in campaign effect

As we outlined in Chapter 1 (see Figure 1.3), there are a range of different types of campaign effects that political actors have in mind when planning their strategies. For instance, they attempt to influence the salience of matters that voters consider when deciding how to vote. They also seek to bring new matters to people's attention. Finally – and certainly the most demanding task – they aim to change the voters' views of the political world.

Undoubtedly, persuasion features most prominently among the effects actually intended by the relevant political actors. As the two chapters on Swiss election (Chapter 3) and referendum campaigns (Chapter 10) suggest, activation of latent predispositions is an important effect brought about by campaigns: this is in line with the classic assertion of Lazarsfeld and his colleagues (Lazarsfeld *et al.* 1968 [1944]). The more they are reached by campaigns, the more those citizens with ideological or partisan affiliations tend to support their own elites, either by electing them or by supporting their positions on referendum proposals. On the other hand, the second message of these studies is that conversion is also possible. In particular, if campaigns are highly intense and non-balanced, in the sense that not all competitors invest equal amounts of resources, they may suitably distract voters from their predispositions.

Several other chapters provide additional evidence of campaign-induced persuasion. For instance, Chapter 4 on the influence of Hungarian public television, shows how government parties used this medium as a campaign tool, and the more citizens were exposed to its coverage the more they tended to like these parties and the better they evaluated their economic record. Yet Popescu and Tóka raise an interesting note of caution: this kind of persuasive effect was observable only in the 1998 election. In 1994, by contrast, there was a backlash effect, actually damaging the prospects of the governing party. Apparently, therefore, if media partisanship becomes too blatant, it may backfire. Chapter 4 demonstrates nicely the complexity of campaign effects: the persuasive impact of a campaign is not always a linear function of the resources which have been mobilized, and in this instance the bias shown by the television coverage in 1994 made it possible for the opposition to turn its onesidedness into an issue in its own right, resulting in a boomerang effect against the government party.

However, this kind of resistance on the part of the target audiences of campaign messages is perhaps restricted to the persuasive potential of blatant 'propaganda'. In the Hungarian case it did not extend to a more subtle mechanism of influence – priming. The voters may have remained unimpressed by public television's onesidedness in evaluative content, but, despite this, they none the less adapted the bases on which they decided their vote in accordance with this medium's issue agenda. Political actors' campaigns aim not only at changing voters' evaluations of them (in a positive direction) and their competitors (in a negative direction), they also seek to get voters to change the considerations – be it issues or candidates – they take into account when forming their preferences. Chapter 5 on Canadian elections, by Gidengil and her colleagues, also provides evidence of this more subtle (and thus more difficult to detect) effect of campaigns.

A third form of intended campaign influence is the classic strategy of promoting voter mobilization, which as we saw in our literature review in Chapter 1 is most closely associated with local campaign activities. Denver and Hands's account in Chapter 7 of campaign trends in the 1997 British election shows that this practice is still very much alive and kicking even in a 'post-Fordist' age – and, as their findings suggest, it works.

There is also evidence in this volume of a fourth type of intentional effect. Campaigns focusing on individual candidates instead of party organizations and their leaders are often confronted with a specific problem, namely that candidates unknown to the public are standing against well known incumbents who earn a lot of 'free' media through parliamentary and other political activities. American primaries are a classic case of where such patterns are notorious (Bartels 1988). For newcomers, the first aim must be to gain visibility and make themselves known to electors. As Chapter 6 by Ruostetsaari and Mattila suggests, investing resources in campaigning may, indeed, help candidates to overcome the drawback of low 'name recognition', thus mastering a crucial precondition for being considered at all as a viable alternative by voters.

The contingent nature of campaign effects

The third main conclusion to be drawn from the studies in this volume is that campaigns may matter, but not necessarily for all voters, all the time, or regardless of circumstances. Campaigning has its limits. The fact is that, for all the efforts a political actor like a party might put into a campaign, for all the resources it might bring to bear in selling itself, its candidates and its policies to the voters, if the voters are not buying then there is not much a campaign can do about it. Such a dilemma was neatly illustrated by the 2001 election campaign of the British Conservative Party. By general consensus it fought the best campaign: for the most part controlling the agenda, on most days setting the 'issue of the day', keeping the media coverage on the party's preferred issues (such as taxation and Europe). The party flung everything it had into the campaign, using all the latest campaign gimmickry, deploying the most professional of strategists, borrowing the best from recent US Republican campaigns, outspending all the other parties. Yet, for all this exhaustive effort, the campaign proved utterly useless in raising the party's vote. From day one of the four-week campaign the Conservatives' poll rating stubbornly refused to budge from the historically low level it had maintained throughout the lifetime of the Parliament; the yawning gap between their vote and that of the Labour incumbents simply refused to close. The outcome of all this was a miniscule rise of 1.0 per cent in the Conservative vote on polling day and a net seat gain of one.

As discussed in Chapter 1 the shape of a campaign – its strategies, its messages and appeals, its communication channels, its length, as well as its 'loudness' and corresponding penetration power – depends on a broad variety of factors, including features of political systems as well as situational circumstances. We have seen throughout the chapters of this volume that the nature of the effects a campaign may have is also highly contingent. Campaigns matter in ways that are dependent on a multitude of factors, often interacting with each other in complex patterns. Some of these factors concern the campaigns themselves, others concern the campaigns' recipients – the electorates and the individuals of which they are composed.

Campaign-related factors

One of the core findings of this book, most notably of Chapter 9, is that campaigns may matter very differently depending on the type of decision event. On the whole, referendum campaigns can be expected to be more effective than election campaigns. As LeDuc suggests, we can look at this distinction in terms of a continuum of stability versus volatility, with elections being located closer to the end-point of stability. Referendum campaigns, however, vary significantly, depending on the degree to which the referendum proposal is related to the socio-political cleavage structures of organized party conflict. In the cases of campaigns for elections and those referendums over established issues with clear partisan connotations, the story is mostly one of activation, as is shown by the Swiss referendum campaigns analysed by Bützer and Marquis in Chapter 10. Towards the other (volatility) end-point of the continuum, we find referendum campaigns over new, unclear and complex issues without inherent and obvious underpinnings in traditional cleavage structures. In such cases opinions cannot be activated but must be formed, and there is considerable scope for conversion through campaign information, leading to unpredictable outcomes. Where parties are internally divided and appear positioned on opposing sides of a referendum, there is even greater potential for this kind of persuasion through campaigns.

Several chapters demonstrate how campaign intensity or loudness can also be important. Lachat and Sciarini's analysis in Chapter 3 compares three Swiss cantonal campaigns that vary by intensity, as expressed in advertising expenditures. It turns out that campaigns of low intensity influence almost no one. A certain minimum intensity seems necessary to influence apartisans. High-intensity campaigns have the capacity to influence apartisans and even some partisans. In general, the findings in Chapters 6, 7 and 10 support the notion that the amount of resources invested in campaigns can matter.

Campaigns may use a number of different channels for communicating to voters. Chapter 7 explores how direct contact with voters, in British constituency campaigns, can affect mobilization. The research in Chapter 6, on the Finnish case, suggests that a range of campaign activities applied simultaneously is important: campaigners should not restrict themselves to too few channels for addressing the electorate. The chapters by Ruostetsaari and Mattila, Lachat and Sciarini and Bützer and Marquis indicate that, at least in the European context where campaigners have very restricted opportunities for purchasing air time on the broadcast media, advertising resources may deliver returns if invested in ads in the printed press. This, again, points to the crucial importance of sufficient resources for the success of campaigns.

As a functional equivalent to advertising, the mass media's political reporting – seen as 'free media' compensating for insufficient resources for 'paid media' – plays a central role in contemporary campaign strategies, providing a key channel of campaign communication, and a focus of effort by campaign organizations to influence the reporting of events. Chapter 4 in particular, focusing on Hungarian public television, indicates that such strategies may actually bear fruit. However, this case may be exceptional and probably cannot be generalized beyond the realm of new democracies. In established democracies, the media usually cannot be fitted quite so neatly into campaign strategies; they prefer to give their own, independent (if not anti-party-political), angle to the presentation of politics, as discussed by Norris in Chapter 8. Either reflecting campaign agendas or their own criteria of news value, the media's agendas are prominent sources of priming effects, determining what voters think of when they make up their minds about how to vote (cf. Chapter 5).

Finally, campaign themes also featured in a number of our chapters. This is most notable in Chapter 5, where, in their analysis of three Canadian elections, Gidengil and her colleagues demonstrate how campaign-specific the themes can be; in some cases with candidate image featuring strongly, in other cases one or more issues playing a stronger role. As they put it, election campaigns 'are not all of a piece' (p. 87). Such differences between campaigns are of consequence with regard to priming effects. While candidate priming seems to take place quite regularly in campaigns, issue priming occurs only in cases of highly concentrated issue agendas in which one dramatically new issue features highly prominently. Agenda structures may not necessarily be under the control of campaigners, however. Issue contexts are also important because they may colour the way campaign messages are interpreted by voters. The 1994 Hungarian general election took place amidst a 'media war' about the issue of government control over broadcast media. This specific context contributed to the 'boomerang effect' of public television's slanted reporting (cf. Chapter 4).

One of the most pressing issues in the study of the consequences of campaigns concerns the theme, raised in several chapters (most notably Chapters 1, 7 and 8), of how campaigns have been going through a process of modernization, towards a form of campaigning which we describe in Chapter 1 as 'stage III' campaigning (see Table 1.1). Implicit in much of this discussion is the notion that (*pace* the British Conservatives in 2001) more modern campaigns are, somehow, more influential, not least because they are more sophisticated and professional and because they perhaps better suit the needs of a more fragmented, and at the same time more available, electorate. Among campaigners, and especially among the consultants who make a living from this, such a belief is common currency. As discussed in Chapter 1, it is the core rationale behind the 'arms race' for ever more sophisticated tools and techniques of campaigning. Although this hypothesis is in desperate need of empirical validation, it would be premature to draw any firm conclusions about it here. With regard to constituency-level campaigns, there is some evidence in Chapter 7 that what Denver and Hands refer to as 'post-Fordist' local campaigning in the constituency may be no less (but equally also no more) effective than more traditional forms of campaigning. In short, then, the jury is still out on this matter: plausible as it may seem to hypothesize that more sophisticated campaigns are more effective, the matter clearly needs further study before a definite assessment can be given.

Factors related to voters

Many models of political behaviour implicitly assume that all citizens base their decisions in similar ways using the same variables. In recent years this view has been challenged by the notion that not all voters are the same, and that correspondingly their political behaviour does not follow the same regularities (Rivers 1988). A number of chapters suggest that this general idea is also important when thinking about the effects of political campaigns. The scope for campaign influence can vary dramatically depending on the types of voters involved. One obvious conditioning factor is, for instance, whether voters are at all available to be influenced by campaigns. This is not the case if they have taken their decisions long before the start of a campaign, as Lachat and Sciarini demonstrate for Swiss voters in Chapter 3. As they show, campaigns can only be expected to have effects on late deciders (see also Chapter 2).

In *The Nature and Origins of Mass Opinion*, John Zaller (1992) places great stress on two features of relevance here, namely the political predispositions of voters and their degrees of political awareness. A number of chapters confirm the importance of both variables. Predispositions like ideology and, above all, partisanship feature as important moderating factors for campaign influence. Referendum campaigns inform partisans about the positions of their parties' elites and help to align their votes accordingly. Depending on the degree of consensus or division between the elites, this leads to a 'mainstream' or a 'polarization effect' in referendum voting, as Bützer and Marquis show in Chapter 10. However, as Chapter 9 by LeDuc suggests, this kind of activating role of predispositions presupposes that the referendum issue bears a relationship to existing cleavage structures and organized party conflict. However; if the issue is new, unclear and/or complex, predispositions may give voters little guidance, thus enabling campaigns to influence different types of voters more evenly.

Zaller (1992) also attaches importance to the mediating role of individual voters' degrees of political awareness, in the sense of a person's intellectual engagement with public affairs, including both 'the extent to which an individual pays attention to current political events and understands what he or she has encountered' (Zaller 1990: 126). Again several chapters in this volume provide evidence of how this affects campaign influence. The more sophisticated voters are more inclined to receive campaign information, as can be seen in Chapters 2 and 10. Those voters who experience higher levels of media exposure, in turn, are more likely to be primed about issues and candidate images, as shown in Chapter 5. However, when it comes to persuasion, the moderating effect of political awareness is more complex. It decreases the likelihood that partisans will be pulled by a campaign towards decisions deviating from their predispositions, and not in line with the campaigns of 'their' elite (Chapter 10). It also reduces the likelihood that (late-deciding) apartisans will vote contrary to their ideological predispositions. Political awareness thus increases the likelihood of activation while inhibiting the likelihood of conversion (Chapter 3).

Political campaigns in perspective

As we noted in Chapter 1, the study of the effects of political campaigns is located at the intersection of various sub-disciplines of political science, thus making it methodologically demanding. To arrive at a credible answer to the question of whether campaigns have effects requires an approach combining different perspectives and using data from various sources. Certainly, the chapters collected in this book represent a broad range of different methodological approaches, although surveys clearly dominate. The groups surveyed include voters (Chapters 2, 3, 4, 5, 8 and 10), candidates (Chapter 6) and party activists (Chapter 7). Some chapters also combine survey data with data from other sources, such as electoral records (Chapters 6 and 7), campaign expenditure records (Chapters 3 and 6) and media content analyses (Chapter 10). In addition, comparisons of different campaigns appear as a particularly promising path towards a better understanding of campaign effects. The chapters include comparisons of various local or regional campaigns for the same election (Chapters 3, 6 and 7), as well as comparisons of national campaigns across various elections or referendums within the same country (Chapters 4, 5, 8 and 10) or even across different countries (Chapters 2 and 9). Although quite varied in their methodological approaches, the studies in this volume do not exhaust the range of research techniques that are available. In particular, experimental methods, applying both laboratory experiments (e.g. Kaid and Holtz-Bacha 1993; Iyengar and Petrocik 2000) and field experiments (e.g. Gerber and Green 2000), appear as a fruitful option that is not represented in this volume.

The findings in this book indicate that research in this area is not a futile effort, and certainly much more is needed. Indeed, if it is the case that, as we have seen, campaigns can matter, then it seems reasonable to propose that they will matter even more in the future. Electorates continue to change in ways that make them more responsive to campaign communications. In many democracies, partisan dealignment makes increasing portions of the electorate susceptible to conversion through campaigns. In new democracies partisanship generally tends to be weak, and unlikely ever to build up to the levels found traditionally in the established democracies. There is thus a far greater potential for campaign effects from the start.

Parallel to these transformations of the electorate, campaigning itself is developing increasingly in the direction of 'stage III', 'post-modern' or 'post-Fordist' styles of permanent, highly intense, sophisticated and targeted operations. Gone are the days when political parties could rely on the support of particular categories of voters; indeed, gone also are the days when the established, mainstream political actors had the electoral field to themselves.

The political market has become much more competitive, and the parties, as well as other relevant actors (such as media and interest groups) have had to adapt their modes of operation if only to keep up with the extent of change, and with adaptations by their competitors. And there is little sign of this abating as the 'arms race' of campaign modernization continues apace.

Whether all the changes connected with the emergence of 'stage III' campaigning actually make for more effective campaigns in comparison with the more traditional ways of conducting campaigns of old is one of the questions for which we are still lacking evidence. Yet some assumptions can safely be made, based on the evidence assembled in this book. For instance, the trend towards the 'permanent' campaign undermines the relevance of the timing of the vote, since in the long run it neutralizes the inhibiting potential of early deciding. As McAllister demonstrates in Chapter 2, partisan dealignment is likely to move the average time when voting decisions are cast closer to the day when elections or referendums are held. In addition, if campaigning is no longer restricted to short periods of intense communication efforts immediately preceding elections or referendums, the campaigns should also start reaching those electors who still take their decisions long in advance. As campaigns start earlier, more and more voters mutate, by definition, from early deciders to campaign deciders.

Furthermore, a proliferation of campaigns is likely, due to the growing number of organizations that are becoming active in the crowded and differentiated landscape of 'post-modern' politics, and due to the increasing propensity of political actors of all sorts to rely on campaigns to promote their causes. As political parties transform into 'cartel parties', increasingly making use of state resources for the purpose of campaigning and removing restrictions and shaping the legal framework of campaigning in their common interest (Katz and Mair 1995), and as campaign organizations develop improved skills at fund raising, campaigns are also likely to be more intense in the future. Campaigns of higher intensity, in turn, are more likely to be effective.

Finally, as we have seen, referendum campaigns are likely to influence more voters than are election campaigns. Hence the general trend towards more plebiscitary politics in contemporary democracies, brought about by the 'participatory revolution' (Kaase 1984), which spawned a spreading institutionalization of the means of direct democracy and an increase in their use (Butler and Ranney 1994; Bowler and Donovan 1998), will also contribute to a growing importance of political campaigns for the processes of democratic governance.

Bibliography

Abramowitz, Alan I. (1978) 'The Impact of a Presidential Debate on Voter Rationality', *American Journal of Political Science* 22: 680–90.

Abramson, Paul (1983) *Political Attitudes in America*. San Francisco: Freeman.

Achille, Yves and Jacques I. Bueno (1994) *Les télévisions publiques en quête d'avenir*. Grenoble: Presses Universitaires de Grenoble.

Ahopelto-Marjamäki, Niina (1999) 'Vuoden 1996 EU-vaalikampanjointi'. (Master's thesis in political science.) Tampere: Department of Political Science, University of Tampere.

Alvarez, R. Michael and Jonathan Nagler (1998) 'When Politics and Models Collide: Estimating Models of Multiparty Elections', *American Journal of Political Science* 42: 55–96.

Amin, Ash (ed.) (1994) *Post-Fordism. A Reader*. Oxford: Blackwell.

Ansolabehere, Stephen and Shanto Iyengar (1995) *Going Negative. How Political Advertisements Shrink and Polarize the Electorate*. New York: Free Press.

Ansolabehere, Stephen, Roy Behr and Shanto Iyengar (1991) 'Mass Media and Elections: An Overview', *American Politics Quarterly* 19: 109–39.

Ansolabehere, Stephen, Roy Behr and Shanto Iyengar (1993) *The Media Game*. New York: Macmillan.

Appleton, Andrew (1992) 'Maastricht and the French Party System: Domestic Implications of the Treaty Referendum', *French Politics and Society* 10: 1–18.

Bartels, Larry M. (1988) *Presidential Primaries and the Dynamics of Public Choice*. Princeton, NJ: Princeton University Press.

Bartels, Larry M. (1992) 'The Impact of Electioneering in the United States', in David Butler and Austin Ranney (eds) *Electioneering. A Comparative Study of Continuity and Change*. Oxford: Clarendon Press, pp. 244–77.

Bartels, Larry M. (2000) 'Partisanship and Voting Behavior, 1952–1996', *American Journal of Political Science* 44: 35–50.

Bartolini, Stefano and Peter Mair (1990) *Identity, Competition and Electoral Availability*. New York: Cambridge University Press.

Bean, Clive (1993) 'The Electoral Influence of Party Leader Images in Australia and New Zealand', *Comparative Political Studies* 26: 111–32.

Bean, Clive and Anthony Mughan (1989) 'Leadership Effects in Parliamentary Elections in Australia and Britain', *American Political Science Review* 83: 1165–79.

Bennett, Stephen E. (1988) '"Know-Nothings" Revisited: The Meaning of Political Ignorance Today', *Social Science Quarterly* 69: 476–90.

Bennett, Stephen Earl, Staci L. Rhine, Richard S. Flickinger and Linda L.M. Bennett (1999) 'Videomalaise Revisited: Reconsidering the Relation between the Public's View of the Media and Trust in Government', *Harvard International Journal of Press/Politics* 4 (4): 8–23.

Bentele, Günter, Tobias Lieber and Michael Vogt (eds) (2001) *PR für Verbände und Organisationen*. Neuwied: Luchterhand.

Berelson, Bernard, Paul F. Lazarsfeld and William N. McPhee (1954) *Voting. A Study of Opinion Formation in a Presidential Campaign*. Chicago: University of Chicago Press.

Bieber, Christoph (1999) *Politische Projekte im Internet. Online-Kommunikation und politische Öffentlichkeit*. Frankfurt: Campus.

Bjørklund, Tor (1982) 'The Demand for Referendum: When Does It Arise and When Does It Succeed?', *Scandinavian Political Studies* 5: 237–59.

Blais, André, Elisabeth Gidengil, Richard Nadeau and Neil Nevitte (1999) 'Measuring Party Identification: Canada, Britain, and the United States'. Paper presented at the annual meeting of the American Political Science Association, Atlanta, GA.

Blais, André, Neil Nevitte, Elisabeth Gidengil and Richard Nadeau (forthcoming) 'Do people Have Feelings Towards Leaders About Whom They Say They Know Nothing?', *Public Opinion Quarterly*.

Blumler, Jay G. and Michael Gurevitch (1995) *The Crisis of Public Communication*. London: Longman.

Blumler, Jay G. and Elihu Katz (eds) (1974) *The Uses of Mass Communications: Current Perspectives on Gratifications Research*. Beverly Hills, CA: Sage.

Bowen, Lawrence (1994) 'Time of Voting Decision and the Use of Political Advertising: The Gorton–Slade Adams–Brock Senatorial Campaign', *Journalism Quarterly* 71: 665–75.

Bowler, Shaun and Todd Donovan (1998) *Demanding Choices. Opinion, Voting, and Direct Democracy*. Ann Arbor, MI: University of Michigan Press.

Bowler, Shaun and David Farrell (eds) (1992a) *Electoral Strategies and Political Marketing*. New York: St Martin's Press.

Bowler, Shaun and David Farrell (1992b) 'The Study of Election Campaigning', in Shaun Bowler and David Farrell (eds) *Electoral Strategies and Political Marketing*. New York: St Martin's Press, pp. 1–23.

Bowler, Shaun and David Farrell (2000) 'The Internationalization of Campaign Consultancy', in James Thurber and Candice Nelson (eds) *Campaign Warriors. Political Consultants in Elections*. Washington, DC: Brookings Institution, pp. 153–74.

Broughton, David (1998) 'The Welsh Devolution Referendum of 1997', *Representation* 35: 200–9.

Brunner, Wolfram (1999) 'Bundestagswahlkämpfe und ihre Effekte. Der Traditionsbruch 1998', *Zeitschrift für Parlamentsfragen* 30: 268–96.

Budge, Ian and Dennis J. Farlie (1983) *Explaining and Predicting Elections. Issue Effects and Party Strategies in Twenty-three Democracies*. London: Allen & Unwin.

Burnell, Peter and Andrew Reeves (1984) 'Persuasion as a Political Concept', *British Journal of Political Science* 14: 393–410.

Butler, David E. (1952) *The British General Election of 1951*. London: Macmillan.

Butler, David E. and Dennis Kavanagh (1984) *The British General Election of 1983*. London: Macmillan.

Butler, David E. and Austin Ranney (eds) (1992) *Electioneering. A Comparative Study of Continuity and Change*. Oxford: Clarendon Press.

Butler, David E. and Austin Ranney (eds) (1994) *Referendums Around the World. The Growing Use of Direct Democracy*. Basingstoke: Macmillan.

Butler, David E. and Donald Stokes (1974) *Political Change in Britain*. London: Macmillan.

Bütschi, Danielle (1993) 'Compétence pratique', in Hanspeter Kriesi (ed.) *Citoyenneté et démocratie directe*. Zurich: Seismo, pp. 99–109.

Buzan, Barry and Eric Herring (1998) *The Arms Dynamic in World Politics*. Boulder, CO: Lynne Rienner.

Campbell, Angus, Philip E. Converse, Warren E. Miller and Donald E. Stokes (1960) *The American Voter*. New York: Wiley.

Campbell, James E. (2000) *The American Campaign. US Presidential Campaigns and the National Vote*. College Station, TX: Texas A&M University Press.

Cappella, Joseph N. and Kathleen H. Jamieson (1996) 'News Frames, Political Cynicism and Media Cynicism', in Kathleen Hall Jamieson (ed.) *The Media and Politics. Annals of the American Academy of Political and Social Science* 546: 23–30.

Cappella, Joseph N. and Kathleen H. Jamieson (1997) *Spiral of Cynicism. The Press and the Public Good*. New York: Oxford University Press.

Chaffee, Steven H. and J. Dennis (1979) 'Presidential Debates: An Empirical Assessment', in Austin Ranney (ed.) *The Past and Future of Presidential Debates*, Washington, DC: American Enterprise Institute.

Chaffee, Steven H. and Joan Schleuder (1986) 'Measurement and Effects of Attention to Media News', *Human Communication Research* 13: 76–107.

Chaiken, Shelly (1980) 'Heuristic Versus Systematic Information Processing and the Use of Source versus Message Cues in Persuasion', *Journal of Personality and Social Psychology* 39: 752–66.

Clarke, Harold D., Jane Jenson, Lawrence LeDuc and Jon H. Pammett (1979) *Political Choice in Canada*. Toronto: McGraw-Hill Ryerson.

Clarke, Harold D. and Allan Kornberg (1994) 'The Politics and Economics of Constitutional Choice: Voting in Canada's 1992 National Referendum', *Journal of Politics* 56: 940–62.

Clarke, Harold D. and Allan Kornberg (1996) 'Choosing Canada? The 1995 Quebec Sovereignty Referendum', *PS* 29: 676–82.

Clarke, Harold D., Jane Jenson, Lawrence LeDuc and Jon H. Pammett (1991) *Absent Mandate: Interpreting Change in Canadian Elections*. Second edition, Toronto: Gage.

Cloutier, Edouard, Jean H. Guay and Daniel Latouche (1992) *Le Virage: l'évolution de l'opinion publique au Québec depuis 1960*. Montreal: Quebec/Amerique.

Converse, Philip E. (1964) 'The Nature of Belief Systems in Mass Publics', in David E. Apter (ed.) *Ideology and Discontent*. New York: Free Press, pp. 206–61.

Copeland, Gary W. (1983) 'Activating Voters in Congressional Elections', *Political Behavior* 5: 391–401.

Crewe, Ivor (1983) 'The Electorate: Partisan Dealignment Ten Years On', *West European Politics* 6: 183–215.

Crewe, Ivor and David Denver (eds) (1985) *Electoral Change in Western Democracies*. London: Croom Helm.

Crewe, Ivor and Anthony King (1994) 'Did Major Win? Did Kinnock Lose? Leadership Effects in the 1992 Election', in Anthony Heath, Roger Jowell and John Curtice (eds) *Labour's Last Chance?* Aldershot: Dartmouth University Press, pp. 125–48.

Crewe, Ivor and Anthony King (1995) *SDP. The Birth, Life and Death of the Social Democratic Party*. Oxford: Oxford University Press.

Cronin, Tomas E. (1989) *Direct Democracy. The Politics of Initiative, Referendum, and Recall*. Cambridge, MA: Harvard University Press.

Curtice, John, Rüdiger Schmitt-Beck and Peter Schrott (1998) 'Do the Media Matter?' Paper presented at the Annual Meeting of the Mid-West Political Science Association, Chicago.

Dahlgren, Peter (1995) *Television and the Public Sphere*. London: Sage.

Dalton, Russell J. (1996) *Citizen Politics. Public Opinion and Political Parties in Advanced Industrial Democracies*. New York: Chatham House.

Dalton, Russell J. and Martin P. Wattenberg (eds) (2000) *Parties Without Partisans. Political Change in Advanced Industrial Democracies*. Oxford: Oxford University Press.

Dalton, Russell J., Paul Allen Beck and Scott Flanagan (eds) (1984) *Electoral Change in Advanced Industrial Societies*. Princeton, NJ: Princeton University Press.

Dalton, Russell J., Ian McAllister and Martin P. Wattenberg (2000) 'The Consequences of Partisan Dealignment', in Russell J. Dalton and Martin P. Wattenberg (eds) *Parties Without Partisans. Political Change in Advanced Industrial Democracies*. Oxford: Oxford University Press, pp. 37–63.

Darcy, Robert and Michael Laver (1990) 'Referendum Dynamics and the Irish Divorce Amendment', *Public Opinion Quarterly* 54: 4–20.

Dautrich, Kenneth and Thomas H. Hartley (1998). *How the News Media Fail American Voters. Causes, Consequences and Remedies*. New York: Columbia University Press.

Denver, David and Gordan Hands (1997) *Modern Constituency Electioneering*. London: Frank Cass.

Denver, David and Gordan Hands (1998a) 'Constituency Campaigning in the 1997 General Election: Party Effort and Electoral Effect', in Ivor Crewe, Brian Gosschalk and John Bartle (eds) *Political Communications. Why Labour Won the General Election of 1997*. London: Frank Cass, pp. 75–92.

Denver, David and Gordan Hands (1998b) 'Triumph of Targeting? Constituency Campaigning in the 1997 Election', *British Elections and Parties Review* 8: 171–90.

Downs, Anthony (1957) *An Economic Theory of Democracy*. New York: Harper.

Dubois, Philip L. and Floyd Feeney (1998) *Lawmaking by Initiative. Issues, Options and Comparisons*. New York: Agathon Press.

Edelman, Murray (1985) *The Symbolic Uses of Politics*. Second edition, Urbana: University of Illinois Press.

Edelman, Murray (1988) *Constructing the Political Spectacle*. Chicago and London: University of Chicago Press.

Eijk, Cees van der, Mark Franklin and Michael Marsh (1995) 'What Voters Teach Us about Europe-wide Elections: What Europe-wide Elections Teach Us about Voters', *Electoral Studies* 14: 149–66.

Fallows, James (1996) *Breaking the News*. New York: Pantheon Books.

Fan, David P. (1988) *Predictions of Public Opinion from the Mass Media. Computer Content Analysis and Mathematical Modelling*. New York: Greenwood Press.

Farrell, David (1996) 'Campaign Strategies and Tactics', in Lawrence LeDuc, Richard Niemi and Pippa Norris (eds) *Comparing Democracies*. London: Sage, pp. 160–83.

Farrell, David (2002) 'Shopping in the US Political Market: Campaign Modernization and the West European Party', in Kurt Richard Luther and Ferdinand

Müller-Rommel (eds) *Political Parties and Democracy in Western Europe* Oxford: Oxford University Press (in press).

Farrell, David and Paul Webb (2000) 'Political Parties as Campaign Organizations', in Russell J. Dalton and Martin P. Wattenberg (eds) *Parties Without Partisans.* Oxford: Oxford University Press, pp. 102–28.

Farrell, David, Robin Kolodny and Stephen Medvic (2001) 'Political Parties and Campaign Professionals in a Digital Age: Political Consultants in the US and their Counterparts Overseas', *Press/Politics* 6: 11–30.

Finger, Matthias and Pascal Sciarini (1991) 'Integrating "New Politics" into "Old Politics": The Swiss Party Elite', *West European Politics* 14: 98–112.

Finkel, Steven E. (1993) 'Reexamining the "Minimal Effects" Model in Recent Presidential Campaigns', *Journal of Politics* 55: 1–21.

Finkel, Steven E. and Peter Schrott (1995) 'Campaign Effects on Voter Choice in the German Election of 1990', *British Journal of Political Science* 25: 349–77.

Flanagan, Scott C. and Russell J. Dalton (1984) 'Parties under Stress: Realignment and Dealignment in Advanced Industrial Societies', *West European Politics* 7: 7–23.

Fowler, Brigid (1998) 'Hungarian Parliamentary Elections, May 1998', *Electoral Studies* 17: 257–68.

Franklin, Bob (1994) *Packaging Politics*. London: Edward Arnold.

Franklin, Mark, Cees van der Eijk and Michael Marsh (1995) 'Referendum Outcomes and Trust in Government: Public Support for Europe in the Wake of Maastricht', *West European Politics* 18: 101–17.

Franklin, Mark, Michael Marsh and Lauren McLaren (1994a) 'Uncorking the Bottle: Popular Opposition to European Unification in the Wake of Maastricht', *Journal of Common Market Studies*. 32: 455–72.

Franklin, Mark, Michael Marsh and Christopher Wlezien (1994b) 'Attitudes Toward Europe and Referendum Votes: a Response to Siune and Svensson', *Electoral Studies* 13: 117–21.

Gallagher, Michael and Pier Vincenzo Uleri (eds) (1996) *The Referendum Experience in Europe*. London: Macmillan.

Gallagher, Michael, Michael Laver and Peter Mair (1992) *Representative Government in Western Europe*. New York: McGraw-Hill.

Gallagher, Michael, Michael Laver and Peter Mair (2001) *Representative Government in Modern Europe: Institutions, Parties, and Governments*. Third edition, New York: McGraw-Hill.

Galligan, Brian (1990) 'The 1988 Referendums and Australia's Record on Constitutional Change', *Parliamentary Affairs* 43: 497–506.

Gamson, William A. and Andre Modigliani (1966) 'Knowledge and Foreign Policy Opinions: Some Models for Consideration', *Public Opinion Quarterly* 30 (2): 187–99.

Geer, John G. (1996) *From Tea Leaves to Opinion Polls. A Theory of Democratic Leadership*. New York: Columbia University Press.

Gerber, Elisabeth R. (1999) *The Populist Paradox. Interest Group Influence and the Promise of Direct Legislation*. Princeton, NJ: Princeton University Press.

Gerber, Alan S. and Donald P. Green (2000) 'The Effects of Canvassing, Telephone Calls, and Direct Mail on Voter Turnout: A Field Experiment', *American Political Science Review* 94: 653–63.

Gidengil, Elisabeth, André Blais, Richard Nadeau and Neil Nevitte (2000) 'Are Leaders Becoming More Important to Vote Choice in Canada?' Paper presented at the annual meeting of the American Political Science Association, Washington, DC.

Gopoian, J. David (1994) 'Late Deciding Voters in Presidential Elections', *Political Behaviour* 16: 55–78.

Gosnell, Harold F. (1927) *Getting Out the Vote. An Experiment in the Stimulation of Voting.* Chicago: University of Chicago Press.

Graetz, Brian and Ian McAllister (1987) 'Party Leaders and Election Outcomes in Britain, 1974–1983', *Comparative Political Studies* 19: 484–507.

Granberg, Donald and Sören Holmberg (1988) 'Preferences, Expectations and Voting in Sweden's Referendum on Nuclear Power', *Social Science Quarterly* 67: 379–91.

Gujarati, Damodar N. (1995) *Basic Econometrics.* Third edition, New York: McGraw-Hill.

Gunther, Richard and Anthony Mughan (2000) *Democracy and the Media.* Cambridge: Cambridge University Press.

Heath, Anthony and Bridget Taylor (1999) 'Were the Scottish and Welsh Referendums Second Order Elections?', in Bridget Taylor and Katarina Thomson, *Scotland and Wales. Nations Again?* Cardiff: University of Wales Press, pp. 149–68.

Hefferman, Richard and Stanyer, James (1997) 'The Enhancement of Leadership Power: The Labour Party and the Impact of Political Communications', in Charles Pattie, David Denver, Justin Fisher and Steve Ludlam (eds) *British Elections and Parties Yearbook*, VII. London: Frank Cass, pp. 168–84.

Helander, Voitto (1997a) 'Ehdokkaat ja heidän eväänsä. Turun eteläisen vaalipiirin ehdokkaat vuoden 1995 eduskuntavaaleissa', in Voitto Helander, Soile Kuitunen and Lauri Paltemaa (eds) *Kansalaisesta aktiiviksi, aktiivista edustajaksi.* Research reports in Political Science 51. Turku: University of Turku, pp. 142–65.

Helander, Voitto (1997b) 'Finland', in Pippa Norris (ed.) *Passages to Power. Legislative Recruitment in Advanced Democracies.* Cambridge: Cambridge University Press, pp. 56–75.

Helander, Voitto and Soile Kuitunen (1997) 'Johdanto', in Voitto Helander, Soile Kuitunen and Lauri Paltemaa (eds) *Kansalaisesta aktiiviksi, aktiivista edustajaksi.* Research Reports in Political Science 51. Turku: University of Turku, pp. 7–27.

Herbst, Susan (1993) *Numbered Voices. How Opinion Polling Has Shaped American Politics.* Chicago: University of Chicago Press.

Hertig, Hans Peter (1982) 'Sind Abstimmungserfolge käuflich? Elemente der Meinungsbildung bei eidgenössischen Abstimmungen', in *Schweizerisches Jahrbuch für politische Wissenschaft* 22. Berne: Haupt, pp. 35–57.

Herz, John H. (1950) 'Idealist Internationalism and the Security Dilemma', *World Politics* 2: 157–80.

Hill, Kevin A. and John E. Hughes (1998) *Cyberpolitics.* New York: Rowman & Littlefield.

Holbrook, Thomas M. (1996) *Do Campaigns Matter?* Thousand Oaks, CA: Sage.

Holt, Robert T. and John Turner (1968) *Political Parties in Action*, New York: Free Press.

Holtz-Bacha, Christina (1990) 'Videomalaise Revisited: Media Exposure and Political Alienation in West Germany', *European Journal of Communication* 5: 73–85.

Huckfeldt, Robert and John Sprague (1987) 'Networks in Context: the Social Flow of Political Information', *American Political Science Review* 81: 1197–216.

Huckfeldt, Robert and John Sprague (1992) 'Political Parties and Electoral Mobilization: Political Structure, Social Structure, and the Party Canvass', *American Political Science Review* 86: 70–86.

Huckfeldt, Robert and John Sprague (1995) *Citizens, Politics and Social Communication: Information and Influence in an Election Campaign*. Cambridge: Cambridge University Press.

Hughes, Colin (1994) 'Australia and New Zealand', in David Butler and Austin Ranney (eds) *Referendums Around the World*. London: Macmillan.

Inglehart, Ronald (1997) *Modernization and Postmodernization: Cultural, Economic and Political Change in Forty-three Societies*. Princeton, NJ: Princeton University Press.

Initiative and Referendum Institute, Washington, DC [http://www.iandrinstitute.org].

Iyengar, Shanto (1990) 'The Accessibility Bias in Politics: Television News and Public Opinion', *International Journal of Public Opinion Research* 2 (1): 1–15.

Iyengar, Shanto (1991) *Is Anyone Responsible? How Television Frames Political Issues*. Chicago: Chicago University Press.

Iyengar, Shanto and Donald R. Kinder (1987) *News that Matters: Television and American Opinion*. Chicago: University of Chicago Press.

Iyengar, Shanto and John R. Petrocik (2000) '"Basic Rule" Voting: Impact of Campaigns on Party- and Approval-based Voting', in James A. Thurber, Candice J. Nelson and David A. Dulio (eds) *Crowded Airwaves. Campaign Advertising in Elections*. Washington, DC: Brookings Institution, pp. 113–48.

Jacobson, Gary (1978) 'The Effects of Campaign Spending in Congressional Elections', *American Political Science Review* 72: 469–91.

Jacobson, Gary (1980) *Money in Congressional Elections*. New Haven, CT: Yale University Press.

Jahn, Detlef and Ann-Sofie Storsved (1995) 'Legitimacy Through Referendum: the Nearly Successful Domino Strategy of the EU Referendums in Austria, Finland, Sweden and Norway', *West European Politics* 18: 18–37.

Jahn, Detlef, Pertti Pesonen, Tore Slaatta and Leif Åberg (1998) 'The Actors and the Campaigns', in Anders Jenssen, Pertti Pesonen and Mikael Gilljam (eds) *To Join or Not to Join: Three Nordic Referendums on Membership in the European Union*. Oslo: Scandinavian University Press.

Jenssen, Anders Todal, Pertti Pesonen and Mikael Gilljam (eds) (1998) *To Join or Not to Join: Three Nordic Referendums on Membership in the European Union*. Oslo: Scandinavian University Press.

Johnston, R. J. and Charles Pattie (1995) 'The Impact of Spending on Party Constituency Campaigns at recent British General Elections', *Party Politics* 1 (2): 261–73.

Johnston, Richard, André Blais, Henry E. Brady and Jean Crête (1992) *Letting the People Decide. Dynamics of a Canadian Election*. Montreal: McGill-Queen's University Press.

Johnston, Richard, André Blais, Elisabeth Gidengil and Neil Nevitte (1996) *The Challenge of Direct Democracy. The 1992 Canadian Referendum*. Montreal: McGill-Queen's University Press.

Johnston, Richard, André Blais, Elisabeth Gidengil, Neil Nevitte and Henry Brady (1994) 'The Collapse of a Party System? The 1993 Canadian General Election'. Paper presented at the Annual Meeting of the American Political Science Association, New York.

Jones, Nicholas (1995) *Soundbites and Spin Doctors*. London: Cassell.

Joslyn, Mark R. and Steve Ceccoli (1996) 'Attentiveness to Television News and Opinion Change in the Fall 1992 Presidential Campaign', *Political Behavior* 18: 141–70.

Kaase, Max (1984) 'The Challenge of the "Participatory Revolution" in Pluralist Democracies', *International Political Science Review* 5: 299–318.

Kaase, Max (2000) 'Germany', in Richard Gunther and Anthony Mughan (eds) *Democracy and the Media. A Comparative Perspective*. New York: Cambridge University Press.

Kahn, Kim Fridkin and Patrick J. Kenney (1999) *The Spectacle of US Senate Campaigns*. Princeton, NJ: Princeton University Press.

Kaid, Lynda Lee (1981) 'Political Advertising', in Dan Nimmo and Keith R. Sanders (eds) *The Handbook of Political Communication*. Beverly Hills, CA: Sage, pp. 249–71.

Kaid, Lynda Lee and Christina Holtz-Bacha (1993) 'Die Beurteilung von Wahlspots im Fernsehen. Ein Experiment mit Teilnehmern in den alten und neuen Bundesländern', in Christina Holtz-Bacha and Lynda Lee Kaid (eds) *Die Massenmedien im Wahlkampf. Untersuchungen aus dem Wahljahr 1990*. Opladen: Westdeutscher Verlag, pp. 185–207.

Kaid, Lynda Lee and Christina Holtz-Bacha (eds) (1995) *Political Advertising in Western Democracies. Parties and Candidates on Television*. Thousand Oaks, CA: Sage.

Katz, Eliku and J. J. Feldman (1962) 'The Debates in the Light of Research: A Survey of Surveys', in Sidney Kraus(ed.) *The Great Debates*. Bloomington, IN: Indiana University Press.

Katz, Richard S. (1980) *A Theory of Parties and Electoral Systems*. Baltimore, MD: Johns Hopkins University Press.

Katz, Richard S. and Peter Mair (1995) 'Changing Models of Party Organization and Party Democracy: The Emergence of the Cartel Party', *Party Politics* 1: 5–28.

Kavanagh, Dennis (1995) *Election Campaigning. The New Marketing of Politics*. Oxford: Blackwell.

Kavanagh, Dennis (1996) 'Speaking Truth to Power? Pollsters as Campaign Advisers', *European Journal of Marketing* 30: 112–21.

Kelley, Stanley (1956) *Professional Public Relations and Political Power*. Baltimore. MD: Johns Hopkins University Press.

Kerr, Henry H. (1987) 'The Swiss Party System: Steadfast and Changing', in Hans Daalder (ed.) *Party Systems in Denmark, Austria, Switzerland, the Netherlands and Belgium*. London: Pinter, pp. 107–92.

Klöti, Ulrich (1998) 'Kantonale Parteiensysteme. Bedeutung des kantonalen Kontexts für die Positionierung der Parteien', in Hanspeter Kriesi, Wolf Linder and Ulrich Klöti (eds) *Schweizer Wahlen 1995*. Berne: Haupt, pp. 45–72.

Klöti, Ulrich and Wolf Linder (1998) 'Vergleichende Perspektiven', in Hanspeter Kriesi, Wolf Linder and Ulrich Klöti (eds) *Schweizer Wahlen 1995*. Berne: Haupt, pp. 297–314.

Krasno, Jonathan S. (1994) *Challengers, Competition, and Reelection: Comparing Senate and House Elections*. New Haven, CT: Yale University Press.

Kriesi, Hanspeter (1980) *Entscheidungsstrukturen und Entscheidungsprozessen in der Schweizer Politik*. Frankfurt: Campus.

Kriesi, Hanspeter (1994) 'Akteure, Medien, Publikum. Die Herausforderung direkter Demokratie durch die Transformation der Öffentlichkeit', in Friedhelm Neidhart (ed.) *Öffentlichkeit, öffentliche Meinung, soziale Bewegungen*. Opladen: Westdeutscher Verlag, pp. 234–60.

Kriesi, Hanspeter (1998a) 'The transformation of cleavage politics: The 1997 Stein Rokkan lecture', *European Journal of Political Research* 33: 165–85.

Kriesi, Hanspeter (1998b) 'Einleitung', in Hanspeter Kriesi, Wolf Linder and Ulrich Klöti (eds) *Schweizer Wahlen 1995*. Berne: Haupt, pp. 1–16.

Krosnick, Jon A. and Laura A. Brannon (1993) 'The Impact of the Gulf War on the Ingredients of Presidential Evaluations: Multidimensional Effects of Political Involvement', *American Political Science Review* 87: 963–75.

Krosnick, Jon A. and Donald R. Kinder (1990) 'Altering the Foundations of Support for the President Through Priming', *American Political Science Review* 84: 497–512.

Kuusela, Kimmo (1995) 'The Finnish Electoral System: Basic Features and Developmental Tendencies', in Sami Borg and Risto Sänkiaho (eds) *The Finnish Voter*. Helsinki: Finnish Political Science Association, pp. 23–44.

Ladd, Everett Carll, and Karlyn H. Bowman (1998) *What's Wrong? A Survey of American Satisfaction and Complaint*. Washington, DC: AEI Press.

Lang, Kurt and Gladys Lang (1966) 'The Mass Media and Voting', in Bernard Berelson and Morris Janowitz (eds) *Reader in Public Opinion and Communication*. New York: Free Press.

Lange, Bernd-Peter (1994) 'The 1994 Hungarian Parliamentary Elections. Monitoring of the Election Coverage in the Hungarian Mass Media: Final Report', Düsseldorf: European Institute for the Media.

Lanoue, David J. (1991) 'The "Turning Point": Viewers' Reactions to the Second 1988 Presidential Debate', *American Politics Quarterly* 19: 80–95.

Lanoue, David J. and Peter Schrott (1989) 'The Effects of Primary Season Debates on Public Opinion', *Political Behavior* 11: 289–306.

Lau, Richard R., Lee Sigelman, Caroline Heldman and Paul Babbitt (1999) 'The Effects of Negative Political Advertisements: A Meta-analytic Assessment', *American Political Science Review* 93: 851–75.

Lazarsfeld, Paul F., Bernard Berelson and Hazel Gaudet (1968 [1944]) *The People's Choice. How the Voter makes up his Mind in a Presidential Campaign*. Third edition, New York: Columbia University Press.

LeDuc, L. and Jon H. Pammett (1995) 'Referendum Voting: Attitudes and Behaviour in the 1992 Constitutional Referendum', *Canadian Journal of Political Science* 28: 3–33.

Lemert, James B., William R. Elliott, William L. Rosenberg and James M. Bernstein (1996) *The Politics of Disenchantment. Bush, Clinton, Perot, and the Press*. Cresskill, NJ: Hampton Press.

Lenart, Silvo (1994) *Shaping Political Attitudes. The Impact of Interpersonal Communication and Mass Media*. Thousand Oaks, CA: Sage.

Liao, Tim Futing (1994) *Interpreting Probability Models. Logit, Probit, and Other Generalized Linear Models*. Sage University Paper Series on Quantitative Application in the Social Sciences 07–101. Thousand Oaks, CA: Sage.

Lijphart, Arend (1999) *Patterns of Democracy. Government Forms and Performance in Thirty-six Countries*, New Haven, CT and London: Yale University Press.

Linder, Wolf (1998) *Schweizerische Demokratie. Insitutionen, Prozesse, Perspektiven*. Berne: Haupt.

Listhaug, Ola, Sören Holmberg and Risto Sänkiaho (1998) 'Partisanship and EU Choice', in Anders Jenssen, Pertti Pesonen and Mikael Gilljam (eds) *To Join or Not to Join: Three Nordic Referendums on Membership in the European Union*. Oslo: Scandinavian University Press.

Long, J. Scott (1997) *Regression Models for Categorical and Limited Dependent Variables.* Thousand Oaks, CA: Sage.

Lull, James and Stephen Hinerman (1997) *Media Scandals.* Oxford: Polity Press.

Lupia, Arthur (1994) 'Shortcuts vs. Encyclopedias: Information and Voting Behavior in California's Insurance Reform Elections', *American Political Science Review* 88: 63–76.

Lupia, Arthur and Matthew McCubbins (1998) *The Democratic Dilemma. Can Citizens Learn What They Need to Know?* New York: Cambridge University Press.

Luskin, Robert C. (1994) 'Political Psychology, Political Behavior, and Politics. Questions of Aggregation, Causal Distance, and Taste'. Revision of paper presented at the Political Psychology Conference at the University of Illinois at Urbana-Champaign, 17–20 June 1993.

McAllister, Ian (1996) 'Leaders', in Lawrence LeDuc, Richard G. Niemi and Pippa Norris (eds) *Comparing Democracies. Elections and Voting in Global Perspective.* Thousand Oaks, CA: Sage, pp. 280–98.

McAllister, Ian (2000) 'Elections Without Cues: The 1999 Australian Republic Referendum'. Paper, Research School of Social Sciences, Australian National University.

McCloskey, Herbert (1964) 'Consensus and Ideology in American Politics', *American Political Science Review* 58: 361–82.

McCombs, Maxwell E. and Donald L. Shaw (1972) 'The Agenda-setting Function of the Mass Media', *Public Opinion Quarterly* 36: 176–87.

McDonough, Peter and Antonio López Pina (1984) 'Continuity and Change in Spanish Politics', in Russell J. Dalton, Scott C. Flanagan and Paul Allen Beck (eds) *Electoral Change in Advanced Industrial Democracies. Realignment or Dealignment?* Princeton, NJ: Princeton University Press, pp. 365–96.

McGuire, William J. (1969) 'The Nature of Attitudes and Attitude Change', in Gardner Lindzey and Elliot Aronson (eds) *The Handbook of Social Psychology* III. Second edition, Reading, MA: Addison-Wesley, pp. 136–314.

Mackerras, Malcolm and Ian McAllister (1999) 'Compulsory Voting, Party Stability and Electoral Advantage in Australia', *Electoral Studies* 18: 217–33.

MacKuen, Michael and Courtney Brown (1987) 'Political Context and Attitude Change', *American Political Science Review* 81: 471–90.

Maheswaran, Durairaj and Shelly Chaiken (1991) 'Promoting Systematic Processing in Low-motivation Settings: Effect of Incongruent Information on Processing and Judgment', *Journal of Personality and Social Psychology* 61: 13–25.

Mancini, Paolo and David L. Swanson (1996) 'Politics, Media, and Modern Democracy: Introduction', in David L. Swanson and Paolo Mancini (eds) *Politics, Media, and Modern Democracy. An International Study of Innovations in Electoral Campaigning and Their Consequences.* Westport, CT: Praeger, pp. 1–26.

Margolis, Michael, David Resnick and Joel D. Wolfe (1999) 'Party Competition on the Internet in the United States and Britain', *Harvard International Journal of Press/Politics* 4: 24–47.

Marquis, Lionel and Pascal Sciarini (1999) 'Opinion Formation in Foreign Policy: the Swiss Experience', *Electoral Studies* 18: 453–71.

Medvic, Stephen (2002) *Political Consultants in US Congressional Elections.* Columbus, OH: Ohio State University Press.

Menard, Scott (1995) *Applied Logistic Regression Analysis*. Sage University Paper series on Quantitative Applications in the Social Sciences 07–106. Thousand Oaks, CA: Sage.

Mendelsohn, Matthew (1993) 'Television's Frames in the 1988 Canadian Election', *Canadian Journal of Communication* 18: 149–71.

Mendelsohn, Matthew (1994) 'The Media's Persuasive Effects: The Priming of Leadership in the 1988 Canadian Election', *Canadian Journal of Political Science* 27: 81–97.

Mendelsohn, Matthew (1996a) 'The Media and Interpersonal Communications: The Priming of Issues, Leaders, and Party Identification', *Journal of Politics* 58: 112–25.

Mendelsohn, Matthew (1996b) 'Television News frames in the 1993 Canadian Election', in Helen Holmes and David Taras (eds) *Seeing Ourselves. Media Power and Policy in Canada*. Second edition, Toronto: Harcourt Brace.

Merton, Robert K. (1968) *Social Theory and Social Structure*, New York: Free Press.

Miller, Arthur H. and Martin P. Wattenberg (1985) 'Throwing the Rascals Out: Policy and Performance Evaluations of Presidential Candidates, 1952–1980', *American Political Science Review* 79: 359–72.

Miller, Joanne M. and Jon A. Krosnick (2000) 'News Media Impact on the Ingredients of Presidential Evaluations: Politically Knowledgeable Citizens Are Guided by a Trusted Source', *American Journal of Political Science* 44: 295–309.

Milton, Andrew K. (2000) *The Rational Politician. Exploiting the Media in New Democracies*. Aldershot: Ashgate.

Mishler, William, Marilyn Hoskin and Roy Fitzgerald (1989) 'British Parties in the Balance: A Time-series Analysis of Long-term Trends in Labour and Conservative Support', *British Journal of Political Science* 19: 211–36.

Mitchell, James, David Denver, Charles Pattie and Hugh Bochel (1998) 'The 1997 Devolution Referendum in Scotland', *Parliamentary Affairs* 51: 166–81.

Morel, Laurence (1993) 'Party Attitudes Toward Referendums in Western Europe', *West European Politics* 16: 225–43.

Morris, Dick (1997) *Behind the Oval Office. Winning the Presidency in the Nineties*. New York: Random House.

Müller, Albrecht (1997) *Willy wählen '72. Siege kann man machen*. Annweiler: Plöger.

Murdock, Graham and Peter Golding (1989) 'Information Poverty and Political Inequality: Citizenship in the Age of Privatised Communications', *Journal of Communication* 39: 180–93.

Mutz, Diana C. (1992) 'Impersonal Influence: Effects of Representations of Public Opinion on Political Attitudes', *Political Behavior* 14: 89–122.

Mutz, Diana C., Paul M. Sniderman and Richard A. Brody (eds) (1996) *Political Persuasion and Attitude Change*. Ann Arbor, MI: University of Michigan Press.

Nadeau, Richard, Richard G. Niemi and Timothy Amato (1996) 'Prospective and Comparative or Retrospective and Individual? Party Leaders and Party Support in Great Britain', *British Journal of Political Science* 26: 245–58.

Nadeau, Richard, André Blais, Elisabeth Gidengil and Neil Nevitte (2000a) 'Perceptions of Party Competence in the 1997 Election', in Hugh Thorbum and Alan Whitehom (eds) *Party Politics in Canada*. Eighth edition, Toronto: Prentice-Hall, pp. 413–30.

Nadeau, Richard, André Blais, Neil Nevitte and Elisabeth Gidengil (2000b) 'It's Unemployment, Stupid! Why Perceptions about the Job Situation Hurt the Liberals in the 1997 Election', *Canadian Public Policy* 26: 77–94.

National Media Archive (1993) 'Election '93: What Role Did Television Play in the Outcome?', *On Balance* 6: 1–8.

Neuman, W. Russel (1986) *The Paradox of Mass Politics. Knowledge and Opinion in the American Electorate.* Cambridge, MA: Harvard University Press.

Nevitte, Neil, André Blais, Elisabeth Gidengil and Richard Nadeau (2000) *Unsteady State. The 1997 Canadian Federal Election.* Toronto: Oxford University Press.

Newton, Kenneth (1997) 'Politics and the News Media: Mobilisation or Video-malaise?', in Roger Jowell, John Curtice, Alison Park, Katarina Thomson and Lindsay Brook (eds) *British Social Attitudes. The Fourteenth Report, 1997/8.* Aldershot: Ashgate, pp. 151–68.

Newton, Kenneth (1999) 'Mass Media Effects: Mobilization or Media Malaise?' *British Journal of Political Science* 29: 577–99.

Newton, Kenneth (2000) 'Versagt politisches Marketing?', in Oskar Niedermayer and Bettina Westle (eds) *Demokratie und Partizipation.* Wiesbaden: Westdeutscher Verlag, pp. 177–91.

Nicholas, Herbert G. (1951) *The British General Election of 1950.* London: Macmillan.

Nie, Norman H., Jane Junn and Kenneth Stehlik-Barry (1996) *Education and Democratic Citizenship in America.* Chicago: University of Chicago Press.

Nie, Norman H., Sidney Verba and John R. Petrocik (1976) *The Changing American Voter.* Cambridge, MA: Harvard University Press

Noponen, Martti (ed.) (1989) *Suomen kansanedustusjärjestelmä.* Helsinki: WSOY.

Norris, P. (1997a) 'Political Communications', in Patrick Dunleavy, Andrew Gamble, Ian Holliday and Gillian Peele (eds) *Developments in British Politics V.* Basingstoke: Macmillan, pp. 75–88.

Norris, Pippa (1997b) *Pathways to Power. Legislative Recruitment in Advanced Democracies.* Cambridge: Cambridge University Press.

Norris, Pippa (1997c) 'Introduction: Theories of Recruitment', in Pippa Norris (ed.) *Passages to Power. Legislative Recruitment in Advanced Democracies.* Cambridge: Cambridge University Press, pp. 1–14.

Norris, Pippa, (1997d) 'Conclusion: Comparing Passages to Power', in Pippa Norris (ed.) *Passages to Power. Legislative Recruitment in Advanced Democracies.* Cambridge: Cambridge University Press, pp. 209–31.

Norris, Pippa (1999) *Critical Citizens. Global Support for Democratic Governance.* Oxford: Oxford University Press.

Norris, Pippa (2000) *A Virtuous Circle. Political Communications in Postindustrial Societies.* Cambridge: Cambridge University Press.

Norris, Pippa (2001a) *Digital Divide. Civic Engagement, Information Poverty and the Internet Worldwide.* New York: Cambridge University Press.

Norris, Pippa (2001b) 'Civic Engagement and Campaign 2000', *Harvard International Journal of Press/Politics* 6(1) (in press).

Norris, Pippa (2001c) 'US Campaign 2000: Of Pregnant Chads, Bulletfly Ballots and Partisan Vitriol', *Government and Opposition* 36 (1): 3–26.

Norris, Pippa (2002) *A Virtuous Circle.* New York: Cambridge University Press.

Norris, Pippa and Joni Lovenduski (1995) *Political Recruitment. Gender, Race and Class in the British Parliament.* Cambridge: Cambridge University Press.

Norris, Pippa and Joni Lovenduski (1997) 'United Kingdom', in Pippa Norris (ed.) *Passages to Power. Legislative Recruitment in Advanced Democracies.* Cambridge: Cambridge University Press, pp. 158–86.

Norris, Pippa, John Curtice, David Sanders, Margaret Scammell and Holli Semetko (1999) *On Message. Communicating the Campaign.* Thousand Oaks, CA: Sage.

Nye, Joseph, Jr, Philip Zelikow and David King (1997) *Why People Don't Trust Government.* Cambridge, MA: Harvard University Press.

OPCS (Office of Population Censuses and Surveys) (1978) *The General Household Survey 1975.* London: HMSO.

OPCS (Office of Population Censuses and Surveys) (1994) *Living in Britain. Results for the 1994 General Household Survey.* London: HMSO.

O'Shaughnessy, Nicholas J. (1990) *The Phenomenon of Political Marketing.* London: Macmillan.

Ottati, Victor C. and Robert S. Wyer Jr (1990) 'The Cognitive Mediators of Political Choice: Toward a Comprehensive Model of Political Information Processing', in John A. Ferejohn and James H. Kuklinski (eds) *Information and Democratic Processes.* Urbana: University of Illinois Press, pp. 186–216.

Owen, Diane and Richard Davis (1998) *New Media and American Politics.* New York: Oxford University Press.

Page, Benjamin I. and Robert Y. Shapiro (1992) *The Rational Public.* Chicago: University of Chicago Press.

Pammett, Jon H. and Lawrence LeDuc (1998) 'Attitudes Toward Sovereignty and the Vote Decision in the 1995 Quebec Referendum'. Paper presented to the annual meeting of the Canadian Political Science Association, Ottawa.

Patterson, Thomas E. (1993) *Out of Order.* New York: Vintage.

Patterson, Thomas E. and Robert McClure (1976) *The Unseeing Eye: The Myth of Television Power in National Elections.* New York: Putnam.

Pattie, Charles J., Ronald J. Johnston and Edward Fieldhouse (1995) 'Winning the Local Vote: The Effectiveness of Constituency Campaign Spending in Great Britain, 1983–1992', *American Political Science Review* 89 (4): 969–83.

Pattie, Charles J., Paul F. Whiteley, Ronald J. Johnston and Patrick Seyd (1994) 'Measuring Local Campaign Effects: Labour Party Constituency Campaigning at the 1987 General Election', *Political Studies* 42: 469–79.

Pedersen, Mogens (1983) 'Changing Patterns of Electoral Volatility in European Party Systems, 1948–1977: Explorations in Explanation', in Hans Daalder and Peter Mair (eds) *Western European Party Systems. Continuity and Change.* London: Sage, pp. 67–94.

Pesonen, Pertti (1998) 'Voting Decisions', in Anders T. Jenssen, Pertti Pesonen and Mikael Gilljam, *To Join or Not to Join. Three Nordic Referendums on Membership in the European Union.* Oslo: Scandinavian University Press, pp. 127–46.

Pesonen, Pertti, Risto Sänkiaho and Sami Borg (1993) *Vaalikansan äänivalta.* Helsinki: WSOY.

Petrocik, John R. (1996) 'Issue Ownership in Presidential Elections, with a 1980 Case Study', *American Journal of Political Science* 40: 825–50.

Petty, Richard E. and John T. Cacioppo (1986) *Communication and Persuasion. Central and Peripheral Routes to Attitude Change.* New York: Springer.

Pfetsch, Barbara (1996) 'Convergence through Privatization? Changing Media Environments and Televised Politics in Germany', *European Journal of Communication* 8 (3): 425–50.

Pharr, Susan J. and Robert D. Putnam (eds) (2000) *Disaffected Democrats: What's Troubling the Trilateral Countries*. Princeton, NJ: Princeton University Press.

Plasser, Fritz, Christian Scheucher and Christian Senft (1999) 'Is There a European Style of Political Marketing?', in Bruce I. Newman (ed.) *The Handbook of Political Marketing*. Thousand Oaks, CA: Sage.

Popkin, Samuel L. (1991) *The Reasoning Voter. Communication and Persuasion in Presidential Campaigns*. Chicago and London: University of Chicago Press.

Popkin, Samuel L. (1994) *The Reasoning Voter. Communication and Persuasion in Presidential Campaigns*. Second edition, Chicago: University of Chicago Press.

Powell, G. Bingham (1982) *Contemporary Democracies*. New Haven, CT: Yale University Press.

Putnam, Robert D. (1993) *Making Democracy Work: Civic Traditions in Modern Italy*. Princeton, NJ: Princeton University Press.

Putnam, Robert D. (2000) *Bowling Alone*. New York: Simon & Schuster.

Qvortrup, Mads (1997) 'Uruguay's Constitutional Referendum 8 December 1996', *Electoral Studies* 17: 549–54.

Rahn, Wendy M., John Brehm and Neil Carlson (1999) 'National Elections as Institutions for Generating Social Capital', in Theda Skocpol and Morris P. Fiorina (eds) *Civic Engagement in American Society*. Washington, DC: Brookings Institution, pp. 111–62.

Rallings, Colin and Michael Thrasher (1995) *Media Guide to the New Constituencies*. Local Government Chronicle Election Centre, University of Plymouth.

Reif, Karlheinz and Hermann Schmitt (1980) 'Nine Second-Order Elections: a Conceptual Framework for the Analysis of European Election Results', *European Journal of Political Research* 8: 3–44.

Riddell, Peter (1996) *Honest Opportunism. How We Get the Politicians We Deserve*. London: Indigo.

Rivers, Douglas (1988) 'Heterogeneity in Models of Electoral Choice', *American Journal of Political Science* 32: 737–57.

Robinson, Michael (1976) 'Public Affairs Television and the Growth of Political Malaise: The Case of "the Selling of the President"', *American Political Science Review* 70 (3): 409–32.

Rose, Richard (1967) *Influencing Voters*. London: Faber.

Rosenbaum, Martin (1997) *From Soapbox to Soundbite. Party Political Campaigning in Britain since 1945*. Basingstoke: Macmillan.

Rosenstone, Steven and Mark Hansen (1993) *Mobilization, Participation and Democracy in America*. New York: Macmillan.

Röttger, Ulrike (ed.) (1997) *PR-Kampagnen. Über die Inszenierung von Öffentlichkeit*. Opladen: Westdeutscher Verlag.

Ruostetsaari, Ilkka (1998) *Politiikan professionalisoituminen ja poliittisen luokan muotoutuminen Suomessa*. Research Reports 3. Tampere: Department of International Relations, University of Tampere.

Ruostetsaari, Ilkka (2000) 'From Political Amateur to Professional Politician and Expert Representative: Recruitment of the Parliamentary Elite in Finland 1863–1995', in Heinrich Best and Maurizio Cotta (eds), *The European Representative. 150 Years of Parliamentary Recruitment in Comparative Perspective, 1848–1998*. Oxford: Oxford University Press, pp. 51–87.

Ruostetsaari, Ilkka (2001) 'In the Euro-elite or in the Wilderness of Politics? Recruitment of MEPs from a new Member State to the European Parliament'. Paper prepared for presentation at the twenty-ninth joint session of the European Consortium for Political Research, Grenoble, 6–11 April.

Salmore, Barbara G. and Stephen A. Salmore (1989) *Candidates, Parties, and Campaigns. Electoral Politics in America.* Second edition, Washington, DC: Congressional Quarterly Press.

Sarcinelli, Ulrich (ed.) (1987) *Politikvermittlung. Beiträge zur politischen Kommunikationskultur.* Bonn: Bundeszentrale für politische Bildung.

Sarcinelli, Ulrich (ed.) (1998) *Politikvermittlung und Demokratie in der Mediengesellschaft. Beiträge zur politischen Kommunikationskultur.* Bonn: Bundeszentrale für politische Bildung.

Saris, Willem E. (1997) 'The Public Opinion about EU can easily be Swayed in Different Directions', *Acta politica* 32: 406–35.

Savoie, Donald (1999) *Governing from the Centre. The Concentration of Power in Canadian Politics.* Toronto: University of Toronto Press.

Scammell, Margaret (1995) *Designer Politics. How Elections are Won.* Basingstoke: Macmillan.

Schmitt-Beck, Rüdiger (1996a) 'Mass Media, the Electorate, and the Bandwagon: A Study of Communication Effects on Vote Choice in Germany', *International Journal of Public Opinion Research* 8: 266–91.

Schmitt-Beck, Rüdiger (1996b) 'Medien und Mehrheiten. Massenmedien als Informationsvermittler über die Wahlchancen der Parteien', *Zeitschrift für Parlamentsfragen* 27: 127–44.

Schmitt-Beck, Rüdiger (2001) 'Soziale Bewegungen und Öffentlichkeit. Theoretische Anmerkungen zu Bedeutung, Formen und Problemen der Öffentlichkeitsarbeit nicht-etablierter Kollektivakteure', in Günter Bentele, Tobias Liebert and Michael Vogt (eds) *PR für Verbände und Organisationen.* Neuwied: Luchterhand, pp. 15–35.

Schmitt-Beck, Rüdiger (2002) 'Ein Sieg der "Kampa"? Politische Symbolik im Wahlkampf der SPD und ihre Resonanz in der Wählerschaft', in Hans-Dieter Klingemann and Max Kaase (eds) *Wahlen und Wähler. Analysen aus Anlaß der Bundestagswahl 1998.* Wiesbaden: Westdeutscher Verlag (in press).

Schmitt-Beck, Rüdiger and Barbara Pfetsch (1994) 'Politische Akteure und die Medien der Massenkommunikation. Zur Generierung von Öffentlichkeit in Wahlkämpfen', in Friedhelm Neidhardt (ed.) *Öffentlichkeit, öffentliche Meinung, soziale Bewegungen.* Opladen: Westdeutscher Verlag, pp. 106–38.

Schrott, Peter R. and David J. Lanou (1992) 'How to Win a Televised Debate: Candidate Strategies and Voter Response in Germany, 1972–87', *British Journal of Political Science* 22: 445–67.

Schulz, Winfried (1997) 'Changes of Mass Media and the Public Sphere', *Javost – The Public* 4 (2): 57–90.

Schumpeter, Joseph A. (1994 [1942]) *Capitalism, Socialism and Democracy.* London: Routledge.

Sciarini, Pascal and Lionel Marquis (2000) 'La formation des opinions dans les votes de politique extérieure: le cas de la Suisse', *International Political Science Review* 21 (2): 149–71.

Sears, David O. and Steven H. Chaffee (1979) 'Uses and Effect of the 1976 Debates: An Overview of Empirical Studies', in Sidney Kraus (ed.) *The Great Debates. Carter vs. Ford, 1976.* Bloomington: Indiana University Press.

Semetko, Holli A. (1996) 'The Media', in Lawrence LeDuc, Richard G. Niemi and Pippa Norris (eds) *Comparing Democracies: Elections and Voting in Global Perspective.* Thousand Oaks, CA: Sage, pp. 254–79.

Seyd, Patrick and Paul Whiteley (1994) 'The Influence of Local Campaigning on the Conservative Vote in the 1992 General Election', in David Broughton, David M. Farrell, David Denver and Colin Rallings (eds) *British Elections and Parties Yearbook, 1994.* London: Frank Cass, pp. 92–119.

Shaw, Daron R. (1999) 'The Effects of TV Ads and Candidate Appearances on State-wide Presidential Votes, 1988–96', *American Political Science Review* 93: 345–61.

Shaw, Daron R. and Brian E. Roberts (2000) 'Campaign Events, the Media and the Prospects of Victory: The 1992 and 1996 US Presidential Elections', *British Journal of Political Science* 30: 259–89.

Siune, Karen (1998) 'Is Broadcasting Policy Becoming Redundant?', in Kees Brants, Joke Hermes and Lizbet van Zoonen (eds) *The Media in Question.* London: Sage.

Siune, Karen, Palle Svensson and Ole Tonsgaard (1994) 'The European Union: Why the Danes said NO in 1992 but YES in 1993', *Electoral Studies* 13: 107–15.

Smith, Denis (1977) 'President and Parliament: The Transformation of Parliamentary Government in Canada', in Thomas A. Hockin (ed.) *The Apex of Power. The Prime Minister and Political Leadership in Canada.* Scarborough, ONT: Prentice-Hall, 308–25.

Smith, Eric R.A.N. (1989) *The Unchanging American Voter.* Berkeley: University of California Press.

Stewart, Marianne C. and Harold D. Clarke (1992) 'The (Un)Importance of Party Leaders: Leader Images and Party Choice in the 1987 British Election', *Journal of Politics* 54: 447–70.

Stöss, Richard (1997) *Stabilität im Umbruch. Wahlbeständigkeit und Parteienwettbewerb im "Superwahljahr" 1994.* Opladen: Westdeutscher Verlag.

Sullivan, John L., Amy Fried and Mary G. Dietz (1992) 'Patriotism, Politics, and the Presidential Election of 1988', *American Journal of Political Science* 36: 200–34.

Sullivan, John L., James Piereson and George E. Marcus (1982) *Political Tolerance and American Democracy.* Chicago: University of Chicago Press.

Sundberg, Jan (1995) 'Organizational Structure of Parties, Candidate Selection and Campaigning', in Borg Samiand Risto Sänkiaho (eds) *The Finnish Voter.* Helsinki: Finnish Political Science Association, pp. 45–65.

Sundberg, Jan (1996) *Partier och partisystem i Finland.* Espoo: Schilds.

SVT (1999) *Elections 1999:1. Parliamentary Rlections.* Helsinki: Statistics Finland.

Swanson, David L. and Paolo Mancini (eds) (1996) *Politics, Media, and Modern Democracy. An International Study of Innovations in Electoral Campaigning and their Consequences.* Westport, CT: Praeger.

Teixeira, Roy (1992) *The Disappearing American Voter.* Washington, DC: Brookings Institution.

Thurber, James A. and Candice J. Nelson (eds) (2000) *Campaign Warriors. Political Consultants in Elections.* Washington, DC: Brookings Institition.

Tóka, Gábor and Zsolt Enyedi (eds) (1999) *Elections to the Hungarian National Assembly 1994.* Berlin: Sigma.

Tonsgaard, Ole (1992) 'A Theoretical Model of Referendum Behaviour', in Peter Gundelach and Karen Siune (eds) *From Voters to Participants.* Aarhus: Institute of Political Science, University of Aarhus.

Topf, Richard (1995) 'Electoral Participation', in Hans-Dieter Klingemann and Dieter Fuchs (eds) *Citizens and the State*. Oxford: Oxford University Press, pp. 24–51.

Trechsel, Alexandre H. und Hanspeter Kriesi (1996) 'Switzerland: the Referendum and Initiative as a Centrepiece of the Political System', in Michael Gallagher and Piervincenzo Uleri (eds) *The Referendum Experience in Europe*. London and New York: Macmillan, pp. 185–208.

Vaalikysely 1998, Helsinki: Taloustutkimus Oy.

Venho, Tomi (1999) 'Tutkimus vuoden 1999 eduskuntavaaliehdokkaiden kampanjarahoituksesta', in *KM 1999:6. Vaalirahoituskomitean mietintö*. Helsinki, pp. 95–171.

Wattenberg, Martin (1991) *The Rise of Candidate-centered Politics. Presidential Elections of the 1980s*. Cambridge, MA: Harvard University Press.

Wattenberg, Martin P. (2000) 'The Decline of Party Mobilization', in Russell J. Dalton and Martin P. Wattenberg (eds) *Parties Without Partisans. Political Change in Advanced Industrial Democracies*. Oxford: Oxford University Press, pp. 64–78.

Weaver, David (1991) 'Issue Salience and Public Opinion: Are There Consequnces of Agenda-setting?' *International Journal of Public Opinion Research* 3: 53–68.

Weber, Max (1980 [1921/22]) *Wirtschaft und Gesellschaft*. Fifth edition, Tübingen: Mohr.

Weir, Blair T. (1985) 'The American Tradition of the Experimental Treatment of Elections: A Review Essay', *Electoral Studies* 4: 125–33.

Westlye, Mark C. (1991) *Senate Elections and Campaign Intensity*. Baltimore, MD: Johns Hopkins University Press.

Whiteley, Paul and Patrick Seyd (1992) 'Labour's Vote and Local Activism', *Parliamentary Affairs* 45 (4): 582–95.

Whiteley, Paul and Patrick Seyd (1998) 'Labour's Grassroots Campaign', *British Elections and Parties Review* 8: 191–207.

Whiteley, Paul, Patrick Seyd and Jeremy Richardson (1994) *True Blues: The Politics of Conservative Party Membership*. Oxford: Clarendon Press.

Zaller, John R. (1990) 'Political Awareness, Elite Opinion Leadership, and the Mass Survey Response', *Social Cognition* 1: 125–53.

Zaller, John R. (1992) *The Nature and Origins of Mass Opinion*. New York: Cambridge University Press.

Zaller, John R. (1993) 'The Converse McGuire Model of Attitude Change and the Gulf War Opinion Rally', *Political Communication* 10: 369–88.

Zaller, John R. (1996) 'The Myth of Massive Media Impact Revived: New Support for a Discredited Idea', in D. Mutz, P. Sniderman and R. Brody (eds) *Political Persuasion and Attitude Change*. Ann Arbor: University of Michigan Press, pp. 17–78.

Zaller, John R. (1998) 'The Rule of Product Substitution in Presidential Campaign News', *Annals of the American Academy of Political and Social Science* 560: 111–28.

Index

214   *Index*